General Assembly
Official Records
Seventy-eighth Session
Supplement No. 10

A/78/10

Report of the International Law Commission

Seventy-fourth session
(24 April–2 June and 3 July–4 August 2023)

United Nations • New York, 2023

Note

Symbols of United Nations documents are composed of capital letters combined with figures. Mention of such a symbol indicates a reference to a United Nations document.

The word *Yearbook* followed by suspension points and the year (e.g. *Yearbook ... 1971*) indicates a reference to the *Yearbook of the International Law Commission*.

A typeset version of the report of the Commission will be included in Part Two of volume II of the *Yearbook of the International Law Commission 2023.*

ISSN 0251-822X

Print ISBN: 978-92-1-003326-8

Summary of contents

Contents

Chapter I
Introduction

1. The International Law Commission held the first part of its seventy-fourth session from 24 April to 2 June 2023 and the second part from 3 July to 4 August 2023 at its seat at the United Nations Office at Geneva. The session was opened by Mr. Marcelo Vázquez-Bermúdez, Second Vice-Chair of the seventy-third session of the Commission.

A. Membership

2. The Commission consists of the following members:

Mr. Dapo Akande (United Kingdom of Great Britain and Northern Ireland)

Mr. Carlos J. Argüello Gómez (Nicaragua)

Mr. Masahiko Asada (Japan)

Mr. Bogdan Aurescu (Romania)

Mr. Yacouba Cissé (Côte d'Ivoire)

Mr. Ahmed Amin Fathalla (Egypt)

Mr. Rolf Einar Fife (Norway)

Mr. Mathias Forteau (France)

Mr. George Rodrigo Bandeira Galindo (Brazil)

Ms. Patrícia Galvão Teles (Portugal)

Mr. Claudio Grossman Guiloff (Chile)

Mr. Huikang Huang (China)

Mr. Charles Chernor Jalloh (Sierra Leone)

Mr. Ahmed Laraba (Algeria)

Mr. Keun-Gwan Lee (Republic of Korea)

Ms. Vilawan Mangklatanakul (Thailand)

Mr. Andreas D. Mavroyiannis (Cyprus)

Mr. Ivon Mingashang (Democratic Republic of the Congo)

Mr. Giuseppe Nesi (Italy)

Mr. Hong Thao Nguyen (Viet Nam)

Ms. Phoebe Okowa (Kenya)

Ms. Nilüfer Oral (Türkiye)

Mr. Hassan Ouazzani Chahdi (Morocco)

Mr. Mario Oyarzábal (Argentina)

Mr. Mārtiņš Paparinskis (Latvia)

Mr. Bimal N. Patel (India)

Mr. August Reinisch (Austria)

Ms. Penelope Ridings (New Zealand)

Mr. Juan José Ruda Santolaria (Peru)

Mr. Alioune Sall (Senegal)

Mr. Louis Savadogo (Burkina Faso)

Mr. Munkh-Orgil Tsend (Mongolia)

Mr. Marcelo Vázquez-Bermúdez (Ecuador)

Mr. Evgeny Zagaynov (Russian Federation)

B. Officers and the Enlarged Bureau

3. At its 3613th meeting, on 25 April 2023, the Commission elected the following officers:

Chair:	Ms. Nilüfer Oral (Türkiye),[1] then Ms. Patrícia Galvão Teles (Portugal)[2]
First Vice-Chair:	Mr. Marcelo Vázquez-Bermúdez (Ecuador)
Second Vice-Chair:	Mr. Charles Chernor Jalloh (Sierra Leone)
Chair of the Drafting Committee:	Mr. Mārtiņš Paparinskis (Latvia)
Rapporteur:	Mr. Hong Thao Nguyen (Viet Nam)

4. The Enlarged Bureau of the Commission was composed of the officers of the present session, the Special Rapporteurs[3] and the Co-Chairs of the Study Group on sea-level rise in relation to international law.[4]

5. On 27 April 2023, the Planning Group was constituted, composed of the following members: Mr. Marcelo Vázquez-Bermúdez (Chair); Mr. Dapo Akande, Mr. Masahiko Asada, Mr. Bogdan Aurescu, Mr. Rolf Einar Fife, Mr. Mathias Forteau, Mr. George Rodrigo Bandeira Galindo, Mr. Claudio Grossman Guiloff, Mr. Huikang Huang, Mr. Charles Chernor Jalloh, Mr. Keun-Gwan Lee, Ms. Vilawan Mangklatanakul, Mr. Andreas D. Mavroyiannis, Mr. Giuseppe Nesi, Ms. Phoebe Okowa, Mr. Hassan Ouazzani Chahdi, Mr. Mario Oyarzábal, Mr. Mārtiņš Paparinskis, Mr. Bimal N. Patel, Mr. August Reinisch, Ms. Penelope Ridings, Mr. Juan José Ruda Santolaria, Mr. Louis Savadogo, Mr. Evgeny Zagaynov and Mr. Hong Thao Nguyen (*ex officio*).

C. Drafting Committee

6. At its 3618th, 3620th, 3625th, and 3633rd meetings, on 3, 9, 16 and 26 May 2023, the Commission established a Drafting Committee, composed of the following members for the topics indicated:

(*a*) *Settlement of disputes to which international organizations are parties*: Mr. Mārtiņš Paparinskis (Chair), Mr. August Reinisch (Special Rapporteur), Mr. Dapo Akande, Mr. Masahiko Asada, Mr. Ahmed Amin Fathalla, Mr. Rolf Einar Fife, Mr. Mathias Forteau, Mr. George Rodrigo Bandeira Galindo, Ms. Patrícia Galvão Teles, Mr. Claudio Grossman Guiloff, Mr. Huikang Huang, Mr. Charles Chernor Jalloh, Mr. Keun-Gwan Lee, Ms. Vilawan Mangklatanakul, Mr. Andreas D. Mavroyiannis, Mr. Ivon Mingashang, Mr. Giuseppe Nesi, Ms. Phoebe Okowa, Ms. Nilüfer Oral, Mr. Hassan Ouazzani Chahdi, Mr. Mario Oyarzábal, Mr. Bimal N. Patel, Ms. Penelope Ridings, Mr. Juan José Ruda Santolaria, Mr. Alioune Sall, Mr. Louis Savadogo, Mr. Marcelo Vázquez-Bermúdez and Mr. Hong Thao Nguyen (*ex officio*);

(*b*) *General principles of law*: Mr. Mārtiņš Paparinskis (Chair), Mr. Marcelo Vázquez-Bermúdez (Special Rapporteur), Mr. Dapo Akande, Mr. Carlos J. Argüello Gómez,

---

[1] Elected as Chair for the duration of the first part of the session.

[2] Elected at its 3634th meeting on 2 June 2023 as Chair for the remainder of the seventy-fourth session.

[3] Mr. Yacouba Cissé, Mr. Claudio Grossman Guiloff, Mr. Charles Chernor Jalloh, Mr. August Reinisch and Mr. Marcelo Vázquez-Bermúdez.

[4] Mr. Bogdan Aurescu, Mr. Yacouba Cissé, Ms. Patrícia Galvão Teles, Ms. Nilüfer Oral and Mr. Juan José Ruda Santolaria.

Mr. Masahiko Asada, Mr. Rolf Einar Fife, Mr. Mathias Forteau, Mr. George Rodrigo Bandeira Galindo, Ms. Patrícia Galvão Teles, Mr. Claudio Grossman Guiloff, Mr. Huikang Huang, Mr. Charles Chernor Jalloh, Mr. Keun-Gwan Lee, Ms. Vilawan Mangklatanakul, Mr. Andreas D. Mavroyiannis, Mr. Ivon Mingashang, Mr. Giuseppe Nesi, Ms. Nilüfer Oral, Mr. Hassan Ouazzani Chahdi, Mr. Mario Oyarzábal, Mr. Bimal N. Patel, Mr. August Reinisch, Ms. Penelope Ridings, Mr. Juan José Ruda Santolaria, Mr. Alioune Sall, Mr. Louis Savadogo, Mr. Munkh-Orgil Tsend and Mr. Hong Thao Nguyen (*ex officio*);

(*c*) *Prevention and repression of piracy and armed robbery at sea*: Mr. Mārtiņš Paparinskis (Chair), Mr. Yacouba Cissé (Special Rapporteur), Mr. Dapo Akande, Mr. Masahiko Asada, Mr. Ahmed Amin Fathalla, Mr. Rolf Einar Fife, Mr. George Rodrigo Bandeira Galindo, Mr. Claudio Grossman Guiloff, Mr. Huikang Huang, Mr. Charles Chernor Jalloh, Mr. Keun-Gwan Lee, Mr. Andreas D. Mavroyiannis, Mr. Ivon Mingashang, Mr. Giuseppe Nesi, Ms. Nilüfer Oral, Mr. Hassan Ouazzani Chahdi, Mr. Mario Oyarzábal, Mr. Bimal N. Patel, Mr. August Reinisch, Ms. Penelope Ridings, Mr. Juan José Ruda Santolaria, Mr. Louis Savadogo and Mr. Hong Thao Nguyen (*ex officio*);

(*d*) *Subsidiary means for the determination of rules of international law*: Mr. Mārtiņš Paparinskis (Chair), Mr. Charles Chernor Jalloh (Special Rapporteur), Mr. Dapo Akande, Mr. Carlos J. Argüello Gómez, Mr. Masahiko Asada, Mr. Ahmed Amin Fathalla, Mr. Rolf Einar Fife, Mr. Mathias Forteau, Mr. George Rodrigo Bandeira Galindo, Ms. Patrícia Galvão Teles, Mr. Huikang Huang, Mr. Keun-Gwan Lee, Ms. Vilawan Mangklatanakul, Mr. Andreas D. Mavroyiannis, Mr. Ivon Mingashang, Mr. Giuseppe Nesi, Ms. Phoebe Okowa, Mr. Mario Oyarzábal, Mr. Bimal N. Patel, Mr. August Reinisch, Ms. Penelope Ridings, Mr. Juan José Ruda Santolaria, Mr. Alioune Sall, Mr. Louis Savadogo, Mr. Marcelo Vázquez-Bermúdez, Mr. Evgeny Zagaynov and Mr. Hong Thao Nguyen (*ex officio*).

7. The Drafting Committee held a total of 28 meetings on the four topics indicated above.

D. Working Groups and Study Group

8. On 28 April 2023, the Planning Group established the following Working Groups:

(*a*) *Working Group on the long-term programme of work*: Mr. Marcelo Vázquez-Bermúdez (Chair), Mr. Dapo Akande, Mr. Carlos J. Argüello Gómez, Mr. Masahiko Asada, Mr. Bogdan Aurescu, Mr. Rolf Einar Fife, Mr. Mathias Forteau, Mr. George Rodrigo Bandeira Galindo, Mr. Claudio Grossman Guiloff, Mr. Huikang Huang, Mr. Charles Chernor Jalloh, Mr. Keun-Gwan Lee, Ms. Vilawan Mangklatanakul, Mr. Andreas D. Mavroyiannis, Mr. Ivon Mingashang, Mr. Giuseppe Nesi, Ms. Phoebe Okowa, Ms. Nilüfer Oral, Mr. Hassan Ouazzani Chahdi, Mr. Mario Oyarzábal, Mr. Mārtiņš Paparinskis, Mr. Bimal N. Patel, Mr. August Reinisch, Ms. Penelope Ridings, Mr. Juan José Ruda Santolaria, Mr. Alioune Sall, Mr. Louis Savadogo, Mr. Evgeny Zagaynov and Mr. Hong Thao Nguyen (*ex officio*);

(*b*) *Working Group on methods of work*: Mr. Charles Chernor Jalloh (Chair), Mr. Dapo Akande, Mr. Carlos J. Argüello Gómez, Mr. Masahiko Asada, Mr. Bogdan Aurescu, Mr. Ahmed Amin Fathalla, Mr. Mathias Forteau, Mr. George Rodrigo Bandeira Galindo, Mr. Claudio Grossman Guiloff, Mr. Huikang Huang, Mr. Keun-Gwan Lee, Ms. Vilawan Mangklatanakul, Mr. Andreas D. Mavroyiannis, Mr. Ivon Mingashang, Mr. Giuseppe Nesi, Ms. Phoebe Okowa, Ms. Nilüfer Oral, Mr. Hassan Ouazzani Chahdi, Mr. Mario Oyarzábal, Mr. Mārtiņš Paparinskis, Mr. Bimal N. Patel, Mr. August Reinisch, Ms. Penelope Ridings, Mr. Juan José Ruda Santolaria, Mr. Louis Savadogo, Mr. Marcelo Vázquez-Bermúdez, Mr. Evgeny Zagaynov and Mr. Hong Thao Nguyen (*ex officio*).

9. At its 3614th meeting, on 26 April 2023, the Commission established a Study Group on sea-level rise in relation to international law, composed of the following members: Mr. Bogdan Aurescu (Co-Chair, and Chair at the current session), Mr. Yacouba Cissé (Co-Chair), Ms. Patrícia Galvão Teles (Co-Chair), Ms. Nilüfer Oral (Co-Chair, and Chair at the current session), Mr. Juan José Ruda Santolaria (Co-Chair), Mr. Dapo Akande,

Mr. Carlos J. Argüello Gómez, Mr. Masahiko Asada, Mr. Ahmed Amin Fathalla, Mr. Rolf Einar Fife, Mr. Mathias Forteau, Mr. George Rodrigo Bandeira Galindo, Mr. Claudio Grossman Guiloff, Mr. Huikang Huang, Mr. Charles Chernor Jalloh, Mr. Ahmed Laraba, Mr. Keun-Gwan Lee, Ms. Vilawan Mangklatanakul, Mr. Andreas D. Mavroyiannis, Mr. Ivon Mingashang, Mr. Giuseppe Nesi, Ms. Phoebe Okowa, Mr. Hassan Ouazzani Chahdi, Mr. Mario Oyarzábal, Mr. Mārtiņš Paparinskis, Mr. Bimal N. Patel, Mr. August Reinisch, Ms. Penelope Ridings, Mr. Louis Savadogo, Mr. Munkh-Orgil Tsend, Mr. Marcelo Vázquez-Bermúdez and Mr. Hong Thao Nguyen (*ex officio*).

10. At its 3621st meeting, on 10 May 2023, the Commission established an open-ended Working Group on "Succession of States in respect of State responsibility" chaired by Mr. August Reinisch.

11. At its 3638th meeting, on 13 July 2023, the Commission established an open-ended Working Group on "Commentaries submitted for the topic on prevention and repression of piracy and armed robbery at sea" chaired by Ms. Nilüfer Oral.

E. Secretariat

12. Mr. Miguel de Serpa Soares, Under-Secretary-General for Legal Affairs and United Nations Legal Counsel, represented the Secretary-General. Mr. Huw Llewellyn, Director of the Codification Division of the Office of Legal Affairs, acted as Secretary to the Commission and, in the absence of the Legal Counsel, represented the Secretary-General. Mr. Arnold Pronto, Principal Legal Officer, served as Principal Assistant Secretary to the Commission. Ms. Patricia Georget, Mr. Carlos Ivan Fuentes, Ms. Carla Hoe and Ms. Paola Patarroyo, Legal Officers, and Mr. Alexey Bulatov and Ms. Raissa Urquiza, Associate Legal Officers, served as Assistant Secretaries to the Commission.

F. Agenda

13. The Commission adopted an agenda for its seventy-fourth session consisting of the following items:

1. Organization of the work of the session.
2. Succession of States in respect of State responsibility.
3. General principles of law.
4. Sea-level rise in relation to international law.
5. Settlement of disputes to which international organizations are parties.
6. Prevention and repression of piracy and armed robbery at sea.
7. Subsidiary means for the determination of rules of international law.
8. Programme, procedures and working methods of the Commission and its documentation.
9. Date and place of the seventy-fifth session.
10. Cooperation with other bodies.
11. Other business.

Chapter II
Summary of the work of the Commission at its seventy-fourth session

14. With regard to the topic **"General principles of law"**, the Commission received and considered the report of the Drafting Committee (A/CN.4/L.982), following the completion by the Drafting Committee of the first reading of the draft conclusions on the topic. The Commission adopted, on first reading, 11 draft conclusions on general principles of law, together with commentaries thereto. The Commission decided, in accordance with articles 16 to 21 of its statute, to transmit the draft conclusions, through the Secretary-General, to Governments for comments and observations, with the request that such comments and observations be submitted to the Secretary-General by 1 December 2024 (chap. IV).

15. With respect to the topic **"Settlement of disputes to which international organizations are parties"**, the Commission had before it the first report of the Special Rapporteur on the topic (A/CN.4/756), which addressed the scope of the topic and provided an analysis of the subject matter of the topic in light of previous relevant work of the Commission and of other international bodies. The report also addressed certain definitional issues. Following the debate in plenary, the Commission decided to refer draft guidelines 1 and 2, as proposed in the first report, to the Drafting Committee, taking into account the comments and observations made in plenary. Upon consideration of the report of the Drafting Committee (A/CN.4/L.983), the Commission provisionally adopted draft guidelines 1 and 2 and decided to change the title of the topic from "Settlement of international disputes to which international organizations are parties" to "Settlement of disputes to which international organizations are parties" (chap. V).

16. With regard to the topic **"Prevention and repression of piracy and armed robbery at sea"**, the Commission had before it the first report of the Special Rapporteur (A/CN.4/758), which discussed the historical, socioeconomical and legal aspects of the topic; reviewed the national legislation and judicial practice of States concerning the definition of piracy and the implementation of conventional and customary international law; and discussed the future programme of work on the topic. The Commission also had before it a memorandum prepared by the Secretariat providing elements in the previous work of the Commission that could be particularly relevant for its future work on the topic and the views expressed by States; as well as information on resolutions adopted by the Security Council and by the General Assembly relevant to the topic (A/CN.4/757). Following the debate in plenary, the Commission decided to refer draft articles 1, 2 and 3, as contained in the first report of the Special Rapporteur, to the Drafting Committee, taking into account the views expressed in the plenary debate. The Commission considered the report of the Drafting Committee (A/CN.4/L.984) on the topic and provisionally adopted draft articles 1 to 3, which had been provisionally adopted by the Drafting Committee at the present session. An open-ended Working Group under the chairpersonship of Ms. Nilüfer Oral was established to assist the Special Rapporteur in the preparation of the draft commentaries to draft articles 1 to 3. The Working Group held one meeting, on 18 July 2023 (chap. VI).

17. With respect to the topic **"Subsidiary means for the determination of rules of international law"**, the Commission had before it the first report of the Special Rapporteur (A/CN.4/760), as well as a memorandum by the Secretariat providing information on previous work of the Commission that could be of relevance to the future work of the Commission (A/CN.4/759). The first report addressed, *inter alia*, the scope of the topic and the main issues to be addressed in the course of the work of the Commission, the drafting history of Article 38, paragraph 1 (*d*) of the Statute of the International Court of Justice and the previous work of the Commission related to subsidiary means. Following the debate in plenary, the Commission decided to refer draft conclusions 1, 2, 3, 4 and 5, as presented in the first report, to the Drafting Committee, taking into account the comments made in plenary. The Commission received the report of the Drafting Committee on the consolidated text of draft conclusions 1 to 3, provisionally adopted by the Drafting Committee (A/CN.4/L.985), and provisionally adopted draft conclusions 1, 2 and 3, together with commentaries. Furthermore, the Commission took note of draft conclusions 4 and 5,

provisionally adopted by the Drafting Committee at the present session, which was contained in an additional report of the Committee (A/CN.4/L.985/Add.1) (chap. VII).

18. With respect to the topic "**Sea-level rise in relation to international law**", the Commission reconstituted the Study Group on sea-level rise in relation to international law. The Study Group had before it the additional paper to the first issues paper (A/CN.4/761 and Add.1), prepared by two of the Co-Chairs of the Study Group, Mr. Bogdan Aurescu and Ms. Nilüfer Oral, which addressed the following issues and principles: meaning of "legal stability" in relation to sea-level rise, with a focus on baselines and maritime zones; immutability and intangibility of boundaries; fundamental change of circumstances (*rebus sic stantibus*); effects of the potential situation whereby overlapping areas of the exclusive economic zones of opposite coastal States, delimited by bilateral agreement, no longer overlap; effects of the situation whereby an agreed land boundary terminus ends up being located out at sea; principle that "the land dominates the sea"; historic waters, title and rights; equity; permanent sovereignty over natural resources; possible loss or gain of benefits by third States; nautical charts and their relationship to baselines, maritime boundaries and the safety of navigation; and relevance of other sources of law. The Study Group had an exchange of views on the additional paper, with a focus on the preliminary observations prepared by the Co-Chairs. It also held a discussion on the future programme of work on the topic (chap. VIII).

19. With respect to the topic "**Succession of States in respect of State responsibility**", the Commission established a Working Group on the topic, chaired by Mr. August Reinisch, in order to consider the way forward in relation to the topic. Upon receiving the oral report of the Working Group, the Commission took note of the Working Group's recommendations, *inter alia*, that the Commission should not proceed with the appointment of a new Special Rapporteur, and that the Working Group should be re-established at the seventy-fifth session with a view to undertaking further reflection, and making a recommendation, on the way forward for the topic (chap. IX).

20. Concerning "**Other decisions and conclusions of the Commission**", the Commission decided to include the topic "Non-legally binding international agreements" in its programme of work and to appoint Mr. Mathias Forteau as Special Rapporteur (chap. X, sect. B). The Commission re-established a Planning Group to consider its programme, procedures and working methods, which in turn decided to re-establish the Working Group on the long-term programme of work, chaired by Mr. Marcelo Vázquez-Bermúdez, and the Working Group on methods of work, chaired by Mr. Charles Chernor Jalloh (chap. X, sect. D).

21. The Commission decided to hold a seventy-fifth anniversary commemorative event during its seventy-fifth session in Geneva in 2024. The Commission also agreed that during the first part of the seventy-fifth session there should be a solemn meeting of the Commission to which dignitaries, and representatives of the host Government should be invited, and one and a half days of meetings with legal advisers of Ministries of Foreign Affairs dedicated to the work of the Commission. Moreover, Member States, in association with regional organizations, professional associations, academic institutions and members of the Commission concerned, were to be encouraged to convene national or regional meetings, which would be dedicated to the work of the Commission (chap. X, sect. D).

22. The Commission recommended the possible convening of the first part of its annual session in New York in 2026, subject to availability of conference servicing and other resources, and in that regard, it requested the Secretariat to proceed with the necessary administrative and organizational arrangements to facilitate such convening (chap. X, sect. D).

23. Judge Joan E. Donoghue, President of the International Court of Justice, addressed the Commission on 18 July 2023. The Commission continued its traditional exchanges of information with the African Union Commission on International Law; the Asian-African Legal Consultative Organization; the Committee of Legal Advisers on Public International Law of the Council of Europe; and the Inter-American Juridical Committee. Members of the Commission also held an informal exchange of views with the International Committee of the Red Cross on 4 July 2023 (chap. X, sect. F).

24. The Commission decided that its seventy-fifth session would be held in Geneva from 15 April to 31 May and from 1 July to 2 August 2024 (chap. X, sect. E).

Chapter III
Specific issues on which comments would be of particular interest to the Commission

A. Prevention and repression of piracy and armed robbery at sea

25. The Commission considers as still relevant the request for information on the topic "Prevention and repression of piracy and armed robbery at sea" contained in chapter III of the report of its seventy-third session (2022) and would welcome any additional information, by 1 December 2023,[5] concerning:

(*a*) the legislation, case law and practice of States relevant to the topic, including in relation to articles 100 to 107 of the United Nations Convention on the Law of the Sea;

(*b*) the agreements entered into by States under which persons accused of piracy or armed robbery at sea are transferred with a view to prosecution; and

(*c*) the role of international, regional and subregional organizations regarding the prevention and repression of acts of piracy and armed robbery at sea.

B. Subsidiary means for the determination of rules of international law

26. The Commission considers as still relevant the request for information on the topic "Subsidiary means for the determination of rules of international law" contained in chapter III of the report of its seventy-third session (2022) and would also welcome any updates to information already submitted pursuant to such request, by 1 February 2024,[6] concerning:

(*a*) decisions of national courts, legislation and any other relevant practice at the domestic level that draw upon judicial decisions and the teachings of the most highly qualified publicists of the various nations in the process of determination of rules of international law, namely: international conventions, whether general or particular; international custom, as evidence of a general practice accepted as law; and the general principles of law recognized by the community of nations;

(*b*) statements made in international organizations, international conferences and other forums, including pleadings before international courts and tribunals, concerning subsidiary means for the determination of rules of international law.

C. Sea-level rise in relation to international law

27. The Commission would welcome any information that States, international organizations and other relevant entities could provide on their practice, as well as other pertinent information concerning sea-level rise in relation to international law, and reiterates its requests made in chapter III of its reports on the work of its seventy-first (2019),[7] seventy-second (2021)[8] and seventy-third (2022)[9] sessions.

28. At the seventy-fifth session (2024), the Study Group will focus on the subject of sea-level rise in relation to statehood and protection of persons affected by sea-level rise. In this connection, the Commission reiterates that it would appreciate receiving the following information, or any updates to information already submitted, by 1 December 2023:

---

[5] *Official Records of the General Assembly, Seventy-seventh Session, Supplement No. 10* (A/77/10), para. 30.

[6] *Ibid.*, para. 29.

[7] *Ibid.*, *Seventy-fourth Session, Supplement No. 10* (A/74/10), paras. 31–33.

[8] *Ibid.*, *Seventy-sixth Session, Supplement No. 10* (A/76/10), para. 26.

[9] *Ibid.*, *Seventy-seventh Session, Supplement No. 10* (A/77/10), para. 28.

(*a*) in relation to the subtopic of statehood, information on the practice of States, international organizations and other relevant entities, and other pertinent information concerning:

(i) appraisals and/or practice on the requirements for the configuration of a State as a subject of international law and for the continuance of its existence in the context of the phenomenon of sea-level rise;

(ii) appraisals and/or practice regarding the nature of the territory of a State, including therein the land surface and the jurisdictional maritime zones, particularly in the context of the sea-level rise;

(iii) practice related to the protection of the rights of peoples and communities, as well as to the preservation of their identity, that may contribute with elements or be considered by analogy when addressing the phenomenon of sea-level rise;

(iv) practice regarding measures of a different nature adopted by States in relation to sea-level rise in order to provide for their conservation and with respect to international cooperation on the subject;

(*b*) in relation to the subtopic on protection of persons affected by sea-level rise, information on the practice of States, international organizations and other relevant entities, as well as other pertinent information concerning:

(i) measures relating to risk reduction specific to the mitigation of the adverse impacts of sea-level rise;

(ii) human rights implications of the adverse impacts of sea-level rise;

(iii) regulation of the displacement of persons affected by sea-level rise;

(iv) prevention of statelessness arising from the displacement of persons affected by sea-level rise;

(v) international cooperation regarding humanitarian assistance to persons affected by sea-level rise.

D. Immunity of State officials from foreign criminal jurisdiction

29. The Commission recalls that it completed the first reading of the draft articles on the topic “Immunity of State officials from foreign criminal jurisdiction” in 2022 and had decided, in accordance with articles 16 to 21 of its statute, to transmit the draft articles, through the Secretary-General, to Governments for comments and observations, with the request that such comments and observations be submitted to the Secretary-General by 1 December 2023.[10] Bearing in mind the importance of the topic for States in international relations, the Commission reiterates the importance it attaches to receiving such comments and observations from as many Governments as possible.

[10] *Ibid.*, chap. VI.

Chapter IV
General principles of law

A. Introduction

30. The Commission, at its seventieth session (2018), decided to include the topic "General principles of law" in its programme of work and appointed Mr. Marcelo Vázquez-Bermúdez as Special Rapporteur. The General Assembly, in paragraph 7 of its resolution 73/265 of 22 December 2018, subsequently took note of the decision of the Commission to include the topic in its programme of work.

31. At its seventy-first session (2019), the Commission considered the Special Rapporteur's first report (A/CN.4/732), which set out his approach to the topic's scope and outcome, as well as the main issues to be addressed in the course of the Commission's work. Following the debate in plenary, the Commission decided to refer draft conclusions 1 to 3, as contained in the Special Rapporteur's first report, to the Drafting Committee. The Commission subsequently took note of the interim report of the Chair of the Drafting Committee regarding draft conclusion 1, provisionally adopted by the Committee in English only, which was presented to the Commission for information.[11]

32. Also at its seventy-first session, the Commission requested the Secretariat to prepare a memorandum surveying the case law of inter-State arbitral tribunals and international criminal courts and tribunals of a universal character, as well as treaties, which would be particularly relevant for its future work on the topic.

33. At its seventy-second session (2021), the Commission considered the Special Rapporteur's second report (A/CN.4/741 and Corr.1), in which the Special Rapporteur addressed the identification of general principles of law in the sense of Article 38, paragraph 1 (*c*), of the Statute of the International Court of Justice. The Commission also had before it the memorandum it had requested from the Secretariat (A/CN.4/742) at its seventy-first session. Following the debate in plenary, the Commission decided to refer draft conclusions 4 to 9, as presented in the second report, to the Drafting Committee. The Commission provisionally adopted draft conclusions 1, 2 and 4, together with commentaries, and took note of draft conclusion 5, as contained in the report of the Drafting Committee.[12]

34. At the seventy-third session (2022), the Commission considered the Special Rapporteur's third report (A/CN.4/753), in which the Special Rapporteur discussed the issue of transposition, general principles of law formed within the international legal system, and the functions of general principles of law and their relationship with other sources of international law. Following the debate in plenary, the Commission decided to refer draft conclusions 10 to 14, as presented in the Special Rapporteur's third report, to the Drafting Committee. The Commission provisionally adopted draft conclusions 3, 5 and 7, together with commentaries, and took note of draft conclusions 6, 8, 9, 10 and 11, as contained in the report of the Drafting Committee.[13]

B. Consideration of the topic at the present session

35. The Commission had no new report of the Special Rapporteur at the present session. The Drafting Committee finalized its consideration of the draft conclusions referred to it

---

[11] The interim report of the Chair of the Drafting Committee is available under the analytical guide to the work of the International Law Commission: http://legal.un.org/ilc/guide/1_15.shtml.

[12] *Official Records of the General Assembly, Seventy-sixth Session, Supplement No. 10* (A/76/10), paras. 169–172 and 238–239. See also A/CN.4/L.955 and Add.1.

[13] *Ibid., Seventy-seventh Session, Supplement No. 10* (A/77/10), paras. 94–149. See also A/CN.4/L.971.

previously by the Commission, and which had already been provisionally adopted by the Committee.[14]

36. At its 3628th meeting, on 19 May 2023, the Commission received and considered the report of the Drafting Committee (A/CN.4/L.982), and adopted the draft conclusions on general principles of law on first reading (see sect. C.1 below).

37. At its 3643rd to 3646th meetings, from 24 to 26 July 2023, the Commission adopted the commentaries to the aforementioned draft conclusions (see sect. C.2 below).

38. At its 3646th meeting, on 26 July 2023, the Commission decided, in accordance with articles 16 to 21 of its statute, to transmit the draft conclusions (see sect. C below), through the Secretary-General, to Governments for comments and observations, with the request that such comments and observations be submitted to the Secretary-General by 1 December 2024.

39. At its 3646th meeting, on 26 July 2023, the Commission expressed its deep appreciation for the outstanding contribution of the Special Rapporteur, Mr. Marcelo Vázquez-Bermúdez, which had enabled the Commission to bring to a successful conclusion its first reading of the draft conclusions on general principles of law.

C. Text of the draft conclusions on general principles of law adopted by the Commission on first reading

1. Text of the draft conclusions

40. The text of the draft conclusions adopted by the Commission on first reading is reproduced below.

General principles of law

Conclusion 1
Scope

The present draft conclusions concern general principles of law as a source of international law.

Conclusion 2
Recognition

For a general principle of law to exist, it must be recognized by the community of nations.

Conclusion 3
Categories of general principles of law

General principles of law comprise those:

(a) that are derived from national legal systems;

(b) that may be formed within the international legal system.

Conclusion 4
Identification of general principles of law derived from national legal systems

To determine the existence and content of a general principle of law derived from national legal systems, it is necessary to ascertain:

(a) the existence of a principle common to the various legal systems of the world; and

(b) its transposition to the international legal system.

[14] At the seventy-third session, the Drafting Committee provisionally adopted the consolidated text of draft conclusions 1 to 11, as contained in the report of the Committee for that session (A/CN.4/L.971).

Conclusion 5
Determination of the existence of a principle common to the various legal systems of the world

1. To determine the existence of a principle common to the various legal systems of the world, a comparative analysis of national legal systems is required.

2. The comparative analysis must be wide and representative, including the different regions of the world.

3. The comparative analysis includes an assessment of national laws and decisions of national courts, and other relevant materials.

Conclusion 6
Determination of transposition to the international legal system

A principle common to the various legal systems of the world may be transposed to the international legal system insofar as it is compatible with that system.

Conclusion 7
Identification of general principles of law formed within the international legal system

1. To determine the existence and content of a general principle of law that may be formed within the international legal system, it is necessary to ascertain that the community of nations has recognized the principle as intrinsic to the international legal system.

2. Paragraph 1 is without prejudice to the question of the possible existence of other general principles of law formed within the international legal system.

Conclusion 8
Decisions of courts and tribunals

1. Decisions of international courts and tribunals, in particular of the International Court of Justice, concerning the existence and content of general principles of law are a subsidiary means for the determination of such principles.

2. Regard may be had, as appropriate, to decisions of national courts concerning the existence and content of general principles of law, as a subsidiary means for the determination of such principles.

Conclusion 9
Teachings

Teachings of the most highly qualified publicists of the various nations may serve as a subsidiary means for the determination of general principles of law.

Conclusion 10
Functions of general principles of law

1. General principles of law are mainly resorted to when other rules of international law do not resolve a particular issue in whole or in part.

2. General principles of law contribute to the coherence of the international legal system. They may serve, *inter alia*:

(a) to interpret and complement other rules of international law;

(b) as a basis for primary rights and obligations, as well as a basis for secondary and procedural rules.

Conclusion 11
Relationship between general principles of law and treaties and customary international law

1. General principles of law, as a source of international law, are not in a hierarchical relationship with treaties and customary international law.

2. A general principle of law may exist in parallel with a rule of the same or similar content in a treaty or customary international law.

3. Any conflict between a general principle of law and a rule in a treaty or customary international law is to be resolved by applying the generally accepted techniques of interpretation and conflict resolution in international law.

2. Text of the draft conclusions and commentaries thereto

41. The text of the draft conclusions and commentaries thereto adopted by the Commission on first reading at its seventy-fourth session is reproduced below.

General principles of law

Conclusion 1
Scope

The present draft conclusions concern general principles of law as a source of international law.

Commentary

(1) Draft conclusion 1 is introductory in nature. It provides that the draft conclusions concern general principles of law as a source of international law. The term "general principles of law" is used throughout the draft conclusions to refer to "the general principles of law recognized by civilized nations" listed in Article 38, paragraph 1 (*c*), of the Statute of International Court of Justice, analysed in the light of the practice of States, the jurisprudence of courts and tribunals, and teachings.[15]

(2) Draft conclusion 1 reaffirms that general principles of law constitute one of the sources of international law. The legal nature of general principles of law as such is confirmed by their inclusion in Article 38, paragraph 1 (*c*), of the Statute of the International Court of Justice, together with treaties and customary international law, as part of the "international law" that shall be applied by the Court to decide the disputes submitted to it. The predecessor of that provision, Article 38, paragraph 3, of the Statute of the Permanent Court of International Justice, was the result of lengthy discussions in 1920 within the League of Nations, and in particular the Advisory Committee of Jurists established by the Council of the League, which sought to codify the practice that existed prior to the adoption of the Statute. Since then, general principles of law as a source of international law have been referred to in State practice, including in bilateral and multilateral treaties, as well as in the decisions of different courts and tribunals.[16]

(3) The term "source of international law" refers to the legal process and form through which a general principle of law comes into existence. The draft conclusions aim to clarify the scope of general principles of law, the method for their identification, and their functions and relationship with other sources of international law.

Conclusion 2
Recognition

For a general principle of law to exist, it must be recognized by the community of nations.

---

[15] Taking into consideration recent practice of States and jurisprudence, the French and Spanish texts of draft conclusion 1 refer, respectively, to "*principes généraux du droit*" and "*principios generales del derecho*". It was understood that the use of "*du droit*" and "*del derecho*" did not change, nor imply a change to, the substance of Article 38, paragraph 1 (*c*), of the Statute of the International Court of Justice.

[16] See, for example, A/CN.4/732 (first report by the Special Rapporteur) and A/CN.4/742 (memorandum by the Secretariat).

Commentary

(1) Draft conclusion 2 reaffirms a basic element of Article 38, paragraph 1 (*c*), of the Statute of the International Court of Justice, namely, that for a general principle of law to exist, it must be "recognized" by the community of nations.

(2) Recognition features widely in the practice of States, the jurisprudence of courts and tribunals and in teachings as the essential condition for the emergence of a general principle of law. This means that, to determine whether a general principle of law exists at a given point in time, it is necessary to examine all the available evidence showing that its recognition has taken place. The specific criteria for this determination are objective and are developed in subsequent draft conclusions.

(3) Draft conclusion 2 employs the term "community of nations" as a substitute for the term "civilized nations" found in Article 38, paragraph 1 (*c*), of the Statute of the International Court of Justice, because the latter term is anachronistic.[17] The term "community of nations" is found in article 15, paragraph 2, of the International Covenant on Civil and Political Rights, a treaty to which 173 States are parties and which is thus widely accepted.[18] The term used in the authentic languages of the Covenant is replicated in the different language versions of draft conclusion 2. For example, "l'ensemble des nations" in French and "communidad internacional" in Spanish. By employing this formulation, the draft conclusion aims to stress that all nations participate equally, without any kind of distinction, in the formation of general principles of law, in accordance with the principle of sovereign equality set out in Article 2, paragraph 1, of the Charter of the United Nations.

(4) The use of the term "community of nations" is not intended to modify the scope or content of Article 38, paragraph 1 (*c*), of the Statute of the International Court of Justice. In particular, the term does not seek to suggest that there is a need for a unified or collective recognition of a general principle of law, nor does it suggest that general principles of law can only arise within the international legal system. Furthermore, the term "community of nations" should not be confused with the term "international community of States as a whole" found in article 53 of the Vienna Convention on the Law of Treaties,[19] relating to peremptory norms of general international law (*jus cogens*).

(5) The use of the term "community of nations" does not preclude that, in certain circumstances, international organizations may also contribute to the formation of general principles of law.

Conclusion 3
Categories of general principles of law

General principles of law comprise those:

(a) that are derived from national legal systems;

(b) that may be formed within the international legal system.

Commentary

(1) Draft conclusion 3 addresses the two categories of general principles of law in the sense of Article 38, paragraph 1 (*c*), of the Statute of the International Court of Justice. The term "categories" is employed to indicate two groups of general principles of law in light of their origins and thus the process through which they may emerge. In contrast with subparagraph (*a*) of the draft conclusion, which uses the phrase "are derived from",

---

[17] Other terms considered included "States", "community of States", "the international community", "nations", "nation States" and "nations as a whole".

[18] The provision reads: "Nothing in this article shall prejudice the trial and punishment of any person for any act or omission which, at the time when it was committed, was criminal according to the general principles of law recognized by the community of nations." International Covenant on Civil and Political Rights (New York, 16 December 1966), United Nations, *Treaty Series*, vol. 999, No. 14668, p. 171. See United Nations, *Status of Multilateral Treaties*, chap. IV.4.

[19] Vienna Convention on the Law of Treaties (Vienna, 23 May 1969), United Nations, *Treaty Series*, vol. 1155, No. 18232, p. 331.

subparagraph (*b*) uses the phrase "may be formed". The phrase "may be formed" was considered appropriate to introduce a degree of flexibility to the provision, acknowledging that there is a debate as to whether a second category of general principles of law exists.

(2) Subparagraph (*a*) of the draft conclusion refers to the general principles of law that are derived from national legal systems. That general principles of law in the sense of Article 38, paragraph 1 (*c*), of the Statute of the International Court of Justice include those derived from national legal systems is established in the jurisprudence of courts and tribunals[20] and teachings,[21] and is confirmed by the *travaux préparatoires* of the Statute.[22] Draft conclusions 4 to 6 deal in greater detail with the methodology for the identification of these general principles of law.

(3) Subparagraph (*b*) of draft conclusion 3 refers to the general principles of law that may be formed within the international legal system. The existence of this category of general principles of law in the sense of Article 38, paragraph 1 (*c*), of the Statute of the International Court of Justice, appears to find support in the jurisprudence of courts and tribunals[23] and

---

20 See, for example, the *Fabiani* case (1896) (in H. La Fontaine, *Pasicrisie internationale 1794–1900: Histoire documentaire des arbitrages internationaux* (Berlin, Stämpfli, 1902), p. 356); *Affaire de l'indemnité russe (Russie, Turquie)*, Award of 11 November 1912, *Reports of International Arbitral Awards* (UNRIAA), vol. XI, pp. 421–447, at p. 445; International Court of Justice, *Corfu Channel case, Judgment of 9 April 1949: I.C.J. Reports 1949*, p. 4, at p. 18; International Court of Justice, *South West Africa, Second Phase, Judgment, I.C.J. Reports 1966*, p. 6, para. 88; *Argentine-Chile Frontier Case*, Award of 9 December 1966, UNRIAA, vol. XVI, pp. 109–182, at p. 164; International Court of Justice, *Barcelona Traction, Light and Power Company, Limited, Judgment, I.C.J. Reports 1970*, p. 3, at p. 38, para. 50; Iran-United States Claims Tribunal, *Sea-Land Service, Inc. v. Iran*, Award No. 135-33-1, 20 June 1984, *Iran-United States Claims Tribunal Reports* (IUSCTR), vol. 6, pp. 149 *et seq.*, at p. 168; Iran-United States Claims Tribunal, *Questech, Inc. v. Iran*, Award No. 191-59-1, 25 September 1985, IUSCTR, vol. 9, pp. 107 *et seq.*, at p. 122; Inter-American Court of Human Rights, *Aloeboetoe* et al. *v. Suriname*, Judgment (Reparations and Costs), 10 September 1993, Series C, No. 15, para. 50; International Criminal Tribunal for the Former Yugoslavia, *Prosecutor v. Duško Tadić*, No. IT-94-1-A, Judgment, 15 July 1999, Appeals Chamber, para. 225; *Prosecutor v. Zejnil Delalić* et al., No. IT-96-21-A, Judgment, 20 February 2001, Appeals Chamber, para. 179; World Trade Organization, Appellate Body, *United States – Tax Treatment for "Foreign Sales Corporations"*, Appellate Body Report, 14 January 2002 (WT/DS108/AB/RW), paras. 142–143; Germany, Constitutional Court, Judgment, 4 September 2004 (2 BvR 1475/07), para. 20; Permanent Court of Arbitration, *Award in the Arbitration regarding the delimitation of the Abyei Area between the Government of Sudan and the Sudan People's Liberation Movement/Army*, Case No. 2008-7, Award, 22 July 2009, UNRIAA, vol. XXX, pp. 145–416, at p. 299, para. 401; International Centre for Settlement of Investment Disputes, *El Paso Energy International Company v. The Argentine Republic*, Case No. ARB/03/15, Award, 31 October 2011, para. 622; Philippines, Supreme Court, *Mary Grace Natividad S. Poe-Llamanzares v. COMELEC*, Decision of 8 March 2016 (G.R. No. 221697; G.R. Nos. 221698-700), pp. 19 and 21.

21 See, for example, B. Cheng, *General Principles of Law as Applied by International Courts and Tribunals* (Cambridge, Cambridge University Press, 1953/2006), p. 25; G. Abi-Saab, "Cours général de droit international public", in *Collected Courses of the Hague Academy of International Law*, vol. 207 (1987), pp. 188–189; J. A. Barberis, "Los Principios Generales de Derecho como Fuente del Derecho Internacional", *Revista IIDH*, vol. 14 (1991), pp. 11–41, at pp. 30–31; R. Jennings and A. Watts, *Oppenheim's International Law*, vol. I, 9th ed. (Longman, 1996), pp. 36–37; S. Yee, "Article 38 of the ICJ Statute and applicable law: selected issues in recent cases", *Journal of International Dispute Settlement*, vol. 7 (2016), pp. 472–498, at p. 487; P. Palchetti, "The role of general principles in promoting the development of customary international rules", in M. Andenas *et al.* (eds.), *General Principles and the Coherence of International Law* (Leiden, Brill, 2019), pp. 47–59, at p. 48; A. Pellet and D. Müller, "Article 38", in A. Zimmermann *et al.* (eds.), *The Statute of the International Court of Justice: A Commentary*, 3rd ed. (Oxford, Oxford University Press, 2019), p. 925.

22 Permanent Court of International Justice, Advisory Committee of Jurists, *Procès-verbaux of the Proceedings of the Committee, June 16th – July 24th, 1920* (The Hague, Van Langenhuysen Bros., 1920), pp. 331–336.

23 See, for example, International Court of Justice, *Corfu Channel case* (see footnote 20 above), p. 22; International Court of Justice, *Reservations to the Convention on Genocide, Advisory Opinion, I.C.J. Reports 1951*, p. 15, at p. 23; International Court of Justice, *Case of the monetary gold removed from Rome in 1943 (Preliminary Question), Judgment of June 15th, 1954, I.C.J. Reports 1954*, p. 19, at p. 32; International Court of Justice, *Frontier Dispute, Judgment, I.C.J. Reports 1986*, p. 554, at

teachings.[24] Some members, however, consider that Article 38, paragraph 1 (*c*), does not encompass a second category of general principles of law, or at least remain sceptical of its existence as an autonomous source of international law, and note that the doctrine is divided on this issue.[25] Further aspects about general principles of law formed within the international legal system are explained in the commentary to draft conclusion 7.

Conclusion 4
Identification of general principles of law derived from national legal systems

To determine the existence and content of a general principle of law derived from national legal systems, it is necessary to ascertain:

(a) the existence of a principle common to the various legal systems of the world; and

(b) its transposition to the international legal system.

Commentary

(1) Draft conclusion 4 addresses the requirements for the identification of general principles of law derived from national legal systems. It provides that, to determine the existence and content of a general principle of law, it is necessary to ascertain: (*a*) the

p 565, paras. 20–21; International Criminal Tribunal for the Former Yugoslavia, *Prosecutor v. Anto Furundžija*, No. IT-95-17/1-T, Judgment, Trial Chamber, 10 December 1998 (IT-95-17/1-T), para. 183; International Criminal Tribunal for the Former Yugoslavia, *Prosecutor v. Zoran Kupreškić* et al., No. IT-95-16-T, Judgment, Trial Chamber, 14 January 2000, para. 738.

[24] See, for example, D. Anzilotti, *Cours de droit international* (Editions Panthéon-Assas, 1929/1999), p. 117; L. Siorat, *Le problème des lacunes en droit International: Contribution à l'étude des sources du droit et de la fonction judiciaire* (Paris, Librairie générale de droit et de jurisprudence, 1958), p. 286; P. Reuter, *Principes de droit international public, Collected Courses of the Hague Academy of International Law*, vol. 103 (1961), pp. 425–656, at pp. 466–467; J.G. Lammers, "General principles of law recognized by civilized nations", in F. Kalshoven, P.J. Kuyper and J.G. Lammers (eds.), *Essays on the Development of the International Legal Order in Memory of Haro F. van Panhuys* (Alphen aa den Rijn, Sijthoff & Noordhoff, 1980), pp. 53–75, at p. 67; O. Schachter, "International law in theory and practice: general course in public international law", in *Collected Courses of the Hague Academy of International Law*, vol. 178 (1982), pp. 9–396, at pp. 75, 79–80; R. Kolb, *La bonne foi en droit international public: contribution à l'étude des principes généraux de droit* (Geneva/Paris, Presse Universitaire de France, 2000), pp. 56–57; R. Wolfrum, "General international law (principles, rules, and standards)", in R. Wolfrum (ed.), *Max Planck Encyclopedia of International Law*, vol. IV (entry updated in 2010; Oxford, Oxford University Press, 2012), para. 28; M. Diez de Velasco Vallejo, *Instituciones de Derecho Internacional Público*, 18th ed. (Madrid, Tecnos, 2013), pp. 126–127; A. A. Cançado Trindade, *International Law for Humankind: Towards a New* Jus Gentium, 3rd rev. ed. (Leiden/Boston, Martinus Nijhoff, 2013), pp. 55–86; B. I. Bonafé and P. Palchetti, "Relying on general principles of law", in C. Brölmann and Y. Radi (eds.), *Research Handbook on the Theory and Practice of International Lawmaking* (Cheltenham, Edward Edgar Publishing, 2016), pp. 160–176, at p. 162; R. Yotova, "Challenges in the identification of the 'general principles of law recognized by civilized nations': the approach of the International Court", *Canadian Journal of Comparative and Contemporary Law*, vol. 3. (2017), pp. 269–325, at p. 275, and 291–310; M. Fitzmaurice, "The history of Article 38 of the Statute of the International Court of Justice: the journey from the past to the present", in S. Besson, J. d'Aspremont and S. Knuchel (eds.), *The Oxford Handbook of the Sources of International Law* (Oxford, Oxford University Press, 2017), p. 193; A. Yusuf, "Concluding remarks", in M. Andenas *et al.* (eds.), *General Principles and the Coherence of International Law* (footnote 21 above), p. 450; P. Dumberry, *A Guide to General Principles of Law in International Investment Arbitration* (Oxford, Oxford University Press, 2020), pp. 35–42; F. Francioni, "Custom and general principles of international cultural heritage law", in F. Francioni and A. F. Vrdoljak (eds.), *The Oxford Handbook of International Cultural Heritage Law* (Oxford, Oxford University Press, 2020), pp. 531–550, at pp. 541–544; G. Gaja, "General principles of law", in *Max Planck Encyclopedia of Public International Law* (2020), paras. 17–20; G. Boas, *Public International Law: Contemporary Principles*, 2nd ed. (Cheltenham, Edward Elgar, 2023), pp. 125–126.

[25] Some authors consider that general principles of law are limited to those derived from national legal systems.

existence of a principle common to the various legal systems of the world; and (*b*) the transposition of that principle to the international legal system.

(2) This two-step analysis is widely accepted in practice and the literature and is aimed at demonstrating that a general principle of law has been "recognized" in the sense of Article 38, paragraph 1 (*c*), of the Statute of the International Court of Justice. It is an objective method to be applied by all those called upon to determine whether a given general principle of law exists at a specific point in time and what the content of that general principle of law is.

(3) Subparagraph (*a*) addresses the first requirement for identification, that is, the ascertainment of the existence of a principle common to the various legal systems of the world. This exercise, which is essentially inductive, is necessary to show that a legal principle has been generally recognized by the community of nations. The use of the term "the various legal systems of the world" is aimed at highlighting the requirement that a principle must be found in legal systems of the world generally. It is an inclusive and broad term, covering the variety and diversity of national legal systems of the world. This requirement is further developed in draft conclusion 5.

(4) Subparagraph (*b*) addresses the second requirement for identification, that is, the ascertainment of the transposition of the principle common to the various legal systems of the world to the international legal system. This requirement, which is further elaborated on in draft conclusion 6, is necessary to show that a principle is not only recognized by the community of nations in national legal systems, but that it is also recognized as applicable within the international legal system.

(5) Subparagraph (*b*) employs the term "transposition", understood as the process of determining whether, to what extent and how a principle common to the various legal systems can be applied in the international legal system. The use of this term is not intended to suggest that a formal or express act of transposition is required.

(6) The term "transposition" was preferred to "transposability", which is sometimes used in this context. Transposition necessarily encompasses transposability; the latter term refers to whether or not a principle identified through the process indicated in subparagraph (*a*) can be applied in the international legal system, but does not cover the whole process of ascertainment of transposition.

(7) Owing to the differences between the international legal system and national legal systems, a principle or some elements of a principle identified through the process indicated in subparagraph (*a*) may not be suitable to be applied in the international legal system. Therefore, "transposition" encompasses the possibility that the content of the general principle of law identified through this two-step analysis may not be identical to the principle found in the various national legal systems.

Conclusion 5
Determination of the existence of a principle common to the various legal systems of the world

1. To determine the existence of a principle common to the various legal systems of the world, a comparative analysis of national legal systems is required.

2. The comparative analysis must be wide and representative, including the different regions of the world.

3. The comparative analysis includes an assessment of national laws and decisions of national courts, and other relevant materials.

Commentary

(1) Draft conclusion 5 addresses the first step of the two-step methodology for the identification of general principles of law derived from national legal systems set out in draft conclusion 4, that is, the determination of the existence of a principle common to the various legal systems of the world. Paragraph 1 of the draft conclusion provides that, to determine the existence of such a principle, a comparative analysis is required. Paragraph 2 describes

the comparative analysis by indicating that the latter must be wide and representative, including the different regions of the world. Paragraph 3 explains which materials are relevant for the purposes of this methodology.

(2) Paragraph 1 of draft conclusion 5 states that a "comparative analysis of national legal systems" is required to determine the existence of a principle common to the various legal systems of the world. This formulation is based on a general approach that is found in practice and in the literature, whereby national legal systems are assessed and compared in order to establish that a legal principle is common to them. The "comparative analysis" referred to in the draft conclusion does not require that particular methodologies that exist in the field of comparative law be employed. While such methodologies may, when appropriate, provide some guidance, a degree of flexibility is generally maintained in practice. What is relevant for the purposes of draft conclusion 5 is that a common denominator is found across national legal systems.[26]

(3) What is meant by a legal principle "common" to the various legal systems of the world is not specified in draft conclusion 5. The Commission considered that, since the content and scope of general principles of law derived from national legal systems may vary, it was appropriate not to be overly prescriptive in this regard, thus allowing for a case-by-case analysis. In many cases, the result of the comparative analysis may be the determination of the existence of a legal principle of a general and abstract character.[27] In other cases, however, the comparative analysis can lead to the ascertainment of legal principles with a more concrete or specific character.[28]

(4) The second paragraph of draft conclusion 5 indicates that the comparative analysis for the determination of the existence of a principle common to the various legal systems of the world must be "wide and representative, including the different regions of the world". This description is aimed at clarifying that, while it is not necessary to assess every single legal system of the world to identify a general principle of law, the comparative analysis must nonetheless be sufficiently comprehensive to take into account the legal systems of States in accordance with the principle of sovereign equality of States. The term "different regions of the world" was included to emphasize that it does not suffice to show that a legal principle exists in legal systems representing certain legal families (such as civil law, common law and Islamic law), but that it is also necessary to show that the principle has been recognized widely in the various regions of the world[29] or, as the International Court of Justice indicated

[26] See, for example, International Criminal Tribunal for the Former Yugoslavia, *Furundžija* (footnote 23 above), para. 178; and *Prosecutor v. Dragoljub Kunarac, Radomir Kunac and Zoran Vuković*, Nos. IT-96-23-T & IT-96-23/1-T, Judgment, Trial Chamber, 22 February 2001, para. 439.

[27] A general principle of law that is often referred to in practice and in the literature, and which may be considered to be of a general and abstract character, is the principle of good faith.

[28] Examples of general principles of law that have been invoked or applied in practice, and which may be considered to be of a more specific character (because they present, for instance, precise conditions for their application), include the principles of *res judicata* and *lis pendens*, and the right to lawyer-client confidentiality. See, respectively, International Court of Justice, *Question of the Delimitation of the Continental Shelf between Nicaragua and Colombia beyond 200 Nautical Miles from the Nicaraguan Coast (Nicaragua v. Colombia), Preliminary Objections, Judgment, I.C.J. Reports 2016*, p. 100, at pp. 125–126, paras. 58–61; Permanent Court of International Justice, *Certain German Interests in Polish Upper Silesia, Judgment*, 25 August 1925, *P.C.I.J. Series A*, No. 6, pp. 5 *et seq*., at p. 20; International Court of Justice, *Questions relating to the Seizure and Detention of Certain Documents and Data (Timor-Leste v. Australia), Provisional Measures, Order of 3 March 2014, I.C.J. Reports 2014*, p. 147, at pp. 152–153, paras. 24–28.

[29] Examples of State practice where a wide and representative comparative analysis may be considered to have been conducted include International Court of Justice, *Case concerning Right of Passage over Indian Territory (Merits), Judgment of 12 April 1960: I.C.J. Reports 1960*, p. 6, Observations and Submissions of Portugal on the Preliminary Objections of India, annex 20, pp. 714–752, and Reply of Portugal, annex 194, pp. 858–861 (including the legal systems of Argentina, Australia, Austria, Belgium, Bolivia (Plurinational State of), Brazil, Bulgaria, Canada, Chile, China, Colombia, Costa Rica, Cuba, Denmark, Dominican Republic, Ecuador, Egypt, El Salvador, France, Germany, Ghana, Greece, Guatemala, Haiti, Honduras, India, Indonesia, Ireland, Italy, Japan, Mexico, Myanmar, Netherlands, New Zealand, Nicaragua, Norway, Pakistan, Panama, Paraguay, Peru, Philippines, Poland, Portugal, Republic of Korea, Saudi Arabia, South Africa, Spain, Sri Lanka, Sweden,

in the *Barcelona Traction* case, that a principle has been "generally accepted by municipal legal systems".[30]

(5) Paragraph 3 of draft conclusion 5 provides additional guidance by listing, in a non-exhaustive manner, the sources that may be relied upon to carry out the comparative analysis of national legal systems. The terms "national laws" and "decisions of national courts" are to be understood in a broad way, covering the whole range of materials in national legal

Switzerland, Türkiye, United States of America, Uruguay, Venezuela (Bolivarian Republic of), Yemen and Zambia, and Czechoslovakia and the Soviet Union); International Court of Justice, *Certain Phosphate Lands in Nauru (Nauru v. Australia), Preliminary Objections, Judgment, I.C.J. Reports 1992*, p. 240, Memorial of Nauru, appendix 3 (including the legal systems of Argentina, Australia, Bangladesh, Belgium, Canada, Chile, China, Colombia, Cyprus, Denmark, Ethiopia, Finland, France, Germany, Ghana, Greece, Hungary, India, Ireland, Italy, Japan, Liechtenstein, Mexico, Netherlands, New Zealand, Nigeria, Pakistan, Romania, Senegal, South Africa, Spain, Sri Lanka, Sweden, Switzerland, the United Kingdom and the United States); International Court of Justice, *Questions relating to the Seizure and Detention of Certain Documents and Data (Timor-Leste v. Australia)* (see footnote 28 above), Memorial of Timor-Leste, annexes 22 to 24 (including the legal systems of Australia, Austria, Belgium, Brazil, Bulgaria, China, Cyprus, Czech Republic, Denmark, Estonia, Finland, France, Germany, Greece, Hungary, Indonesia, Ireland, Italy, Japan, Latvia, Lithuania, Luxembourg, Malta, Mexico, Netherlands, New Zealand, Norway, Poland, Portugal, Republic of Korea, Romania, Russian Federation, Saudi Arabia, Singapore, South Africa, Slovakia, Slovenia, Spain, Sweden, Switzerland, Thailand, Türkiye, United Kingdom and the United States, and the European Union, and Hong Kong, China) and Counter-Memorial of Australia, annex 51 (covering the legal systems of Australia, Belgium, Denmark, France, Germany, India, Indonesia, Mexico, Morocco, New Zealand, Russian Federation, Slovakia, Switzerland, Timor-Leste, Uganda, United Kingdom and United States of America). Similar examples are found in the case law. See, for example, International Criminal Tribunal for the Former Yugoslavia, *Delalić*, Appeals Chamber (see footnote 20 above), paras. 584–589 (Australia, Bahamas, Barbados, Croatia, Germany, Italy, Japan, Russian Federation, Singapore, South Africa, Türkiye, United States, England, Scotland, and former Yugoslavia, and Hong Kong, China); International Criminal Tribunal for the Former Yugoslavia, *Prosecutor v. Pavle Strugar*, No. IT-01-42-A, Judgment, Appeals Chamber, 17 July 2008, paras. 52–54 (Australia, Austria, Belgium, Bosnia and Herzegovina, Canada, Chile, Croatia, Germany, India, Japan, Malaysia, Montenegro, Netherlands, Republic of Korea, Russian Federation, Serbia, United Kingdom and United States); International Criminal Tribunal for the Former Yugoslavia, *Prosecutor v. Dražen Erdemović*, Judgment, Appeals Chamber, Case No. IT-96-22-A, Judgment, 7 October 1997, para. 19, referring to the Joint Separate Opinion of Judge McDonald and Judge Vohrah, paras. 59–65 (Australia, Belgium, Canada, Chile, China, Ethiopia, Finland, France, Germany, India, Italy, Japan, Malaysia, Mexico, Morocco, Netherlands, Nicaragua, Nigeria, Norway, Panama, Poland, Somalia, South Africa, Spain, Sweden, Venezuela (Bolivarian Republic of), and England, and former Yugoslavia); *Furundžija* (see footnote 23 above), para. 180 (Argentina, Austria, Bosnia and Herzegovina, Chile, China, France, Germany, India, Italy, Japan, Netherlands, Pakistan, Uganda, Zambia, and England and Wales, former Yugoslavia, and New South Wales (Australia)); *Kunarac* (see footnote 26 above), paras. 437–460 (Argentina, Australia, Austria, Bangladesh, Belgium, Bosnia and Herzegovina, Brazil, Canada, China, Costa Rica, Denmark, Estonia, Finland, France, Germany, India, Italy, Japan, New Zealand, Norway, Philippines, Portugal, Republic of Korea, Sierra Leone, South Africa, Spain, Sweden, Switzerland, Uruguay, United Kingdom, United States and Zambia).

[30] *Barcelona Traction* (see footnote 20 above), p. 38, para. 50. See also *Mary Grace Natividad S. Poe-Llamanzares v. COMELEC* (footnote 20 above), pp. 19 and 21; *El Paso Energy International Company v. The Argentine Republic* (footnote 20 above), para. 622; International Court of Justice, *Ahmadou Sadio Diallo (Republic of Guinea v. Democratic Republic of the Congo), Merits, Judgment, I.C.J. Reports 2010*, p. 639, at p. 675, para. 104; *Abyei Area* (footnote 20 above), p. 299, para. 401; Germany, Constitutional Court, Judgment, 4 September 2004 (footnote 20 above), para. 20; *Kunarac* (see footnote 26 above), para. 439; *Delalić*, Appeals Chamber (footnote 20 above), para. 179; *Tadić* (footnote 20 above), para. 225; International Criminal Tribunal for Rwanda, *Prosecutor v. Jean-Paul Akayesu*, No. ICTR-96-4-T, Judgment, 2 September 1998, para. 46; International Criminal Tribunal for the Former Yugoslavia, *Prosecutor v. Zejnil Delalić* et al., No. IT-96-21-T, Decision on the motion to allow witnesses K, L and M to give their testimony by means of video-link conference, Trial Chamber, 28 May 1997, paras. 7–8; *Aloeboetoe* et al. *v. Suriname* (footnote 20 above), para. 62; *Questech* (footnote 20 above), p. 122; *Sea-Land Service, Inc. v. Iran* (footnote 20 above), p. 168; *Corfu Channel case* (footnote 20 above), p. 18; *Fabiani* case (footnote 20 above), p. 356; and the *Queen* case between Brazil, Norway and Sweden (1871) (reproduced in La Fontaine, *Pasicrisie internationale 1794–1900: Histoire documentaire des arbitrages internationaux* (footnote 20 above)), p. 155.

systems that can be potentially relevant for the identification of a general principle of law, such as constitutions, legislation, decrees and regulations, as well as decisions of national courts from different levels and jurisdictions, including constitutional courts or tribunals, supreme courts, courts of cassation, courts of appeal, courts of first instance, and administrative tribunals. The term "and other relevant materials" was included so as not to preclude other sources of national legal systems that may also be relevant, such as customary law or doctrine.

(6) In preparing draft conclusion 5, paragraph 3, the Commission was mindful that national legal systems are not identical and that each legal system must be analysed in its own context, taking into account its own characteristics. In certain legal systems, for example, the decisions of national courts may be more relevant to determine the existence of a legal principle, while in others written codes and doctrine may have prevalence. The Commission was also in agreement that all branches of national law, including both private and public law, are potentially relevant for the identification of a general principle of law derived from national legal systems.[31]

(7) It should be highlighted that determining the existence of a principle common to the various legal systems of the world is not sufficient to establish the existence and content of a general principle of law in the sense of Article 38, paragraph 1 (*c*), of the Statute of the International Court of Justice. As noted in draft conclusion 4, the ascertainment of the transposition of that principle to the international legal system is also required. This second step of the methodology is addressed in draft conclusion 6.

Conclusion 6
Determination of transposition to the international legal system

A principle common to the various legal systems of the world may be transposed to the international legal system insofar as it is compatible with that system.

Commentary

(1) Draft conclusion 6 concerns the determination of the transposition of a principle common to the various legal systems of the world to the international legal system. It states that such a principle may be so transposed insofar as it is compatible with the international legal system. It ought to be recalled that, as draft conclusion 4 makes clear, determining transposition is the second requirement for purposes of ascertaining the existence and content of a general principle of law derived from national legal systems.

[31] See, for example, *Question of the Delimitation of the Continental Shelf between Nicaragua and Colombia* (footnote 28 above), p. 125, para. 58 (applying the principle of *res judicata*, derived from civil procedure); *Barcelona Traction* (footnote 20 above), p. 38, para. 50 (applying the principle of separation between companies and shareholders, derived from corporate law); *United States–Tax Treatment for "Foreign Sales Corporations"* (footnote 20 above), para. 143 (applying a principle relating to taxation of non-residents, derived from tax law); *Questech* (see footnote 20 above), p. 122 (applying the principle *rebus sic stantibus*, derived from contract law); *Sea-Land Service* (footnote 20 above), p. 168 (applying the principle of unjust enrichment, derived from civil law or the law of obligations); *Furundžija* (see footnote 23 above), paras. 178–182, and *Kunarac* (see footnote 26 above), paras. 439–460 (applying a definition of "rape" derived from criminal law); *Aloeboetoe v. Suriname* (footnote 20 above), para. 62 (applying a principle relating to succession for purposes of compensation, derived from laws on inheritance or succession); *Mary Grace Natividad S. Poe-Llamanzares v. COMELEC* (footnote 20 above), p. 21 (applying a principle of nationality of foundlings, derived from laws on nationality). See also *El Paso Energy International Company v. The Argentine Republic* (footnote 20 above), para. 622 ("'general principles' are rules largely applied *in foro domestico*, in private or public, substantive or procedural matters"); *South West Africa, Second Phase* (footnote 20 above), Dissenting Opinion of Judge Tanaka, p. 250, at p. 294 ("So far as the 'general principles of law' are not qualified, the 'law' must be understood to embrace all branches of law, including municipal law, public law, constitutional and administrative law, private law, commercial law, substantive and procedural law, etc.").

(2) Draft conclusion 6 states that a principle common to the various legal systems of the world "may be" transposed to the international legal system. The words "may be" are used to highlight that transposition does not occur in an automatic fashion.

(3) The relevant test for the purposes of determining transposition is that the principle common to the various legal systems of the world must be shown to be "compatible" with the international legal system. The rationale that underlies this compatibility test is that the international legal system and national legal systems have distinct structures and characteristics that should not be overlooked. Principles that may be common to the various legal systems of the world, adopted first and foremost to meet the needs of a particular society and to apply within a specific legal system, are not necessarily capable of operating at the international level due to those differences.

(4) A principle *in foro domestico* may be considered compatible with the international legal system if it is suitable to apply within the framework of the international legal system, when conditions for its application exist.[32]

(5) An example commonly referred to in this regard is the right of access to courts that invariably exists across national legal systems. Such a right cannot be transposed to international courts and tribunals because it would be incompatible with the fundamental principle of consent to jurisdiction in international law, which underlies the structure and functioning of international courts and tribunals. Transposition of the right of access to courts would not only result in a direct contravention of the principle of consent to jurisdiction – that right would also be incapable of operating at the international level due to the absence of conditions for its application, *i.e.* a judicial body with universal and compulsory jurisdiction to settle disputes.

(6) Draft conclusion 6 indicates that a principle common to the various legal systems of the world may only be transposed "insofar as" it is compatible with the international legal

32 For instance, in the *North Atlantic Coast Fisheries* case, the tribunal did not support the principle of "international servitude" as it was considered as "being but little suited to the principle of sovereignty". *North Atlantic Coast Fisheries Case (Great Britain, United States)*, Award, 7 September 1910, UNRIAA, vol. XI, pp. 167–226, at p. 182. In *North Sea Continental Shelf*, the International Court of Justice did not support the "principle of the just and equitable share" invoked by Germany as a general principle of law, pointing out that this doctrine was "quite foreign to, and inconsistent with, the basic concept of continental shelf entitlement". *North Sea Continental Shelf, Judgment, I.C.J. Reports 1969*, p. 3, at pp. 21–23, paras. 17 and 19–20. In the *Tadić* case, regarding the principle that a tribunal must be established by law, the Appeals Chamber of the International Criminal Tribunal for the Former Yugoslavia observed that "[i]t is clear that the legislative, executive and judicial division of powers which is largely followed in most municipal systems does not apply to the international setting nor, more specifically, to the setting of an international organization such as the United Nations … Consequently the separation of powers element of the requirement that a tribunal be 'established by law' finds no application in an international law setting." Taking into account several human rights conventions and decisions by human rights bodies, the Appeals Chamber considered that "established by law" means "in accordance with the rule of law". *Prosecutor v. Duško Tadić a/k/a "DULE"*, Case No. IT-94-1-AR72, Decision on the defence motion for interlocutory appeal on jurisdiction, 2 October 1995, Appeals Chamber, International Criminal Tribunal for the Former Yugoslavia, paras. 43–45. In *Delalić et al.*, a Trial Chamber of the International Criminal Tribunal for the Former Yugoslavia considered that the "principles of legality [*nullum crimen sine lege and nulla poena sine lege*] exist and are recognised in all the world's major criminal justice systems", but that it was "not certain to what extent they have been admitted as part of international legal practice, separate and apart from the existence of the national legal systems … because of the different methods of criminalisation of conduct in national and international criminal justice systems". As a result, the Trial Chamber found that "the principles of legality in international criminal law are different from their related national legal systems with respect to their application and standards. They appear to be distinctive, in the obvious objective of maintaining a balance between the preservation of justice and fairness towards the accused and taking into account the preservation of world order. To this end, the affected State or States must take into account the following factors, *inter alia*: the nature of international law; the absence of international legislative policies and standards; the *ad hoc* processes of technical drafting; and the basic assumption that international criminal law norms will be embodied into the national criminal law of the various States." *Prosecutor v. Zejnil Delalić et al.*, Case No. IT-96-21-T Judgment, 16 November 1998, Trial Chamber, International Criminal Tribunal for the Former Yugoslavia, paras. 403 and 405.

system. The use of these words ("insofar as") is meant to highlight that there is a degree of flexibility when determining transposition. As indicated in the commentary to draft conclusion 4 above: if only part of that principle is compatible with the international legal system, it may be transposed to that extent only.[33]

(7) Draft conclusion 6 must be read together with draft conclusion 2, which indicates that, for a general principle of law to exist, it must be recognized by the community of nations. Therefore, recognition that a principle common to the various legal systems of the world is transposed to the international legal system is required. In this context, recognition is implicit when the compatibility test is fulfilled. In other words, if a principle common to the various legal systems of the world is suitable for application within the framework of the international legal system, when conditions for that application exist, it can generally be inferred that the community of nations has recognized that it is transposed. No formal act of transposition is required for a general principle of law to emerge.

Conclusion 7
Identification of general principles of law formed within the international legal system

1. To determine the existence and content of a general principle of law that may be formed within the international legal system, it is necessary to ascertain that the community of nations has recognized the principle as intrinsic to the international legal system.

2. Paragraph 1 is without prejudice to the question of the possible existence of other general principles of law formed within the international legal system.

Commentary

(1) Draft conclusion 7 addresses the identification of general principles of law formed within the international legal system.[34]

(2) Paragraph 1 of draft conclusion 7 provides that, to determine the existence and content of a general principle of law that may be formed within the international legal system, it is necessary to ascertain that the community of nations has recognized the principle as intrinsic to that system. The Commission considered that the existence of this type of general principle of law is justified for a number of reasons. First, there are examples in judicial and State practice which appear to support the existence of these general principles of law. Second, the international legal system, like any other legal system, must be able to generate general principles of law that are specific to it, and not have only general principles of law borrowed from other legal systems. Third, nothing in the text of Article 38, paragraph 1 (*c*), of the

---

[33] Owing to the differences between the international and domestic legal systems, sometimes only certain aspects of a principle common to various legal systems can be transposed to the international legal system. As a result of the transposition, general principles of law applied in international settings may not have exactly the same content as the relevant domestic legal principles. See, *e.g.*, *Tadić* (footnote 20 above), paras. 41–45; *Delalić* (footnote 32 above), paras. 403–405; *Furundžija* (footnote 23 above), para. 178; *El Paso Energy International Company v. The Argentine Republic* (footnote 20 above) para. 622; International Court of Justice, *Application of the Interim Accord of 13 September 1995 (the former Yugoslav Republic of Macedonia v. Greece), Judgment of 5 December 2011, I.C.J. Reports 2011*, p. 695, Separate Opinion of Judge Simma, para. 13. It has been noted, in this regard, that a principle *in foro domestico* cannot be transposed "lock, stock and barrel" (International Court of Justice, *International status of South-West Africa, Advisory Opinion, I.C.J. Reports 1950*, p. 128, Separate Opinion of Judge McNair, p. 146, at p. 148).

[34] Examples that were referred to by members of the Commission during the debates of the Commission include the principle of sovereign equality of States, the principle of territorial integrity, the principle of *uti possidetis juris*, the principle of non-intervention in the internal affairs of another State, the principle of consent to the jurisdiction to international courts and tribunals, elementary considerations of humanity, respect for human dignity, the Nürnberg Principles and principles of international environmental law. (Principles of International Law Recognized in the Charter of the Nürnberg Tribunal and in the Judgment of the Tribunal (Nürnberg Principles), are contained in *Yearbook of the International Law Commission, 1950*, vol. II, p. 374, para. 96.)

Statute of the International Court of Justice or in its drafting history limits general principles of law to those derived from national legal systems.

(3) As regards the methodology for the identification of general principles of law formed within the international legal system, the Commission considered that it has similarities to the methodology applicable to the identification of general principles of law derived from national legal systems, addressed in draft conclusions 4 to 6 above. In both cases, an inductive analysis of existing norms is first carried out. In the case of the principles of the first category, rules existing in the various legal systems of the world are analysed comparatively to determine the existence of a principle common to them. For the principles of the second category, in turn, an analysis of existing rules in the international legal system is required in order to find principles reflected in those rules or underlying them, and having an autonomous status. This analysis must take into account all available evidence of the recognition of the principle in question by the community of nations, such as international instruments reflecting the principle, resolutions adopted by international organizations or at intergovernmental conferences, and statements made by States. Paragraphs (6) to (10) refer to decisions of courts and tribunals that illustrate aspects of this methodology.

(4) The methodology is also deductive for both categories. As regards general principles of law derived from national legal systems, their compatibility with the international legal system must be determined. General principles formed within the international legal system, for their part, must be shown to be intrinsic to that system. The term "intrinsic" means that the principle is specific to the international legal system and reflects and regulates its basic features.

(5) The principle of consent to jurisdiction can be considered as a general principle recognized by the community of nations as intrinsic to the international legal system due to the basic features of the latter. It is a consequence of the principle that sovereign States are equal and the fact that a judiciary with universal and compulsory jurisdiction to which any dispute may be submitted does not exist at the international level. This principle inspires and finds reflection in various international instruments, and has been often referred to in decisions of courts and tribunals.[35]

(6) The principle of *uti possidetis* is another general principle that can be considered recognized by the community of nations as intrinsic to the international legal system when the conditions for its application are satisfied. In *Frontier Dispute (Burkina Faso/Mali)*, a Chamber of the International Court of Justice referred to it as a general principle logically connected to the phenomenon of independence, which has been recognized and confirmed by solemn affirmations of States. The Chamber noted:

> it should be noted that the principle of *uti possidetis* seems to have been first invoked and applied in Spanish America, inasmuch as this was the continent which first witnessed the phenomenon of decolonization involving the formation of a number of sovereign States on territory formerly belonging to a single metropolitan State. Nevertheless, the principle is not a special rule which pertains solely to one specific system of international law. It is a general principle, which is logically connected with the phenomenon of the obtaining of independence, wherever it occurs. Its obvious purpose is to prevent the independence and stability of new States being endangered by fratricidal struggles provoked by the challenging of frontiers following the withdrawal of the administering power.[36]

(7) The Chamber further maintained that "[t]he fact that the new African States have respected the administrative boundaries and frontiers established by the colonial powers must be seen not as a mere practice contributing to the gradual emergence of a principle of

---

[35] See, for example, *Case of the monetary gold* (footnote 23 above), p. 32 ("[t]o adjudicate upon the international responsibility of Albania without her consent would run counter to a well-established principle of international law embodied in the Court's Statute, namely, that the Court can only exercise jurisdiction over a State with its consent"); International Court of Justice, *Land, Island and Maritime Frontier Dispute (El Salvador/Honduras), Application to Intervene, Judgment, I.C.J. Reports 1990*, p. 92, at pp. 132–133, para. 94.

[36] *Frontier Dispute* (see footnote 23 above), p. 565, para. 20.

customary international law, limited in its impact to the African continent as it had previously been to Spanish America, but as the application in Africa of a rule of general scope".[37] It similarly recalled that the principle had been reflected in statements by African leaders, the Charter of the Organization of African Unity, and in resolution AGH/Res.16 (I), adopted at the first session of the Conference of African Heads of State in 1964.[38] The Chamber added that the obligation to respect pre-existing boundaries in the event of a State succession "derives from a general rule of international law, whether or not the rule is expressed in the formula of *uti possidetis*. Hence the numerous solemn affirmations of the intangibility of the frontiers existing at the time of the independence of African States … are evidently declaratory rather than constitutive: they recognize and confirm an existing principle".[39] Thus, the principle of *uti possidetis*, considered logically connected to the phenomenon of obtaining independence, has been applied by States and recognized and confirmed through solemn declarations, international instruments, and resolutions.

(8) In the *Corfu Channel* case, the International Court of Justice identified some international obligations on the basis of certain general and well-recognized principles, namely: "elementary considerations of humanity, even more exacting in peace than in war; the principle of the freedom of maritime communication; and every State's obligation not to allow knowingly its territory to be used for acts contrary to the rights of other States".[40]

(9) The Court did not apply Hague Convention No. VIII,[41] which is applicable only in time of war and, in any event, Albania was not a party to it. Instead, it identified certain obligations based on "general and well-recognized principles", which appear to have been deduced from existing rules of conventional and customary international law. These principles may be considered intrinsic to the international legal system.

(10) In *Furundžija*, the Trial Chamber of the International Criminal Tribunal for the Former Yugoslavia identified and applied a "general principle of respect for human dignity" on the basis that "[t]he essence of the whole corpus of international humanitarian law as well as human rights law lies in the protection of the human dignity of every person" and it is "the basic underpinning and indeed the very *raison d'être* of international humanitarian law and human rights law".[42]

(11) The second paragraph of draft conclusion 7 indicates that the draft conclusion is without prejudice to the question of the possible existence of other general principles of law formed within the international legal system. This paragraph was included to reflect the view of some members of the Commission who supported the existence of general principles of law formed within the international legal system, but considered that paragraph 1 of the draft conclusion would be too narrow and would not encompass other possible principles that,

---

[37] *Ibid.*, para. 21. On the relationship between customary international law and general principles of law, see draft conclusion 11 below.

[38] *Ibid.*, pp. 565–566, para. 22.

[39] *Ibid.*, para. 24. See also p. 567, para. 26 ("the applicability of *uti possidetis* in the present case cannot be challenged merely because in 1960, the year when Mali and Burkina Faso achieved independence, the Organization of African Unity which was to proclaim this principle did not yet exist, and the above-mentioned resolution calling for respect for the pre-existing frontiers dates only from 1964").

[40] *Corfu Channel case* (see footnote 20 above), p. 22: "The obligations incumbent upon the Albanian authorities consisted in notifying, for the benefit of shipping in general, the existence of a minefield in Albanian territorial waters and in warning the approaching British warships of the imminent danger to which the minefield exposed them. Such obligations are based, not on the Hague Convention of 1907, No. VIII, which is applicable in time of war, but on certain general and well-recognized principles, namely: elementary considerations of humanity, even more exacting in peace than in war; the principle of the freedom of maritime communication; and every State's obligation not to allow knowingly its territory to be used for acts contrary to the rights of other States." See also International Court of Justice, *Military and Paramilitary Activities in and Against Nicaragua (Nicaragua v. United States), Merits, Judgment, I.C.J. Reports 1986*, p. 14, at p. 112, para. 215; International Tribunal for the Law of the Sea, *M/V "SAIGA" (No. 2) Case (Saint Vincent and the Grenadines v. Guinea)*, Judgment, *ITLOS Reports 1999*, p. 10, at pp. 61–62, para. 155.

[41] Convention (VIII) of 1907 relative to the Laying of Automatic Submarine Contact Mines (The Hague, 18 October 1907), *The Hague Conventions and Declarations of 1899 and 1907*, J.B. Scott, ed. (New York, Oxford University Press, 1915), p. 151.

[42] *Furundžija* (footnote 23 above), para. 183.

while not intrinsic in the international legal system, may nonetheless emerge from within the latter system and not from national legal systems.

(12) Several members, while not excluding that a second category of general principles of law in the sense of Article 38, paragraph 1 (*c*), of the Statute of the International Court of Justice might exist, raised the concern that no sufficient State practice, jurisprudence or teachings are available to fully support the existence of the second category, making it difficult to determine in a clear manner the methodology for their identification.

(13) Some other members were of the view that Article 38, paragraph 1 (*c*), of the Statute of the International Court of Justice is limited to the general principles of law derived from national legal systems. Some members cautioned that the Commission should be careful and not engage in an exercise of progressive development in a topic concerning one of the sources of international law. The view was also expressed that confusion with the other sources of international law should be avoided. In this regard, some members of the Commission considered that the distinction between customary international law and general principles of law formed within the international legal system, within the meaning given in draft conclusion 7, was not clear, and that the Commission should not put forward a methodology for the identification of those general principles of law that could overlap with the conditions for the emergence of rules of customary international law.

Conclusion 8
Decisions of courts and tribunals

1. Decisions of international courts and tribunals, in particular of the International Court of Justice, concerning the existence and content of general principles of law are a subsidiary means for the determination of such principles.

2. Regard may be had, as appropriate, to decisions of national courts concerning the existence and content of general principles of law, as a subsidiary means for the determination of such principles.

Commentary

(1) Draft conclusion 8 concerns the role of decisions of courts and tribunals, both international and national, as an aid in the identification of general principles of law. The approach towards this issue is the same as that adopted by the Commission in its conclusions on the identification of customary international law,[43] which is also, like general principles of law, a source of international law.

(2) Decisions of international courts and tribunals are often relied upon in order to determine the existence or lack thereof of general principles of law, in particular those derived from national legal systems, as well as their content. To cite but a few examples, in the *Corfu Channel* case, the International Court of Justice found that the use of indirect evidence, in addition to being admitted in "all systems of law", was "recognized by international decisions".[44] In *Pedra Branca/Pulau Batu Puteh*, the Court similarly noted that "[i]t is a general principle of law, confirmed by the jurisprudence of this Court, that a party which advances a point of fact in support of its claims must establish that fact".[45] In the *Chagos Marine Protected Area* arbitration, the tribunal noted that the "frequent invocation [of the principle of estoppel] in international proceedings has added definition to the scope of the principle".[46]

(3) The European Court of Human Rights and the Inter-American Court of Human Rights have likewise relied on prior decisions to justify the existence of the principle *iura novit*

[43] *Yearbook ... 2018*, vol. II (Part Two), paras. 65–66.

[44] *Corfu Channel case* (see footnote 20 above), p. 18.

[45] International Court of Justice, *Sovereignty over Pedra Branca/Pulau Batu Puteh, Middle Rocks and South Ledge (Malaysia/Singapore), Judgment, I.C.J. Reports 2008*, p. 12, at p. 31, para. 45.

[46] Permanent Court of Arbitration, *Chagos Marine Protected Area (Mauritius v. United Kingdom)*, Case No. 2011-03, Award of 18 March 2015, UNRIAA, vol. XXXI, p. 543, para. 436.

curia.[47] In international criminal law, prior decisions by international courts and tribunals have also played a significant role in the identification of general principles of law.[48]

(4) Decisions by national courts may also be relied upon in the identification of general principles of law. In this regard, it should be recalled that decisions of national courts serve a dual role in the identification of general principles of law. On the one hand, as draft conclusion 5 indicates, they may be relevant for purposes of the comparative analysis required to determine the existence of a principle common to the various legal systems of the world. On the other hand, decisions by national courts may serve as a subsidiary means for the determination of general principles of law when such decisions themselves examine the existence and content of a general principle of law. Draft conclusion 8 concerns only the latter scenario.

(5) Draft conclusion 8 follows closely the language of Article 38, paragraph 1 (*d*), of the Statute of the International Court of Justice, according to which, while decisions of the Court have no binding force except between the parties and in respect of that particular case, judicial decisions are a subsidiary means for the determination of rules of international law, including general principles of law. The term "subsidiary means" denotes the ancillary role of such decisions in elucidating the law, rather than being themselves a source of international law (unlike treaties, customary international law and general principles of law). The use of the term "subsidiary means" does not, and is not intended to, suggest that such decisions are not important for the identification of general principles of law.

(6) Decisions of courts and tribunals on questions of international law, in particular those decisions in which the existence of general principles of law is considered and such principles are identified and applied, may offer valuable guidance for determining the existence or lack thereof of general principles. The value of such decisions may vary greatly, however, depending both on the quality of the reasoning (including primarily the extent to which it results from an examination of various legal systems of the world and transposition, in the case of general principles derived from national legal systems, and from an analysis of the existing rules in the international legal system, and relevant resolutions adopted by international organizations or at intergovernmental conferences and statements made by States, in the case of general principles formed within the international legal systems), and on the reception of the decision, in particular by States and in subsequent decisions of courts and tribunals.

(7) Paragraph 1 refers to "international courts and tribunals", a term intended to cover any international body exercising judicial powers that is called upon to consider general principles of law. Express mention is made of the International Court of Justice, the principal judicial organ of the United Nations whose Statute is an integral part of the Charter of the United Nations and whose members are elected by the General Assembly and Security Council, in recognition of the significance of its decisions and its particular position as the only standing international court of general jurisdiction. While the International Court of

47 European Court of Human Rights, *Handyside v. the United Kingdom*, 7 December 1976, Series A, No. 24, para. 41; European Court of Human Rights, *Guerra and Others v. Italy*, 19 February 1998, *Reports of Judgments and Decisions* 1998-I, para. 44; on Inter-American Court of Human Rights, see, *inter alia*, *Velásquez Rodríguez v. Honduras*, Judgment (Merits) of 29 July 1988, Series C, No. 4, para. 163.

48 See, for example, International Criminal Tribunal for the Former Yugoslavia, *Prosecutor v. Enver Hadžihasanović, Mehmed Alagić and Amir Kubura*, Case No. IT-01-47-PT, Decision on Joint Challenge to Jurisdiction, Trial Chamber, 12 November 2002, paras. 58–61; Special Court for Sierra Leone, *Prosecutor v. Sam Hinga Norman*, Case No. SCSL-2004-14-AR72(E), Decision on Preliminary Motion Based on Lack of Jurisdiction (Child Recruitment), 31 May 2004, paras. 25–26; Special Court for Sierra Leone, *Prosecutor v. Sam Hinga Norman* et al., Case No. SCSL-04-14-PT, Decision on Prosecution's Motion for Judicial Notice and Admission of Evidence, 2 June 2004, paras. 22–30; Special Court for Sierra Leone, *Prosecutor v. Issa Hassan Sesay* et al., Case No. SCSL-04-15-T, Ruling on the Issue of the Third Accused, Augustine Gbao, to Attend Hearing of the Special Court for Sierra Leone on 7 July 2004 and Succeeding Days, 12 July 2004, paras. 10–11.

Justice has expressly mentioned Article 38, paragraph 1 (*c*), on only a few occasions,[49] it has referred to several general principles of law in its jurisprudence (as the Permanent Court of International Justice did), contributing to the understanding of this source of international law and to the scope of particular principles.[50] The term "international courts and tribunals" also includes (but is not limited to) specialist and regional courts, such as the International Tribunal for the Law of the Sea, the International Criminal Court and ad hoc international criminal tribunals, regional human rights courts and the World Trade Organization Dispute Settlement Body. It also includes inter-State arbitral tribunals and other arbitral tribunals applying international law. The skills and the breadth of evidence usually at the disposal of the international courts and tribunals may lend significant weight to their decisions, subject to the considerations mentioned in the preceding paragraph.

(8) For the purposes of this draft conclusion, the term "decisions" includes judgments, awards and advisory opinions, as well as orders on procedural and interlocutory matters. Separate and dissenting opinions may shed light on the decision and may discuss points not covered in the decision of the court or tribunal concerned, but they need to be approached with caution since they reflect the viewpoint of the individual judge or arbitrator, and may set out points not accepted by the court or tribunal.

(9) Paragraph 2 concerns decisions of national courts (also referred to as domestic or municipal courts). The distinction between international and national courts is not always clear-cut; in the present draft conclusions, the term "national courts" includes courts with an international composition operating within one or more domestic legal systems, such as some "hybrid" courts and tribunals with mixed national and international composition and jurisdiction.

(10) Some caution is called for when seeking to rely on decisions of national courts as a subsidiary means for the determination of general principles of law. This is reflected in the different wording of paragraphs 1 and 2, in particular the use of the words "[r]egard may be had, as appropriate" in paragraph 2. National courts operate within a particular legal system, which may incorporate international law only in a particular way and to a limited extent. Their decisions may reflect a particular national perspective. Unlike most international courts, national courts may sometimes lack international law expertise and may have reached their decisions without the benefit of hearing arguments advanced by States.

Conclusion 9
Teachings

Teachings of the most highly qualified publicists of the various nations may serve as a subsidiary means for the determination of general principles of law.

Commentary

(1) Draft conclusion 9 concerns the role of teachings in the identification of general principles of law. Following closely the language of Article 38, paragraph 1 (*d*), of the Statute of the International Court of Justice, it provides that such works may be resorted to as a

---

[49] *South West Africa, Second Phase* (footnote 20 above), p. 47, para. 88; *North Sea Continental Shelf* (footnote 32 above), pp. 21–22, paras. 17–18; *Avena and Other Mexican Nationals (Mexico v. United States of America), Judgment, I.C.J. Reports 2004*, p. 12, at p. 61, para. 127.

[50] See, for example, *Corfu Channel case* (footnote 20 above), pp. 18 and p. 22; *Reservations to the Convention on Genocide* (footnote 23 above), p. 23; *Effect of awards of compensation made by the U.N. Administrative Tribunal, Advisory Opinion of July 13th,1954: I.C.J. Reports 1954*, p. 47, at p. 53; *Right of Passage* (footnote 29 above), p. 43; *South West Africa, Second Phase* (footnote 20 above), p. 47, para. 88; *North Sea Continental Shelf* (footnote 32 above), pp. 21–22, paras. 17–18; *Barcelona Traction* (footnote 20 above), p. 37, para. 50; *Application for Review of Judgment No. 158 of the United Nations Administrative Tribunal, Advisory Opinion, I.C.J. Reports 1973*, p. 166, at p. 181, para. 36; *Application for Review of Judgment No. 273 of the United Nations Administrative Tribunal, Advisory Opinion, I.C.J. Reports 1982*, p. 325, at pp. 338–339, para. 29; *Question of the Delimitation of the Continental Shelf between Nicaragua and Colombia* (footnote 28 above), p. 100, para. 58; *Maritime Delimitation in the Caribbean Sea and the Pacific Ocean (Costa Rica v. Nicaragua)* and *Land Boundary in the Northern Part of Isla Portillos (Costa Rica v. Nicaragua), Judgment, I.C.J. Reports 2018*, p. 139, at p. 166, para. 68.

subsidiary means for determining general principles of law, that is to say, when ascertaining whether there is a principle common to the various legal systems of the world that may be transposed to the international legal system, or whether there is a principle formed within the international legal system. The term "teachings", often referred to as "writings", is to be understood in a broad sense; it includes teachings in non-written form, such as lectures and audiovisual materials.

(2) As with decisions of courts and tribunals, referred to above in draft conclusion 8, teachings are not themselves a source of international law, but may offer guidance for the determination of the existence and content of general principles of law. This auxiliary role recognizes the value that teachings may have in collecting and assessing national laws and other materials and the compatibility of a principle common to the various legal systems of the world with the international legal system; in weighing up relevant rules in the international legal system and relevant resolutions adopted by international organizations or at intergovernmental conferences and statements made by States to assess the recognition of a general principle of law formed within the international legal system; in identifying divergences and the possible absence or development of general principles of law; and in evaluating the law. Use of teachings may be particularly useful to overcome any linguistic barriers found when conducting a comparative analysis of national legal systems.

(3) There is need for caution when drawing upon writings, since their value for determining the existence and content of a general principle of law varies: this is reflected in the words "may serve as" in the draft conclusion. Teachings sometimes seek not merely to record the state of the law as it is (*lex lata*) but to advocate its development (*lex ferenda*). Furthermore, teachings may reflect the national or other individual viewpoints of their authors. Teachings may moreover differ greatly in quality, and assessing the authority of a given work is thus essential.

(4) The reference to "publicists of the various nations" highlights the importance of having regard, so far as possible, to teachings that are representative of the various legal systems and regions of the world and in various languages. This may acquire particular importance when identifying general principles of law derived from national legal systems.

(5) The output of private international bodies engaged in the codification and development of international law may provide a useful resource in this regard. Such collective bodies include the Institute of International Law (Institut de droit international) and the International Law Association. The value of each output needs to be carefully assessed in the light of the expertise of the body concerned, the extent to which the output seeks to state existing law, the care and objectivity with which it works on a particular issue, the support a particular output enjoys within the body, and the reception of the output by States and others.

(6) Beyond teachings, special attention is warranted, among other subsidiary means, as regards the output of the Commission, in particular considering its unique mandate as a subsidiary organ of the General Assembly to promote the progressive development of international law and its codification. It should also be taken into account that the members of the Commission are from different regions and represent various legal systems of the world, and that the Commission has a close relationship with the General Assembly and States, including the benefit of receiving oral and written comments from States as it proceeds with its work. This understanding is without prejudice to the work of the Commission on the topic "Subsidiary means for the determination of rules of international law".

Conclusion 10
Functions of general principles of law

1. General principles of law are mainly resorted to when other rules of international law do not resolve a particular issue in whole or in part.

2. General principles of law contribute to the coherence of the international legal system. They may serve, *inter alia*:

(a) to interpret and complement other rules of international law;

(b) as a basis for primary rights and obligations, as well as a basis for secondary and procedural rules.

Commentary

(1) Draft conclusion 10 addresses the functions of general principles of law. It states that general principles are mainly resorted to when other rules of international law do not resolve a particular issue in whole or in part. It also indicates that general principles of law contribute to the coherence of the international legal system, and that they may serve, *inter alia*, to interpret and complement other rules of international law, and as a basis for primary rights and obligations, secondary rules and procedural rules. Draft conclusion 10 applies to all general principles of law, regardless of whether they are derived from national legal systems or formed within the international legal system, depending on the general principle in question.

(2) It ought to be recalled that the functions of general principles of law are, in principle, similar to those performed by other sources of international law. Treaties, customary international law and general principles of law are all equally listed in Article 38, paragraph 1, of the Statute of the International Court of Justice, and it is in the light of this and their application in practice that the functions of general principles of law should be understood.

(3) Paragraph 1 of draft conclusion 10 indicates that general principles of law are mainly resorted to when other rules of international law do not resolve a particular issue in whole or in part.[51] This aims to capture the tendency in practice and in doctrine, when assessing a particular issue, to first determine whether there is a treaty rule or rule of customary international law that may provide a solution, and to resort to general principles of law if the two other sources prove insufficient. The words "are mainly resorted to" clarify that this is not the only manner in which one may proceed, and that in some cases general principles of law may be directly resorted to depending on the circumstances. The Commission thereby sought to avoid the misconception that general principles of law play an ancillary role in comparison to treaties or custom.

(4) The term "other rules of international law" refers to treaties and rules of customary international law. The words "do not resolve a particular issue in whole or in part" are meant to clarify that general principles of law may be applied when an issue does not find a solution in treaties or custom at all, or when treaties and custom provide only a partial solution and general principles may serve as a complement.

(5) It ought to be noted that there may not always be a general principle of law filling the *lacunae* left by treaties or customary international law. A general principle of law may be used in the manner described in paragraph 1 of draft conclusion 10 only to the extent that it can be identified in accordance with the present draft conclusions.

(6) Paragraph 2 of draft conclusion 10 begins with the factual proposition that general principles of law contribute to the coherence of the international legal system.[52] While rules

[51] See also Pellet and Müller, "Article 38", pp. 934–935; H. Lauterpacht, *Private Law Sources and Analogies of International Law* (London, Longmans, 1927), p. 85; F. Raimondo, *General Principles of Law in the Decisions of International Criminal Courts and Tribunals* (Leiden, Martinus Nijhoff, 2008), pp. 42–43; M. Bogdan, "General principles of law and the problem of *lacunae* in the law of nations", *Nordic Journal of International Law*, vol. 46 (1977), pp. 37–53, at pp. 37–41; Yee, "Article 38 of the ICJ Statute and applicable law", p. 487; Bonafé and Palchetti, "Relying on general principles in international law"), p. 162.

[52] See statement of H.E. Mr. Abdulqawi Ahmed Yusuf, President of the International Court of Justice before the Sixth Committee of the General Assembly, New York, 1 November 2019, para. 37 ("The question of coherence in international law is an existential one. The lack of a centralized legislator at the international level has often triggered fears about the possible effect of contradictions between international legal norms. It has also raised questions about possible *lacunae* in international law, and its corollary, the potential declaration by the Court of a *non liquet*. General principles have proved effective in helping the Court to address both structural problems of law-making in international society and to promote coherence"). See also H. Thirlway, *The Sources of International Law* (Oxford, Oxford University Press, 2019), p. 113 ("The principles contemplated by [Article 38, paragraph 1 (c), of the Statute of the International Court of Justice] are, or at all events include, those principles

derived from the other sources of international law also contribute to the coherence of the international legal system, certain general principles appear to be aimed at performing this function in a more direct manner. Examples of such general principles of law may include *pacta sunt servanda*, good faith, the principles of *lex specialis* and *lex posterior*, respect for human dignity and elementary considerations of humanity.

(7) Paragraph 2 also refers to two more concrete functions of general principles. The term "*inter alia*" is used to indicate that the functions referred to are not exhaustive, while the words "may serve" indicate that the functions of general principles must be determined on a case-by-case basis depending on their content and scope.

(8) Subparagraph (*a*) states that general principles of law may serve to interpret and complement other rules of international law. That general principles of law may be relied upon for purposes of interpretation is well-established in practice.[53]

(9) That general principles of law are resorted to interpret other rules of international law is confirmed by article 31, paragraph 3 (c), of the Vienna Convention on the Law of Treaties, which requires the interpreter of a treaty to take into account "any relevant rules of

---

without which no legal system can function at all, that are part and parcel of legal reasoning"); R. Kolb, *Theory of International Law* (Oxford, Hart Publishing, 2016), p. 136 ("From the logical point of view, there are some general principles that must be supposed to conceive a legal order. Without these principles, the construction of the sources would fall into a vicious circle"); T. Gazzini, "General principles of law in the field of foreign investment", *Journal of World Investment and Trade*, vol. 10 (2009), p. 106 (General principles of law "lie at the very foundation of the [international] legal system and are indispensable to its operation" (citing B. Cheng, *General Principles of Law as Applied by International Courts and Tribunals*)); M. Andenas and L. Chiussi, "Cohesion, convergence and coherence of international law", in M. Andenas *et al.* (eds.), *General Principles and the Coherence of International Law* (Leiden, Brill, 2019), p. 10 ("principles of law represent a central cohesive force, revealing and reinforcing the systemic nature of the system. Second, they operate as a tool for intra-systemic convergence in the constellation of international courts and tribunals, avoiding or reducing fragmentation in the approaches adopted in different sub-fields of international law by ensuring that they remain part of general international law. Third, principles of law promote inter-systemic coherence by bridging the gap between international law and domestic legal systems").

[53] See, for example, European Court of Human Rights, *Golder v. the United Kingdom*, Judgment of 21 February 1975, Series A No. 18, para. 35 ("Article 31 para. 3 (c) of the Vienna Convention indicates that account is to be taken, together with the context, of 'any relevant rules of international law applicable in the relations between the parties'. Among those rules are general principles of law and especially 'general principles of law recognized by civilized nations' … The principle whereby a civil claim must be capable of being submitted to a judge ranks as one of the universally 'recognised' fundamental principles of law; the same is true of the principle of international law which forbids the denial of justice. Article 6 para. 1 (art. 6-1) must be read in the light of these principles"); World Trade Organization, *United States – Import Prohibition of Certain Shrimp and Shrimp Products*, Appellate Body Report, 6 November 1998 (WT/DS58/AB/R), *Dispute Settlement Reports 1998*, vol. VII, p. 2755, at para. 158 ("The chapeau of Article XX is, in fact, but one expression of the principle of good faith. This principle, at once a general principle of law and a general principle of international law, controls the exercise of rights by states … our task here is to interpret the language of the chapeau, seeking additional interpretative guidance, as appropriate, from the general principles of international law"); *United States – Tax Treatment for "Foreign Sales Corporations"* (footnote 20 above), para. 142 ("Although these instruments do not define 'foreign-source income' uniformly, it appears to us that certain widely recognized principles of taxation emerge from them. In seeking to give meaning to the term 'foreign-source income' in footnote 59 to the *SCM Agreement*, which is a tax-related provision in an international trade treaty, we believe that it is appropriate for us to derive assistance from these widely recognized principles which many States generally apply in the field of taxation"); *Kupreškić* (footnote 23 above), para. 609 ("The Trial Chamber is thus called upon to examine what acts not covered by Article 5 of the Statute of the International Tribunal may be included in the notion of persecution. Plainly, the Trial Chamber must set out a clear-cut notion of persecution, in order to decide whether the crimes charged in this case fall within its ambit. In addition, this notion must be consistent with general principles of criminal law such as the principles of legality and specificity"). See also Central American Court of Justice, *El Salvador v. Nicaragua*, Judgment of 9 March 1917, in *American Journal of International Law*, vol. 11 (1917), pp. 674–730, at p. 728; *Furundžija* (footnote 23 above), para. 180; *Kunarac* (footnote 26 above), paras. 437–460; *Delalić*, Appeals Chamber (footnote 20 above), para. 538.

international law applicable in the relations between the parties". The report of the Commission's Study Group on the fragmentation of international law states that this provision deals with the case where sources external to a treaty are relevant in its interpretation, which may include other treaties, customary rules or general principles of law.[54]

(10) The term "complement" in paragraph 2, subparagraph (*a*), of draft conclusion 10 is meant to cover other cases where a general principle of law is applied simultaneously with a treaty rule or rule of customary international law.[55]

(11) Subparagraph (*b*) indicates that general principles of law may serve as the basis for primary rights and obligations, secondary rules and procedural rules. The term "primary rights and obligations" covers the proposition that, like any other source of international law, general principles of law may give rise to substantive rights and obligations incumbent upon States and other subjects of international law, and that international responsibility may be engaged for a breach thereof.[56] Legal instruments and judicial decisions refer as examples of such general principles to the prohibition of unjust enrichment,[57] the principle of *uti possidetis*,[58] the principle that attribution of territory *ipso facto* carries with it the waters appurtenant to the territory attributed,[59] principles underlying the Convention on the Prevention and Punishment of the Crime of Genocide,[60] the prohibition of crimes under international law,[61] elementary considerations of humanity, freedom of maritime

---

54 Report of the Study Group on the fragmentation of international law, *Yearbook ... 2006*, vol. II (Part Two), para. 251, at p. 180, conclusions (17)–(20).

55 In the *Barcelona Traction* case, for example, the International Court of Justice considered that applying general principles of law was appropriate since the customary rules on diplomatic protection did not address the specific issue of the relationship between companies and shareholders, noting in particular that "international law ha[d] not established its own rules" on the matter (*Barcelona Traction* (see footnote 20 above), pp. 33–34, para. 38. See also *Diallo (Republic of Guinea v. Democratic Republic of the Congo)* (see footnote 30 above), p. 675, para. 104. Similarly, the arbitral tribunal in the *Proceedings concerning the OSPAR Convention* noted, in determining the law applicable to the dispute, that "[i]t should go without saying that the first duty of the Tribunal is to apply the OSPAR Convention [Convention for the Protection of the Marine Environment of the North-East Atlantic]. An international tribunal, such as this Tribunal, will also apply customary international law and general principles unless and to the extent that the Parties have created a *lex specialis*" (*Proceedings pursuant to the OSPAR Convention (Ireland – United Kingdom)*, Decision of 2 July 2003, UNRIAA, vol. XXIII, pp. 59–151, at p. 87, para. 84). See also *Prosecutor v. Dražen Erdemović*, No. IT-96-22-T, Sentencing Judgment, 29 November 1996, para. 26 ("the Trial Chamber notes that the Statute and the Rules provide no further indication as to the length of imprisonment to which the perpetrators of crimes falling within the International Tribunal's jurisdiction, including crimes against humanity, might be sentenced. In order to review the scale of penalties applicable for crimes against humanity, the Trial Chamber will identify the features which characterise such crimes and the penalties associated with them under international law and national laws, which are expressions of general principles of law recognised by all nations").

56 Art. 12 (Existence of a breach of an international obligation) of the 2001 articles on State responsibility for internationally wrongful acts provides that: "There is a breach of an international obligation by a State when an act of that State is not in conformity with what is required of it by that obligation, regardless of its origin". In explaining the meaning of the term "regardless of its origin", the commentary noted that "[i]nternational obligations may be established by a customary rule of international law, by a treaty or by a general principle applicable within the international legal order". See *Yearbook ... 2001*, vol. II (Part Two) and corrigendum, paras. 76–77, at p. 55, para. (3) of the commentary to art. 12. See also *Yearbook ... 1976*, vol. II (Part Two), pp. 80–87.

57 *Sea-Land Service* (see footnote 20 above), p. 169.

58 *Frontier Dispute* (see footnote 23 above), p. 565, paras. 20–21.

59 *Dispute between Argentina and Chile concerning the Beagle Channel*, Decision of 18 February 1977, UNRIAA, vol. XXI, pp. 53–264, at p. 145.

60 *Reservations to the Convention on Genocide* (see footnote 23 above), p. 23 (Convention on the Prevention and Punishment of the Crime of Genocide (Paris, 9 December 1948), United Nations, *Treaty Series*, vol. 78, No. 1021, p. 277).

61 See article 15, paragraph 2, of the International Covenant on Civil and Political Rights ("Nothing in this article shall prejudice the trial and punishment of any person for any act or omission which, at the time when it was committed, was criminal according to the general principles of law recognized by the community of nations"). See also article 7, paragraph 2, of the European

communication, every States obligation not to allow knowingly its territory to be used for acts contrary to the rights of other States,[62] and foundlings' right to be presumed to have been born of nationals of the country in which they are found.[63]

(12) The words "secondary and procedural rules" in subparagraph (*b*) are meant to cover certain general principles of law that may be characterized as performing such specific functions in light of their particular content.

(13) International tribunals have considered that some secondary rules of responsibility are derived from general principles of law; for instance, the principle of *force majeure* as a ground for precluding wrongfulness,[64] the obligation to make reparation for breaches of international law,[65] the obligation to pay moratory or compensatory interests,[66] *rebus sic stantibus*,[67] and principles on succession of individuals for the purposes of compensation.[68]

(14) Procedural rules refer to those regulating the process in international courts and tribunals. A typical example is the principle of *res judicata*, which has been acknowledged on several occasions as a general principle of law by international courts and tribunals.[69] Other such principles referred to by international courts and tribunals include *iura novit curia*,[70] *compétence-compétence*,[71] review of excess of mandate,[72] the principle that no one can be judge in his or her own cause, [73] the rule of burden of proof,[74] the admissibility of indirect evidence,[75] and the possibility of trial *in absentia*.[76]

Convention on Human Rights ("This Article shall not prejudice the trial and punishment of any person for any act or omission which, at the time when it was committed, was criminal according to the general principles of law recognised by civilised nations") (Convention for the Protection of Human Rights and Fundamental Freedoms (European Convention on Human Rights) (Rome, 4 November 1950), United Nations, *Treaty Series*, vol. 213, No. 2889, p. 221).

[62] *Corfu Channel case* (see footnote 20 above), p. 22.

[63] *Mary Grace Natividad S. Poe-Llamanzares v. COMELEC* (see footnote 20 above), p. 21.

[64] See, *e.g.*, European Court of Justice: *Denkavit België NV v. Belgian State*, case 145/85, judgment, 5 February 1987, *European Court Reports 1987*, p. 565; and *Commission of the European Communities v. Italian Republic*, case 101/84, judgment, 11 July 1985, *ibid.*, 1985, p. 2629. See also United Nations Convention on Contracts for the International Sale of Goods (Vienna, 11 April 1980), United Nations, *Treaty Series*, vol. 1489, No. 25567, p. 3, art. 79; P. Schlechtriem (ed.), *Commentary on the UN Convention on the International Sale of Goods*, 2nd ed. (trans. G. Thomas) (Oxford, Clarendon Press, 1998), pp. 600–626; art. 7.1.7 of the UNIDROIT Principles of International Commercial Contracts (Rome, UNIDROIT, 1994), pp. 169–171; and G. H. Aldrich, *The Jurisprudence of the Iran-United States Claims Tribunal* (Oxford, Clarendon Press, 1996), pp. 306–320.

[65] Permanent Court of International Justice, *Case concerning the Factory at Chorzów (Merits)*, Judgment of 13 September 1928, PCIJ Series A, No. 17, p. 29.

[66] *Affaire de l'indemnité russe (Russie, Turquie)*, Award of 11 November 1912, UNRIAA, vol. XI, pp. 421–447, at p. 441.

[67] *Questech* (see footnote 20 above), p. 122.

[68] *Aloeboetoe* v. *Suriname* (see footnote 20 above), paras. 61–62.

[69] *Question of the Delimitation of the Continental Shelf between Nicaragua and Colombia* (see footnote 28 above), p. 100, at pp. 125–126, paras. 58–61.

[70] See footnote 47 above.

[71] Permanent Court of International Justice, *Interpretation of Greco-Turkish Agreement of December 1st, 1926*, Advisory Opinion of 28 August 1928, PCIJ Series B, No. 16, p. 20.

[72] *Abyei Area* (see footnote 20 above), p. 299, paras. 401–406.

[73] Permanent Court of International Justice, *Interpretation of Article 3, Paragraph 2, of the Treaty of Lausanne,* Advisory Opinion of 21 November 1925, PCIJ Series B, No. 12, p. 32 (considering that Article 15, paragraphs 6 and 7, of the Covenant of the League of Nations reflected the "well-known rule that no one can be judge in his own suit").

[74] *Salini Costruttori S.p.A. and Italstrade S.p.A. v. The Hashemite Kingdom of Jordan*, Case No. ARB/02/13, Award of 31 January 2006, paras. 70 *ff*; *Autopista Concesionada de Venezuela, C.A. v. Bolivarian Republic of Venezuela*, Case No. ARB/00/5, Award of 23 September 2003, para. 110; *International Thunderbird Gaming Corporation v. United Mexican States*, UNCITRAL Award of 26 January 2006, para. 95; *Asian Agricultural Products Limited v. Republic of Sri Lanka*, Case No. ARB/87/3, Award of 27 June 1990, para. 56.

[75] *Corfu Channel case* (see footnote 20 above), p. 18.

[76] *Sesay* (see footnote 48 above), paras. 9–10.

Conclusion 11
Relationship between general principles of law and treaties and customary international law

1. General principles of law, as a source of international law, are not in a hierarchical relationship with treaties and customary international law.

2. A general principle of law may exist in parallel with a rule of the same or similar content in a treaty or customary international law.

3. Any conflict between a general principle of law and a rule in a treaty or customary international law is to be resolved by applying the generally accepted techniques of interpretation and conflict resolution in international law.

Commentary

(1) Draft conclusion 11 clarifies certain aspects concerning the relationship between general principles of law, on the one hand, and treaties and customary international law, on the other.

(2) Paragraph 1 of draft conclusion 11 indicates that general principles of law are not in a hierarchical relationship with treaties and customary international law. This statement follows Article 38, paragraph 1, of the Statute of the International Court of Justice, which lists the three sources of international law without indicating the existence of any hierarchy among them. In addition, the conclusions of the work of the Study Group on the fragmentation of international law[77] confirm also that no such hierarchy exists.[78]

(3) It ought to be recalled that, as indicated in paragraph 1 of draft conclusion 10, general principles of law are mainly resorted to when other rules of international law do not resolve a particular issue in whole or in part. As explained in the commentary thereto, this reflects what for the most part, but not always, occurs in practice, which can be explained in terms of legal reasoning, and as a result of the application of the *lex specialis* principle.[79] It was the Commission's understanding, however, that this practice should not be understood as suggesting that a hierarchical relationship exists between general principles of law and treaties and customary international law. The three sources of international law listed in Article 38, paragraph 1, of the Statute of the International Court of Justice enjoy equal status. General principles of law may be applied directly or simultaneously with other rules of international law to interpret or complement them, as indicated in the commentary to draft conclusion 10.

---

[77] Conclusions of the work of the Study Group on the fragmentation of international law, *Yearbook ... 2006*, vol. II (Part Two), p. 182, para. (31) ("The main sources of international law (treaties, custom and general principles of law as laid out in Article 38 of the Statute of the International Court of Justice) are not in a hierarchical relationship *inter se*").

[78] This proposition is also generally accepted in teachings. See, for example, Pellet and Müller, "Article 38", p. 935; J. Dugard and D. Tladi, "Sources of international law" in J. Dugard *et al.* (eds.), *Dugard's International Law: A South African Perspective*, 5th ed. (Cape Town, Juta & Company Ltd., 2018), pp. 28–56, at pp. 28–29; Palchetti, "The role of general principles in promoting the development of customary international rules", p. 49; C. Bassiouni, "A functional approach to 'general principles of international law'", *Michigan Journal of International Law*, vol. 11 (1990), pp. 768–818, at pp. 781–783; Cheng, *General Principles of Law as Applied by International Courts and Tribunals*, pp. 20–22; Raimondo, *General Principles of Law in the Decisions of International Criminal Courts and Tribunals*, p. 20; Díez de Velasco Vallejo, *Instituciones de Derecho Internacional Público* (footnote 24 above), pp. 121–122; V.D. Degan, *Sources of International Law* (The Hague, Martinus Nijhoff, 1997), p. 5; T. Gazzini, "General principles of law in the field of foreign investment", p. 108.

[79] See, for example, *Right of Passage* (footnote 29 above), p. 43 ("Having arrived at the conclusion that the course of dealings between the British and Indian authorities on the one hand and the Portuguese on the other established a practice, well understood between the Parties, by virtue of which Portugal had acquired a right of passage in respect of private persons, civil officials and goods in general, the Court does not consider it necessary to examine whether general international custom or the general principles of law recognized by civilized nations may lead to the same result").

(4) Paragraph 1 of draft conclusion 11 is a statement of general international law. It should be noted, however, that nothing prevents States from establishing, for example, a treaty regime envisaging a different arrangement, such as the Rome Statute of the International Criminal Court,[80] article 21 of which seemingly creates a hierarchy between the different sources to be applied by the Court referred to therein.[81]

(5) In line with the above, paragraph 2 of the draft conclusion states that a general principle of law may exist in parallel with a rule of the same or similar content in a treaty or customary international law. The Commission thereby intended to highlight that general principles of law are a separate source of international law, with their own requirements for identification, and that their existence and applicability as part of general international law is not affected if a treaty rule or a rule of customary international law addresses the same or a similar subject matter.

(6) This situation may arise, for example, when a treaty codifies a general principle of law in its entirety, with the result that a given rule may be found, with identical content, both in the treaty in question and in general principles of law. In such a case, the general principle of law may continue to inform the interpretation and application of the treaty, and it would remain applicable as a matter of general international law between the States parties to the treaty and non-parties, and between States non-parties to the treaty.[82] Similarly, a treaty may codify a general principle of law only in part, in which case the general principle of law would need to be taken into account when interpreting and applying the treaty rule in question, and would furthermore remain applicable between parties and non-parties to the treaty.[83] Analogous considerations apply with respect to customary international law, depending on the specific content of the customary rule in question.[84] A general principle of law may apply in various areas of international law, such as the principle of good faith, which may become a customary rule,[85] but the principle maintains its distinct existence and applicability.

---

[80] Rome Statute of the International Criminal Court (Rome, 17 July 1998), United Nations, *Treaty Series*, vol. 2187, No. 38544, p. 3.

[81] See also art. 61 of the African Charter on Human and People's Rights (Nairobi, 27 June 1981), United Nations, *Treaty Series*, vol. 1520, No. 26363, p. 217.

[82] An example in this regard is the principle *pacta sunt servanda*, reflected in article 26 of the Vienna Convention on the Law of Treaties, which may apply as a treaty rule between the States parties to the Convention, and as a general principle of law between States parties and non-parties to the Convention, as well as between States non-parties to the Convention. The preamble to the Convention notes that "the principles of free consent and of good faith and the *pacta sunt servanda* rule are universally recognized".

[83] The principle of *res judicata*, for example, has been referred to on various occasions by the International Court of Justice as a principle that is at the same time a general principle of law and a rule provided for in its Statute (*Question of the Delimitation of the Continental Shelf between Nicaragua and Colombia* (see footnote 28 above), p. 125, para 58; *Maritime Delimitation in the Caribbean Sea and the Pacific Ocean (Costa Rica v. Nicaragua)* and *Land Boundary in the Northern Part of Isla Portillos (Costa Rica v. Nicaragua)* (see footnote 50 above), p. 166, para. 68). Another instance where the Court seems to have noted the parallel existence of a rule laid down in its Statute and a general principle of law is the *Nottebohm* case, as regards the principle *compétence-compétence* (*Nottebohm case (Preliminary Objection), Judgment of November 18th, 1953: I.C.J. Reports 1953*, p. 111, at p. 120). With respect to the principle *rebus sic stantibus*, the Iran-United States Claims Tribunal noted that "[t]his concept of changed circumstances … has in its basic form been incorporated into so many legal systems that it may be regarded as a general principle of law; it has also found a widely recognized expression in article 62 of the Vienna Convention on the Law of Treaties" (*Questech* (see footnote 20 above), p. 122). A further example is the doctrine of abuse of rights, codified in article 300 of the United Nations Convention on the Law of the Sea ((Montego Bay, 10 December 1982), United Nations, *Treaty Series*, vol. 1833, No. 31363, p. 3), and the general principles of criminal law codified in Part 3 of the Rome Statute of the International Criminal Court.

[84] For example, the "*pacta tertiis nec nocent nec prosunt*" principle, which is codified in article 34 of the Vienna Convention on the Law of Treaties, may be considered a rule of customary international law and a general principle of law at the same time.

[85] The general principle of good faith has been codified, for instance, in the Vienna Convention on the Law of Treaties (*e.g.*, arts. 26 and 31). Conclusion 2, paragraph 1, of the conclusions on subsequent agreement and subsequent practice in relation to the interpretation of treaties, adopted by the

(7) Paragraph 3 of draft conclusion 11 indicates that any conflict between a general principle of law and a rule in treaty or customary international law is to be resolved by applying the generally accepted techniques of interpretation and conflict resolution in international law. This paragraph must be read together with the conclusions of the Study Group on the fragmentation of international law, which it builds upon. The "generally accepted techniques of interpretation and conflict resolution in international law" mentioned in the draft conclusion refer to principles such as *lex specialis derogat legi generali*, *lex posterior derogat legi priori*, the principle of harmonization, as well as to articles 31 to 33 of the Vienna Convention on the Law of Treaties. Furthermore, account must be taken of recognized hierarchical relationships by the substance of the rule (peremptory norms of general international law (*jus cogens*)), and by virtue of a treaty provision (such as Article 103 of the Charter of the United Nations).

Commission, states that the rules set forth in articles 31 and 32 of the Vienna Convention of the Law of Treaties also apply as customary international law (*Yearbook ... 2018*, vol. II (Part Two), para. 51). The principle of good faith is also reflected in the Friendly Relations Declaration.

Chapter V
Settlement of disputes to which international organizations are parties

A. Introduction

42. The Commission, at its seventy-third session (2022), decided to include the topic "Settlement of international disputes to which international organizations are parties" in its programme of work[86] and appointed Mr. August Reinisch as Special Rapporteur for the topic. Also at its seventy-third session,[87] the Commission requested the Secretariat to prepare a memorandum providing information on the practice of States and international organizations which may be of relevance to its future work on the topic, including both international disputes and disputes of a private law character. The Commission also approved the Special Rapporteur's recommendation that the Secretariat contact States and relevant international organizations in order to obtain information and their views for the purposes of the memorandum.

43. The General Assembly, in paragraph 7 of its resolution 77/103 of 7 December 2022, subsequently took note of the decision of the Commission to include the topic in its programme of work.

B. Consideration of the topic at the present session

44. At the present session, the Commission had before it the first report of the Special Rapporteur (A/CN.4/756). In his first report, the Special Rapporteur addressed the scope of the topic and provided an analysis of the subject matter of the topic in light of previous work of the Commission relevant to it and of other international bodies. The report also addressed certain definitional issues. The Special Rapporteur proposed two draft guidelines: one regarding the scope of the draft guidelines, and the other concerning the definitional issues. He also discussed the question of the outcome of the work of the Commission on the topic and made suggestions for the future programme of work.

45. The Commission considered the first report of the Special Rapporteur from its 3613th to 3618th meetings, from 25 April to 3 May 2023. At its 3618th meeting, on 3 May 2023, the Commission decided to refer draft guidelines 1 and 2, as contained in the first report, to the Drafting Committee, taking into account the views expressed in the plenary debate.

46. At its 3631st meeting, on 25 May 2023, the Commission considered the report of the Drafting Committee on the topic (A/CN.4/L.983) and provisionally adopted draft guidelines 1 and 2 (see sect. C.1 below). At the same meeting, the Commission decided to change the title of the topic from "Settlement of international disputes to which international organizations are parties" to "Settlement of disputes to which international organizations are parties".

47. From its 3647th to 3649th meetings, on 26 and 27 July 2023, the Commission adopted the commentaries to the draft guidelines provisionally adopted at the current session (see sect. C.2 below).

---

[86] At its 3582nd meeting, on 17 May 2022. The topic had been included in the long-term programme of work of the Commission during its sixty-eighth session (2016), on the basis of the proposal contained in an annex to the report of the Commission to that session (*Yearbook ... 2016*, vol. II (Part Two), annex I, p. 233).

[87] At its 3612th meeting, on 5 August 2022.

C. Text of the draft guidelines on settlement of disputes to which international organizations are parties provisionally adopted by the Commission at its seventy-fourth session

1. Text of the draft guidelines

48. The text of the draft guidelines provisionally adopted by the Commission at its seventy-fourth session is reproduced below.

Guideline 1
Scope

The present draft guidelines concern the settlement of disputes to which international organizations are parties.

Guideline 2
Use of terms

For the purposes of the present draft guidelines:

(a) "international organization" means an entity possessing its own international legal personality, established by a treaty or other instrument governed by international law, that may include as members, in addition to States, other entities, and has at least one organ capable of expressing a will distinct from that of its members.

(b) "dispute" means a disagreement concerning a point of law or fact in which a claim or assertion is met with refusal or denial.

(c) "means of dispute settlement" refers to negotiation, enquiry, mediation, conciliation, arbitration, judicial settlement, resort to regional agencies or arrangements, or other peaceful means of resolving disputes.

2. Text of the draft guidelines and commentaries thereto provisionally adopted by the Commission at its seventy-fourth session

49. The text of the draft guidelines, together with commentaries, provisionally adopted by the Commission at its seventy-fourth session, is reproduced below.

Guideline 1
Scope

The present draft guidelines concern the settlement of disputes to which international organizations are parties.

Commentary

(1) Draft guideline 1 is concerned with the scope of application of the draft guidelines. The provision should be read together with draft guideline 2, which sets out the use of the terms "international organization", "dispute" and "means of dispute settlement". These terms also contribute to delimiting the scope of the topic.

(2) International organizations may be parties to a variety of disputes both on the international and the national level. Their disputes with members and host States, but also with third States or other international organizations, will most often arise under international law; whereas their disputes with private parties are likely to arise under national law or specifically stipulated applicable rules. Disputes with international organizations may also arise under the rules of the organization.

(3) Examples of the former type of disputes are those concerning rights and obligations under headquarters or seat agreements, such as those addressed in the *UNESCO Tax Regime*[88]

---

[88] *Tax regime governing pensions paid to retired UNESCO officials residing in France (France UNESCO)*, 14 January 2003, *Reports of International Arbitral Awards* (UNRIAA), vol. XXV(Sales No. E.05.V.5), pp. 231–266.

or the *EMBL-Germany* arbitrations,[89] or the issues giving rise to the advisory opinions of the International Court of Justice in the *WHO Regional Office*[90] or the *PLO Mission* cases.[91] Other examples of disputes at the international level are international claims raised by international organizations for injuries suffered by their agents, such as the dispute which formed the background to the International Court of Justice's *Reparation for Injuries* advisory opinion,[92] or claims raised against an international organization by States on behalf of their nationals, such as those addressed in the Belgium-United Nations settlement.[93]

(4) Examples of disputes at the national level are those of a delictual or tort character brought against an international organization by a private party being harmed by an international organization, such as the dispute giving rise to the *Starways* arbitration,[94] or disputes brought by an international organization against private parties for harm occurring, for instance, through the unauthorized use of the organization's logo or internet domain.[95] Furthermore, the most frequent types of disputes to which international organizations are parties – those concerning contractual rights and obligations, which are often governed by a specific national law or general principles of contract law –[96] fall under the category of disputes at the national level. Contractual and tort claims are often seen as giving rise to disputes of a "private law character" in the sense of article VIII, section 29, of the Convention on the Privileges and Immunities of the United Nations[97] or similar treaty provisions.[98]

(5) The former type of disputes may be qualified as "international disputes" and the latter as "non-international" or as disputes arising under "national" law,[99] or as disputes of a

---

[89] *European Molecular Biology Laboratory Arbitration (EMBL v. Germany)*, 29 June 1990, International Law Reports (ILR), vol. 105 (1997), pp. 1–74.

[90] *Interpretation of the Agreement of 25 March 1951 between the WHO and Egypt, Advisory Opinion, I.C.J. Reports 1980*, p. 7.

[91] *Applicability of the Obligation to Arbitrate under Section 21 of the United Nations Headquarters Agreement of 26 June 1947, Advisory Opinion, I.C.J. Reports 1988*, p. 12.

[92] *Reparation for injuries suffered in the service of the United Nations, Advisory Opinion, I.C.J. Reports 1949*, p. 174.

[93] Exchange of Letters Constituting an Agreement between the United Nations and Belgium Relating to the Settlement of Claims Filed against the United Nations in the Congo by Belgian Nationals (New York, 20 February 1965), *United Nations Juridical Yearbook 1965* (United Nations publication, Sales No. 67.V.3), p. 39.

[94] *Starways Limited v. United Nations*, 24 September 1969 (Bachrach, Sole Arbitrator), ILR, vol. 44 (1972), pp. 433–437.

[95] *International Bank for Reconstruction and Development d/b/a The World Bank v. Yoo Jin Sohn*, Case No. 2002-0222, Administrative Panel Decision, 7 May 2002, WIPO [World Intellectual Property Organization] Arbitration and Mediation Center. Available at https://www.wipo.int/amc/en/domains/decisions/html/2002/d2002-0222.html.

[96] See "Legal opinion of the Secretariat of the United Nations on law applicable to contracts concluded by the United Nations with private parties–procedures for settling disputes arising out of such contracts–relevant rules and practices", *United Nations Juridical Yearbook 1976* (United Nations publication, Sales No. E.78.V.5), p. 159, at p. 165; "Legal opinion of the Secretariat of the United Nations on determination of the applicable law to contracts concluded between the United Nations and private parties – "service contracts" and "functional contracts" – UNCITRAL arbitral rules", *United Nations Juridical Yearbook 1988* (United Nations publication, Sales No. E.99.V.1), p. 285. See also August Reinisch, "Contracts between international organizations and private law persons", in Anne Peters and Rüdiger Wolfrum (eds.), *The Max Planck Encyclopedia of Public International Law* (online, Oxford University Press, 2021). Available at http://www.mpepil.com/.

[97] Art. VIII, sect. 29, of the Convention on the Privileges and Immunities of the United Nations (New York, 13 February 1946), United Nations, *Treaty Series*, vol. 1, No. 4, p. 15 ("The United Nations shall make provisions for appropriate modes of settlement of: (a) Disputes arising out of contracts or other disputes of a private law character to which the United Nations is a party").

[98] Art. IX, sect. 31, of the Convention on the Privileges and Immunities of the Specialized Agencies (New York, 21 November 1947), *ibid.*, vol. 33, No. 521, p. 261.

[99] The Commission's terminology has varied. In addition to referring in other topics to "national" law (see, *e.g.*, art. 2, para. 3, and art. 6 of the draft articles on prevention and punishment of crimes against humanity, *Official Records of the General Assembly, Seventy-fourth Session, Supplement No. 10* (A/74/10), paras. 44–45; arts. 14 and 15 of the draft articles on the protection of persons in the event of disasters, *Yearbook of the International Law Commission, 2016*, vol. II (Part Two), p. 26, para. 48), it has used the expressions "municipal" law (see, *e.g.*, draft arts. 29 and 38 of the draft

"private law character". However, such distinctions may be difficult to draw in practice, especially because the nature of a dispute may change. A tort claim for personal injury or property damage, giving rise to a dispute of a "private law character" may be transformed into an international claim through its espousal by the victim's home State exercising diplomatic protection.[100] Similarly, like States, international organizations can choose whether they want to regulate their mutual rights and obligations in the form of an instrument governed by international law or in the form of a private law contract.[101] The relationship between individuals working for an international organization may be governed by a contract or by staff rules and regulations, the latter often considered part of an international organization's internal administrative law.[102]

(6) Furthermore, "non-international" disputes, such as contractual or delictual/tort disputes, may raise important issues determined by international law, such as legal personality, jurisdictional immunity, human rights obligations, in particular the duty to provide for access to justice, or the treaty-based duty to make provision for appropriate modes of settlement of disputes of a private law character.[103]

(7) As a consequence, a sharp distinction between international disputes and non-international ones is often not feasible. To ensure that disputes of a "private law character" and any disputes that may be qualified as "non-international" fall within the scope of the present draft guidelines, the Commission decided not to include the word "international" before "disputes" in the present draft guideline 1. As a result, the Commission also decided, on 25 May 2023, to change the title of the topic by deleting the word "international" before "disputes" to make it clear that the draft guidelines would address all kinds of disputes to which international organizations are parties.[104]

(8) International organizations may be subject to various obligations concerning the settlement of disputes to which they are parties. These may be found in, among others, their constituent instruments,[105] multilateral privileges and immunities treaties,[106] or headquarters agreements.[107] Furthermore, international organizations may have agreed to specific forms of dispute settlement in contracts with third parties.[108] It is thus not feasible to design across-

articles on consular relations, *Yearbook ... 1961*, vol. II, at pp. 109 and 113–114; para. (3) of the commentary to art. 1 of the articles on the responsibility of international organizations, *Yearbook ... 2011*, vol. II (Part Two), paras. 87–88, at p. 47 (see also General Assembly resolution 66/100 of 9 December 2011, annex)), "internal" law (see, *e.g.*, arts. 3, 4 and 32 of the articles on responsibility of States for internationally wrongful acts and commentaries thereto, *Yearbook ... 2001*, vol. II (Part Two) and corrigendum, para. 76, at pp. 36–38, 40–42 and 94 (see also General Assembly resolution 56/83 of 12 December 2001, annex)), as well as "domestic" law (see, *e.g.*, paras. (1), (2) and (4) of the commentary to draft art. 9 of the draft articles on consular relations, *Yearbook ... 1961*, vol. II, at pp. 99–100).

100 Jean-Pierre Ritter, "La protection diplomatique à l'égard d'une organisation internationale", *Annuaire français de droit international*, vol. 8 (1962), pp. 427–456.

101 See para. (3) of the commentary to draft art. 2 of the draft articles on the law of treaties between States and international organizations or between international organizations, *Yearbook ... 1982*, vol. II (Part Two), para. 63, at p. 18.

102 C.F. Amerasinghe, *The Law of the International Civil Service as Applied by International Administrative Tribunals*, 2 vols. (Oxford, Clarendon Press; New York, Oxford University Press, 1988); Henry G. Schermers and Niels M. Blokker, *International Institutional Law: Unity Within Diversity*, 6th ed. (Leiden, Brill Nijhoff, 2018), pp. 382 et seq.

103 See, for the United Nations, Report of the Secretary-General on procedures in place for implementation of article VIII, section 29, of the Convention on the Privileges and Immunities of the United Nations, adopted by the General Assembly on 13 February 1946 (A/C.5/49/65), para. 5.

104 At its 3631st meeting, held on 25 May 2023.

105 Art. XVIII, paragraph (a), of the Agreement relating to the International Telecommunications Satellite Organization "INTELSAT" (Washington, opened for signature 20 August 1971), United Nations, *Treaty Series*, vol. 1220, No. 19677, p. 21.

106 Art. 32 of the Agreement on the Privileges and Immunities of the International Criminal Court (New York, 9 September 2002), *ibid.*, vol. 2271, No. 40446, p. 3.

107 Art. VIII, sect. 21, of the Agreement between the United Nations and the United States of America regarding the Headquarters of the United Nations (Lake Success, 26 June 1947), *ibid.*, vol. 11, No. 147, p. 11.

108 See footnote 103 above.

the-board draft articles that may eventually form the basis for a treaty. Instead, it seems more apt to restate the existing practices of international organizations concerning the settlement of their disputes and to develop recommendations for the most appropriate way of handling them.[109]

(9) For this purpose, the elaboration of a set of draft guidelines appears to be the most suitable form for the Commission's output, which is intended to direct States, international organizations and other users to answers that are consistent with existing rules or that seem most appropriate for contemporary practice.[110] The guidelines will be mainly concerned with the availability and adequacy of means for the settlement of disputes to which international organizations are parties. They are not intended to elaborate detailed sets of procedural rules.

(10) In addition to the guidelines, however, the Commission may also develop a set of model clauses that may be used in treaties or other instruments governed by international law, as well as in contracts or other national law instruments.

Guideline 2
Use of terms

For the purposes of the present draft guidelines:

(a) "international organization" means an entity possessing its own international legal personality, established by a treaty or other instrument governed by international law, that may include as members, in addition to States, other entities, and has at least one organ capable of expressing a will distinct from that of its members.

(b) "dispute" means a disagreement concerning a point of law or fact in which a claim or assertion is met with refusal or denial.

(c) "means of dispute settlement" refers to negotiation, enquiry, mediation, conciliation, arbitration, judicial settlement, resort to regional agencies or arrangements, or other peaceful means of resolving disputes.

Commentary

(1) Draft guideline 2 provides for the use of three core terms found in draft guideline 1. These terms contribute to delimiting the scope of the draft guidelines.

Subparagraph (a)

(2) The definition of "international organization" in draft guideline 2, subparagraph (*a*), builds on the definition contained in article 2, subparagraph (*a*), of the articles on the responsibility of international organizations, adopted by the Commission in 2011. Draft guideline 2, subparagraph (*a*), outlines the commonly accepted characteristic features of an international organization and stresses the possession of its "own international legal personality" as the paramount characteristic relevant for purposes of dispute settlement.

(3) The Commission initially defined "international organizations" merely as "intergovernmental organizations" in its 1966 draft articles on the law of treaties.[111] This definition can be found in several conventions, such as the Vienna Convention on the Law

[109] See para. (2) of the introduction to the Guide to Practice on Reservations to Treaties, *Yearbook ... 2011*, vol II (Part Three), at p. 35 ("The purpose of this Guide is not – or, in any case, not only – to offer the reader a guide to past (and often uncertain) practice in this area, but rather to direct the user towards solutions that are consistent with existing rules (where they exist) or to the solutions that seem most appropriate for the progressive development of such rules").

[110] See para. (1) of the general commentary to the Guide to Provisional Application of Treaties, *Official Records of the General Assembly, Seventy-sixth Session, Supplement No. 10* (A/76/10), para. 52 ("The objective of the Guide is to direct States, international organizations and other users to answers that are consistent with existing rules or that seem most appropriate for contemporary practice").

[111] *Yearbook ... 1966*, vol. II, document A/6309/Rev.1, at pp. 177–274.

of Treaties,[112] the Vienna Convention on the Law of Treaties between States and International Organizations or between International Organizations,[113] the Vienna Convention on the Representation of States in their Relations with International Organizations,[114] and the Vienna Convention on Succession of States in respect of Treaties.[115] This definition mainly served the purpose of excluding non-governmental organizations. However, the question of the adequacy of merely identifying "international organizations" as "intergovernmental organizations", without further defining them, was raised within the Commission.[116]

(4) With the articles on the responsibility of international organizations, the Commission adopted a more elaborate definition.[117] The simple reference to their "intergovernmental" nature in the previous definition was criticized as too narrow because several organizations consisted of members other than States: in particular, other international organizations.[118] Article 2, subparagraph (a), of the articles on the responsibility of international organizations defined an "international organization" as

> an organization established by treaty or other instrument governed by international law and possessing its own international legal personality. International organizations may include as members, in addition to States, other entities.[119]

In this definition, the Commission emphasized that the legal basis of an international organization was to be found on the international level, by referring to an "organization established by treaty or other instrument governed by international law". It did not explicitly refer to the common characteristic feature of organs through which an organization acts; although the existence of "organs" was arguably inherent in the notion of an "organization" and the articles on the responsibility of international organizations even contain a definition

---

[112] Art. 2, para. 1 (*i*), Vienna Convention on the Law of Treaties (Vienna, 23 May 1969), United Nations, *Treaty Series*, vol. 1155, No. 18232, p. 331 ("'international organization' means an intergovernmental organization").

[113] Art. 2, para. 1 (*i*), Vienna Convention on the Law of Treaties between States and International Organizations or between International Organizations (Vienna, 21 March 1986, not yet in force), *Official Records of the United Nations Conference on the Law of Treaties between States and International Organizations or between International Organizations (Documents of the Conference)*, vol. II, document A/CONF.129/15 (reproduced in A/CONF.129/16/Add.1 (Vol. II)) ("'international organization' means an intergovernmental organization").

[114] Art. 1, para. 1, of the Vienna Convention on the Representation of States in their Relations with International Organizations of a Universal Character (Vienna, 14 March 1975, not yet into force), A/CONF.67/16; or *United Nations Juridical Yearbook 1975* (United Nations publication, Sales No. E.77.V.3), p. 87 ("'international organization' means an intergovernmental organization").

[115] Art. 2, para. 1 (n), of the Vienna Convention on Succession of States in respect of Treaties (Vienna, 23 August 1978), United Nations, *Treaty Series*, vol. 1946, No. 33356, p. 3 ("'international organization' means an intergovernmental organization").

[116] Para. (23) to draft art. 2 of the draft articles on the law of treaties between States and international organizations or between international organizations, *Yearbook ... 1982*, vol. II (Part Two), para. 63, at p. 21 ("the Commission has wondered whether the concept of international organization should not be defined by something other than the 'intergovernmental' nature of the organization").

[117] The Commission's Special Rapporteur, Giorgio Gaja, originally suggested the use of the term "international organization" for "an organization which includes States among its members insofar as it exercises in its own capacity certain governmental functions". See *Yearbook ... 2003*, vol. II (Part One), document A/CN.4/532 (first report on responsibility of international organizations), p. 105, para. 34.

[118] Para. (3) of the commentary to art. 2 of the articles on the responsibility of international organizations, *Yearbook ... 2011*, vol. II (Part Two), paras. 87–88, at p. 49 ("First, it is questionable whether by defining an international organization as an intergovernmental organization one provides much information: it is not even clear whether the term 'intergovernmental organization' refers to the constituent instrument or to actual membership. Second, the term 'intergovernmental' is in any case inappropriate to a certain extent, because several important international organizations have been established with the participation also of State organs other than Governments. Third, an increasing number of international organizations include among their members entities other than States as well as States").

[119] Art. 2 (a), *ibid.*, at p. 49.

of organs,[120] which appears to indicate that organs are integral features of international organizations. The definition in the articles on the responsibility of international organizations further expressly reflected the fact that, in addition to States, other entities might become members of international organizations.[121] Finally, it highlighted that a core feature of an international organization is the possession of its own international legal personality, i.e. a legal personality on the international plane distinct from that of its members. This is particularly important for incurring international responsibility.[122]

(5) Most international organizations are established by treaties regardless of how they may be referred to: they include instruments designated as treaties, conventions, charters, constitutions, statutes, or articles of agreement.[123] In order to cover organizations established on the international plane without a treaty, draft guideline 2, subparagraph (*a*), refers, as an alternative to treaties, to any "other instrument governed by international law". Some international organizations have been set up by resolutions adopted by an international organization[124] or by decisions at conferences of States. An example of the former is the establishment of the United Nations Industrial Development Organization (UNIDO)[125] which was originally a subsidiary organ of the General Assembly of the United Nations.[126] After decisions taken within the United Nations in 1979,[127] it became a United Nations specialized agency when the relationship agreement, accepted by the General Assembly in 1985,[128] entered into force. Examples of organizations established by decisions of conferences include the Asian-African Legal Consultative Organization,[129] the Organization of the Petroleum

---

120 Art. 2 (c), *ibid.* ("'organ of an international organization' means any person or entity which has that status in accordance with the rules of the organization").

121 See para. (8) of the commentary to draft guideline 2 below.

122 Para. (10) of the commentary to article 2, *ibid.*, at p. 50.

123 Schermers and Blokker, *International Institutional Law* ... (see footnote 102 above), p. 15.

124 Institute of International Law, resolution of the 7th Commission, "Limits to evolutive interpretation of the constituent instruments of the organizations within the United Nations system by their internal organs", 4 September 2021, first preambular paragraph ("Noting that international organizations are established by multilateral agreements or by decisions of other international organizations").

125 Constitution of the United Nations Industrial Development Organization (Vienna, 8 April 1979), United Nations, *Treaty Series*, vol. 1401, No. 23432, p. 3. See also Abdulqawi A. Yusuf, "The role of the legal adviser in the reform and restructuring of an international organization: the case of UNIDO", in United Nations (ed.), *Collection of Essays by Legal Advisers of States, Legal Advisers of International Organizations and Practitioners in the Field of International Law* (1999), pp. 329–350.

126 General Assembly resolution 2152 (XXI) of 17 November 1966.

127 General Assembly resolution 34/96 of 13 December 1979.

128 General Assembly resolution 40/180 of 17 December 1985; United Nations, *Treaty Series*, vol. 1412, No. 937, p. 305.

129 The Asian-African Legal Consultative Organization (originally known as the Asian-African Legal Consultative Committee) was constituted by the Governments of Burma, Ceylon, India, Indonesia, Iraq, Japan and Syria on 15 November 1956, as an outcome of the Asia-Africa Conference, held in Bandung, Indonesia, in April 1955. Asian Legal Consultative Committee Statutes (1956), in "Asian Legal Consultative Committee: first session – New Delhi: India, April 18 to 27, 1957" (New Delhi, Caxton Press), p. 7, available at https://www.aalco.int/First%20Session%20New%20Delhi.pdf.

Exporting Countries,[130] the Association of Southeast Asian Nations,[131] the Southern African Development Community,[132] or the Nordic Council.[133]

(6) The establishment of international organizations based on an instrument governed by international law is crucial for distinguishing them from non-governmental organizations (NGOs)[134] as well as from transnational corporations or multinational enterprises.[135] NGOs and business entities are created on the basis of national law and usually take the various forms available to non-profit entities, such as associations, foundations or charities,[136] or to corporate entities with a profit-making purpose.[137] These entities are not international

---

[130] See Agreement concerning the creation of the Organization of Petroleum Exporting Countries (OPEC) (Baghdad, 14 September 1960), United Nations, *Treaty Series*, vol. 443, No. 6363, p. 247, Resolution I. 2, para. 1 ("With a view to giving effect to the provisions of Resolution No. I the Conference decides to form a permanent Organization called the Organization of the Petroleum Exporting Countries, for regular consultation among its Members with a view to …").

[131] The Association of Southeast Asian Nations (ASEAN) was established by a declaration of the foreign ministers of five States in 1967 (Bangkok Declaration). ASEAN was transformed into an organization through the Charter of the Association of Southeast Asian Nations (ASEAN Charter) (Singapore, 20 November 2007), United Nations, *Treaty Series*, vol. 2624, No. 46745, p. 223.

[132] The predecessor of the Southern African Development Community was the Southern African Development Co-ordination Conference. The Southern African Development Co-ordination Conference was established through a series of decisions adopted at conferences of States with incremental institutionalization. On 17 August 1992, the Southern African Development Community was founded at a summit held in Windhoek. See Declaration and Treaty of the Southern African Development Community, available at https://www.sadc.int/sites/default/files/2021-11/Declaration__Treaty_of_SADC_0.pdf.

[133] Denmark, Iceland, Norway and Sweden were the founding members of the Nordic Council when it was formed in 1952. See Nordic Co-Operation, "The Nordic Council", available at https://www.norden.org/en/information/nordic-council.

[134] See Economic and Social Council resolution 1996/31 on the arrangements for consultation with non-governmental organizations, para. 12 ("Any such organization that is not established by a governmental entity or intergovernmental agreement shall be considered a non-governmental organization for the purpose of these arrangements").

[135] In United Nations terminology, the notion "transnational corporations" prevails (see Commission on Transnational Corporations, established by the Economic and Social Council, pursuant to its resolution 1913 (LVII) (*Yearbook of the United Nations 1974* (United Nations publication, Sales No. E.76.I.1), vol. 28, part 1, p. 485), whereas the Organisation for Economic Co-operation and Development (OECD) uses the expression "multinational enterprises" (see OECD, *Guidelines for Multinational Enterprises* (2011 ed.)). See also Peter T. Muchlinski, *Multinational Enterprises and the Law*, 3rd ed. (Oxford, Oxford University Press, 2021), pp. 3 et seq.

[136] A useful definition of NGOs is found in article 1 of the European Convention on the Recognition of the Legal Personality of International Non-Governmental Organizations (Strasbourg, 24 April 1986), *European Treaty Series*, No. 124 (NGOs are "associations, foundations and other private institutions which …: (a) have a non-profit-making aim of international utility; (b) have been established by an instrument governed by the internal law of a Party; (c) carry on their activities with effect in at least two States; and (d) have their statutory office in the territory of a Party and the central management and control in the territory of that Party or of another Party"). See also Bas Arts, Math Noortmann and Bob Reinalda (eds.), *Non-State Actors in International Relations* (Aldershot, Ashgate, 2001); Math Noortmann, August Reinisch and Cedric Ryngaert (eds.), *Non-State Actors in International Law* (Oxford, Bloomsbury, 2015); Stephan Hobe, "Non-governmental organizations", in Rüdiger Wolfrum (ed.), *The Max Planck Encyclopedia of Public International Law* vol. VII (Oxford, Oxford University Press, 2012), p. 716.

[137] The Code of Conduct on Transnational Corporations refers to transnational corporations as enterprises "comprising entities in two or more countries, regardless of the legal form and fields of activity of these entities, which operate under a system of decision-making, permitting coherent policies and a common strategy through one or more decision-making centres, in which the entities are so linked, by ownership or otherwise, that one or more of them may be able to exercise a significant influence over the activities of others and, in particular, to share knowledge, resources and responsibilities with the others" (E/1988/39/Add.1, para. 1) and the OECD *Guidelines for Multinational Enterprises* indicate that "multinational enterprises … operate in all sectors of the economy. They usually comprise companies or other entities established in more than one country and so linked that they may coordinate their operations in various ways. While one or more of these entities may be able to exercise a significant influence over the activities of others, their degree of

organizations as understood for the purposes of the present draft guidelines since they are not established by an instrument governed by international law.

(7) Even in the rare instances where an NGO is transformed into an international organization, that international organization is created by an international agreement. For instance, the International Union of Official Travel Organizations was originally a non-governmental organization under Swiss law that was subsequently transformed into the World Tourism Organization.[138] Today, the World Tourism Organization is a specialized agency of the United Nations.[139] It was created by States "whose official tourism organisations are Full Members of [the International Union of Official Travel Organizations] at the time of adoption of these Statutes" through ratifying a treaty.[140]

(8) The reference to "a treaty or other instrument governed by international law" reflects the fact that only States, other *sui generis* subjects of international law, such as the Holy See or the Sovereign Order of Malta, and international organizations which possess treaty-making capacity can be parties to an international organization's constituent treaty. It is not intended to exclude entities other than States from subsequently becoming members of an international organization.

(9) The reference to "other entities" than States as potential members of international organizations affirms that even entities not possessing treaty-making capacity may be accepted as members of an organization if the rules of that organization so provide. In this sense, some – in particular technical – international organizations have members that are not sovereign States, but territories or entities with capacities relevant to the respective organizations. For instance, certain territories have been able to become members of the World Trade Organization[141] or of the World Meteorological Organization.[142]

(10) The fact that subparagraph (*a*) considers that an international organization "may include as members, in addition to States, other entities" does not necessarily imply that a plurality of States as members is required. Thus, an international organization may be established by a State and an international organization, as was the case with the Special Court for Sierra Leone.[143] It is also not meant to imply that it always requires States as members. Although rare in practice, international organizations may be established by and entirely consist of international organizations, as evidenced by the Joint Vienna Institute.[144]

(11) Nevertheless, the most frequent cases of entities other than States becoming members of international organizations are international organizations. This is particularly true for regional (economic) integration organizations. A number of constituent instruments of international organizations expressly provide for such membership.[145]

---

autonomy within the enterprise may vary widely from one multinational enterprise to another. Ownership may be private, State or mixed" (sect. I. Concepts and Principles, para. 4).

138 Statutes of the World Tourism Organization (Mexico City, 27 September 1970), United Nations, *Treaty Series*, vol. 985, No. 14403, p. 339.

139 General Assembly resolution 58/232 of 23 December 2003.

140 Art. 36, Statutes of the World Tourism Organization.

141 Art. XII, para. 1 ("Accession"), of the Marrakesh Agreement establishing the World Trade Organization (Marrakesh, 15 April 1994, entered into force 1 January 1995), United Nations, *Treaty Series*, vol. 1867, No. 31874, p. 3 (permitting membership of "[a]ny separate customs territory possessing full autonomy in the conduct of its external commercial relations").

142 Art. 3 of the Convention of the World Meteorological Organization (Washington D.C., 11 November 1947), *ibid.*, vol. 77, No. 998, p. 143 (permitting membership of "[a]ny territory or group of territories maintaining its own meteorological service").

143 Agreement between the United Nations and the Government of Sierra Leone on the establishment of a Special Court for Sierra Leone (Freetown, on 16 January 2002), *ibid.*, vol. 2178, No. 38342, p. 137.

144 Agreement for the establishment of the Joint Vienna Institute (Vienna, 27 and 29 July 1994 and 10 and 19 August 1994), *ibid.*, vol. 2029, No. 1209, p. 391. The Joint Vienna Institute was established by the Bank for International Settlements, the European Bank for Reconstruction and Development, the International Bank for Reconstruction and Development, the International Monetary Fund and the Organisation for Economic Co-operation and Development. Subsequently, the World Trade Organization also joined.

145 Art. II, para. 3, of the Constitution of the Food and Agriculture Organization of the United Nations (Quebec, 16 October 1945), *British and Foreign State Papers*, vol. 145, p. 910, provides for the

(12) Subparagraph (*a*) further specifically mentions the possession of "at least one organ capable of expressing a will distinct from that of its members". This characteristic feature of an international organization is only implicitly found in the 2011 definition of the Commission.[146]

(13) The inclusion of this element in the text of the definition makes explicit the generally accepted view that an international organization must have at least one organ that is capable of expressing the organization's will ("will of its own" or "*volonté distincte*")[147] in order to perform the tasks or functions entrusted to the organization. The concept of an international organization's own will is closely related to the idea that an international organization has a legal personality separate from its members,[148] or, as the International Court of Justice put it, "a certain autonomy", and that through such organs international organizations can pursue "common goals".[149]

(14) International organizations regularly possess numerous organs, such as plenary organs, in which all members are represented, executive ones with a more restricted composition, secretariats and often expert or judicial organs with individuals serving in their personal capacities.[150] That a minimum of one organ is required to distinguish an organization

possibility "to admit as a Member of the Organization any regional economic integration organization meeting the criteria set out in paragraph 4 of this Article". That paragraph specifies that "a regional economic integration organization must be one constituted by sovereign States, a majority of which are Member Nations of the Organization, and to which its Member States have transferred competence over a range of matters within the purview of the Organization, including the authority to make decisions binding on its Member States in respect of those matters". To date, only the European Union has made use of this option. See *Basic texts of the Food and Agriculture Organization of the United Nations, vols. I and II*, 2017 ed., p. 240. See also art. 4 of the Agreement establishing the Common Fund for Commodities (Geneva, 27 June 1980), United Nations, *Treaty Series*, vol. 1538, No. 26691, p. 3 ("Membership in the Fund shall be open to: … [a]ny intergovernmental organization of regional economic integration which exercises competence in fields of activity of the Fund").

146 See text at footnote 120 above.

147 Éric David, *Droit des Organisations Internationales* (Brussels, Bruylant, 2016), p. 582; Manuel Diez de Velasco Vallejo, *Las Organizaciones Internacionales*, 14th ed. (Madrid, Tecnos, 2006), pp. 46–47; Rosalyn Higgins *et al.*, *Oppenheim's International Law: United Nations* (Oxford University Press, Oxford, 2017), p. 385; Jan Klabbers, *An Introduction to International Organizations Law*, 4th ed. (Cambridge, Cambridge University Press, 2022), p. 12; Shigeru Kozai et al., *Introduction to International Law*, 3rd ed. (Tokyo, Yuhikaku Publishing Co. Ltd., 1988), p. 101; Pierre-Yves Marro, *Rechtsstellung internationaler Organisationen* (Zürich, Dike, 2021), p. 29; Francisco Rezek, *Direito internacional público*, 16th ed. (São Paulo, Editora Saraiva, 2016), pp. 301–302; Matthias Ruffert and Christian Walter, *Institutionalisiertes Völkerrecht. Das Recht der Internationalen Organisationen und seine wichtigsten Anwendungsfelder,* 2nd ed. (Munich, C.H. Beck, 2015), p. 4; Schermers and Blokker, *International Institutional Law …* (see footnote 102 above), pp. 48 and 1031; Kirsten Schmalenbach, "International organizations or institutions, general aspects", in Rüdiger Wolfrum (ed.), *The Max Planck Encyclopedia of Public International Law* vol. V (Oxford, Oxford University Press, 2012), p. 1128; Ignaz Seidl-Hohenveldern and Gerhard Loibl, *Das Recht der Internationalen Organisationen einschließlich der Supranationalen Gemeinschaften*, 7th ed. (Köln, Carl Heymanns, 2000), p. 7.

148 See para. (10) of the commentary to article 2 of the articles on the responsibility of international organizations, *Yearbook … 2011*, vol. II (Part Two), paras. 87–88, at p. 50 (referring to "the requirement in article 2, subparagraph (*a*), that the international legal personality should be the organization's 'own', a term that the Commission considers as synonymous with the phrase 'distinct from that of its member States'").

149 *Legality of the Use by a State of Nuclear Weapons in Armed Conflict*, Advisory Opinion, *I.C.J. Reports 1996*, p. 66, at p. 75, para. 19 (characterizing the object of constituent instruments of international organizations as "to create new subjects of law endowed with a certain autonomy, to which the parties entrust the task of realizing common goals").

150 See Celso D. de Albuquerque Mello, *Curso de Direito Internacional Público*, vol. I, 12th ed. (Rio de Janeiro, Renovar, 2000), pp. 577–579; José E. Alvarez, *International Organizations as Law-makers* (Oxford, Oxford University Press, 2005), p. 9; Jean Combacau and Serge Sur, *Droit international public*, 13th ed. (Paris, LGDJ, 2019), pp. 782 et seq.; Diez de Velasco Vallejo, *Las Organizaciones Internacionales* (footnote 147 above), pp. 101–109.

from a mere treaty-based form of cooperation seems inherent in the notion of "organization".[151]

(15) The will of organizations is formed through the decision-making procedures to be adhered to by their organs pursuant to the rules of the various organizations. These decision-making procedures may range from different forms of majority voting to unanimity, consensus or other techniques. So-called member-driven or forum-like organizations, operating on the basis of unanimity and expressing the collective will of their members, can also be considered to express the organizations' own will.

(16) Subparagraph *(a)* reaffirms the requirement of the possession of international legal personality as found in the 2011 definition of the Commission in the articles on the responsibility of international organizations. Such personality is required for the purposes of entering into treaties, incurring international responsibility or, in the present context, for raising international claims or being the respondent to such claims, or more generally being a party before an international dispute settlement mechanism.

(17) There exists a long-standing scholarly debate about the source of such personality.[152] According to the "will theory",[153] international organizations derive their international legal personality from the express or implied will of the entities creating them. Pursuant to the "objective personality theory", their international legal personality stems from their mere existence.[154] A third, compromise approach[155] asserts that the international legal personality of an international organization can be presumed, when it performs acts that require such separate personality.

(18) In the past, international legal personality was only rarely explicitly conferred upon an international organization in its constituent instrument.[156] Thus, it regularly had to be

---

[151] Antônio Augusto Cançado Trindade, *Princípios do Direito Internacional Contemporâneo*, 2nd ed. (Brasília, Fundação Alexandre de Gusmão, 2017) p. 336; Mathias Forteau and others, *Droit international public*, 9th ed. (Paris, LGDJ, 2022), p. 861; Inés Martínez Valinotti, *Derecho Internacional Público* (Asunción, Colección de Estudios Internacionales, 2012), p. 229.

[152] Heber Arbuet-Vignali, "Las organizaciones internacionales como sujetos del derecho internacional", in Eduardo Jiménez de Aréchaga, Heber Arbuet-Vignali and Roberto Puceiro Ripoll (eds.), *Derecho Internacional Público: Principios, normas y estructuras*, vol. I (Montevideo, Fundación de Cultura Universitaria, 2005), pp. 154–156; David J. Bederman, "The souls of international organizations: legal personality and the lighthouse at Cape Spartel", *Virginia Journal of International Law*, vol. 36, No. 2 (1996), pp. 275–377; Chris Osakwe, "Contemporary Soviet doctrine on the juridical nature of universal international organizations", *American Journal of International Law*, vol. 65, No. 3 (July 1971), pp. 502–521; Manuel Rama-Montaldo, "International legal personality and implied powers of international organizations", *The British Yearbook of International Law*, vol. 44 (1970), pp. 111–155.

[153] Philippe Sands and Pierre Klein, *Bowett's Law of International Institutions*, 6th ed. (London, Sweet and Maxwell, 2009), p. 479; Ruffert and Walter, *Institutionalisiertes Völkerrecht* (see footnote 147 above), p. 58. See also Grigory I. Tunkin, "The legal nature of the United Nations", *Recueil des Cours*, vol. 119 (1966-III), pp. 1–68.

[154] Originally developed in a series of contributions by Finn Seyersted. See Finn Seyersted, "International personality of intergovernmental organizations: do their capacities really depend upon their constitutions?", *Indian Journal of International Law*, vol. 4 (1964), pp. 1–74; "Is the international personality of intergovernmental organizations valid vis-à-vis non-members?", *ibid.*, pp. 233–268; "Objective international personality of intergovernmental organizations: do their capacities really depend upon the conventions establishing them?", *Nordisk Tidsskrift for International Ret*, vol. 34 (1964), pp. 1–112. See also Pierre d'Argent, "La personnalité juridique de l'organisation internationale", in Evelyne Lagrange and Jean-Marc Sorel (eds.), *Droit des organisations internationales* (Paris, LGDJ, 2013), p. 452; Dapo Akande, "International organizations", in Malcolm D. Evans (ed.), *International Law*, 5th ed. (Oxford, Oxford University Press, 2018), pp. 233–234.

[155] Jan Klabbers, "Presumptive personality: the European Union in international law", in Martti Koskenniemi (ed.), *International Law Aspects of the European Union* (The Hague, Kluwer Law International, 1998), p. 231; Angelo Golia Jr and Anne Peters, "The concept of international organization", in Jan Klabbers (ed.), *The Cambridge Companion to International Organizations Law* (Cambridge, Cambridge University Press, 2022), p. 37.

[156] See, *e.g.* art. 10, sect. 1, of the Agreement establishing the International Fund for Agricultural Development (Rome, 13 June 1976), United Nations, *Treaty Series*, vol. 1059, No. 16041, p. 191 ("The Fund shall possess international legal personality"); art. 176 of the United Nations Convention

deduced from the powers conferred upon an international organization. Since the 1990s, however, the practice of including explicit clauses on international legal personality of the organization seems to have become more common.

(19) This was the approach of the International Court of Justice in the *Reparation for Injuries* advisory opinion.[157] Therein, the Court derived the international legal personality of the United Nations from the Charter-based rights of the Organization, which required its Members to assist it, to accept and carry out Security Council decisions, as well as from its privileges and immunities and its powers to conclude international agreements. The Court found that

> the Organization was intended to exercise and enjoy, and is in fact exercising and enjoying, functions and rights which can only be explained on the basis of the possession of a large measure of international personality and the capacity to operate upon an international plane.[158]

Since most international organizations perform at least some similar acts, having been either explicitly or implicitly empowered to do so, it seems safe to conclude that most international organizations enjoy international legal personality as a result. In fact, without possessing such personality, an international organization could not carry out its functions.[159] Therefore, it is generally accepted that international organizations possess international legal personality.[160]

---

on the Law of the Sea (with regard to the International Sea-Bed Authority) (Montego Bay, 10 December 1982), United Nations, *Treaty Series*, vol. 1833, No. 31363, p. 3 ("The Authority shall have international legal personality and such legal capacity as may be necessary for the exercise of its functions and the fulfilment of its purposes"); art. 34 of the Additional Protocol to the Asunción Treaty on the Institutional Structure of Mercosur [Southern Common Market] (Ouro Preto, 17 December 1994), *ibid.*, vol. 2145, annex A, No. A-37341, p. 298 ("Mercosur shall possess legal personality of international law"); art. 4, para. 1, of the Rome Statute of the International Criminal Court (Rome, 17 July 1998), *ibid.*, vol. 2187, No. 38544, p. 3 ("The Court shall have international legal personality"); art. I, para. 2, of the Agreement for the Establishment of the International Anti-Corruption Academy as an International Organization (Vienna, 2 September 2010), *ibid.*, vol. 2751, No. 48545, p. 81 ("The Academy shall possess full international legal personality").

157 *Reparation for injuries suffered in the service of the United Nations* (see footnote 92 above).

158 *Ibid.*, p. 179.

159 See also the opinion of the International Court of Justice in the International Fund for Agricultural Development (IFAD) case, *Judgment No. 2867 of the Administrative Tribunal of the International Labour Organization upon a Complaint Filed against the International Fund for Agricultural Development, Advisory Opinion, I.C.J. Reports 2012*, p. 10, at p. 36, para. 61, in which it found that "the Global Mechanism [of the United Nations Convention to Combat Desertification in Those Countries Experiencing Serious Drought and/or Desertification, Particularly in Africa] had no power and has not purported to exercise any power to enter into contracts, agreements or 'arrangements', internationally or nationally". This led the Court to conclude that in the absence of a separate legal personality, the Global Mechanism had to "identify an organization to house it and to make appropriate arrangements with such an organization for its administrative operations", which included IFAD employing staff members working for the Global Mechanism.

160 See paras. (7) et seq. of the commentary to article 2 of the articles on the responsibility of international organizations, *Yearbook ... 2011*, vol. II (Part Two), paras. 87–88, at p. 50; Schermers and Blokker, *International Institutional Law* ... (see footnote 102 above), pp. 1031 et seq.; James Crawford, *Brownlie's Principles of Public International Law*, 9th ed. (Oxford, Oxford University Press, 2019), p. 157; Paola Gaeta, Jorge E. Viñuales and Salvatore Zappalà, *Cassese's International Law*, 3rd ed. (Oxford, Oxford University Press, 2020), pp. 143–145; Golia Jr and Peters, "The concept of international organization" (see footnote 155 above), p. 37; see also Tarcisio Gazzini, "Personality of international organizations", in Jan Klabbers and Åsa Wallendahl (eds.), *Research Handbook on the Law of International Organizations* (Cheltenham, Edward Elgar Publishing, 2011), p. 33; Zewei Yang (ed.), *Liang Xi's International Organization Law–Principles and Practices*, 7th ed. (Wuhan, Wuhan University Press, 2022), pp. 4–5. There remains controversy over the international legal personality and the status of organizations such as the Organization for Security and Cooperation in Europe (OSCE). See Niels M. Blokker and Ramses A. Wessel, "Revisiting questions of organisationhood, legal personality and membership in the OSCE: the interplay between law, politics and practice", in Manteja Steinbrück Platise, Carolyn Moser and Anne Peters (eds.), *The Legal Framework of the OSCE* (Cambridge, Cambridge University Press, 2019), pp. 135–164.

(20) In the *Reparation for Injuries* advisory opinion, the Court, which was asked whether the United Nations had the power to bring an international claim against a non-Member State, also found that it had "objective international personality",[161] implying that the personality of the United Nations had effect not only for its members, but also for third States. While it was argued that such "objective international personality" appertained only to the United Nations, allowing non-Member States to refuse to recognize other international organizations,[162] recent practice indicates that other international organizations are also generally considered to possess such personality.[163] Nevertheless, formal or implied recognition, *e.g.* through the conclusion of treaties or the establishment of official relations, may serve as supporting evidence of the international legal personality of international organizations.[164]

(21) The existence of organs through which an international organization will perform the powers entrusted to it is usually easier to ascertain than the possession of international legal personality.

(22) In doctrine concerning international organizations, the correlation between the possession of organs and of international legal personality is sometimes regarded as a consequential one, in the sense that the possession of organs permitting an international organization to express an independent will result in its possession of international legal personality.[165] Others take the view that the two should be treated totally separate.[166] The present draft guideline 2, subparagraph (*a*), does not prejudge either position.

Subparagraph (b)

(23) Draft guideline 2, subparagraph (*b*) explaining the term "dispute" builds on the definition contained in the *Mavrommatis Palestine Concessions* judgment[167] and is sufficiently general to encompass legal disputes arising at the international level and under national law whether of a public or private law nature.

---

161 *Reparation for injuries suffered in the service of the United Nations* (see footnote 92 above), p. 185.

162 See, *e.g.*, the Soviet Union's policy of non-recognition of the European Economic Community (EEC). Sands and Klein, *Bowett's Law of International Institutions* (footnote 153 above), p. 480; Schermers and Blokker, *International Institutional Law* ... (see footnote 102 above), pp. 1238 et seq.

163 See Akande, "International organizations", pp. 233–234 ("Thus, international organizations with a membership consisting of the vast majority of the international community possess objective international personality. However, it is important to note that the Court did not say that only such organizations possess objective personality and there are good reasons of practice and principle for concluding that the personality possessed by any international organization is objective and opposable to non-members. In practice, 'no recent instances are known of a non-member State refusing to acknowledge the personality of an organization on the ground that it was not a member State and had not given the organization specific recognition' (Amerasinghe, 2005, p 87)"); Crawford, *Brownlie's Principles of Public International Law* (see footnote 160 above), p. 160 ("Although the Court conditioned its opinion on the quantity and standing of the founding Members of the [United Nations], there are good reasons for applying this proposition to *all* international organizations, and in practice this has occurred").

164 The practice at the United Nations of granting observer status to international organizations can be regarded as a recognition of the status of an entity as an international organization. See Miguel de Serpa Soares, "Responsibility of international organizations", in *Courses of the Summer School on Public International Law*, vol. 7 (Moscow, International and Comparative Law Research Center, 2022), p. 100.

165 C.F. Amerasinghe, *Principles of the Institutional Law of International Organizations*, 2nd ed. (Cambridge, Cambridge University Press, 2005), pp. 10–11; August Reinisch, *International Organizations Before National Courts* (Cambridge, Cambridge University Press, 2000), p. 6.

166 See Fernando Lusa Bordin, *The Analogy between States and International Organizations* (Cambridge, Cambridge University Press, 2018), pp. 72–79.

167 *The Mavrommatis Palestine Concessions*, Judgment No. 2, 1924, P.C.I.J. Series A, No. 2, p. 7.

(24) Pursuant to the *Mavrommatis* definition, endorsed by the International Court of Justice in numerous cases,[168] a legal dispute is "a disagreement on a point of law or fact, a conflict of legal views or of interests between two persons".[169]

(25) The International Court of Justice further clarified that a mere "conflict of … interests" will not necessarily amount to a legal dispute, and that "[i]t must be shown that the claim of one party is positively opposed by the other".[170] Thus, the core element of the *Mavrommatis* definition, a disagreement on a point of law or fact, is coupled with the "opposition of views" which can be generally expressed by "claims" that are met with "refusal" in regard to legal points and "assertions" that are met by "denial" in regard to factual points.[171] Many national legal systems rely on similar concepts when defining "disputes".[172]

(26) As in the *Mavrommatis* definition, draft guideline 2, subparagraph (*b*), only refers to disagreements on a point of law or fact and not to mere policy disputes, although it is acknowledged by the Commission that legal disputes may have policy underpinnings. Likewise, the fact that a dispute on a point of law may have political aspects does not deprive it of its legal character.[173]

(27) A disagreement on a point of fact will amount to a legal dispute if the factual assertions and denials are relevant in a legal context, *i.e.* relate to a point of law.[174]

(28) Given that a dispute implies a disagreement and involves claims and assertions that are positively opposed, it is not necessary to include any reference to potential parties to a dispute. A dispute stems from the fact that at least two persons disagree. Since the topic refers to disputes to which international organizations are parties, it is evident that at least one party to the relevant disagreements will be an international organization. Being a party to a dispute is without prejudice to the question of whether an international organization can be a party

---

168 See, *e.g.*, *Interpretation of Peace Treaties, Advisory Opinion, I.C.J. Reports 1950*, p. 65, at p. 74; *Certain Property (Liechtenstein v. Germany), Preliminary Objections, Judgment, I.C.J. Reports 2005*, p. 6, at p. 18, para. 24; *Armed Activities on the Territory of the Congo (New Application: 2002) (Democratic Republic of the Congo v. Rwanda), Jurisdiction and Admissibility, Judgment, I.C.J. Reports 2006*, p. 6, at p. 40, para. 90; *Territorial and Maritime Dispute between Nicaragua and Honduras in the Caribbean Sea (Nicaragua v. Honduras), Judgment, I.C.J. Reports 2007*, p. 659, at p. 700, para. 130.

169 *The Mavrommatis Palestine Concessions* (see footnote 167 above), p. 11.

170 See *e.g.*, *South West Africa Cases* (*Ethiopia v. South Africa; Liberia v. South Africa*), Preliminary Objections, Judgment, *I.C.J. Reports 1962*, p. 319, at p. 328; *Certain Property (Liechtenstein v. Germany), Preliminary Objections, Judgment, I.C.J. Reports 2005*, p. 6 at p. 18, para. 24 ("for the purposes of verifying the existence of a legal dispute it falls to the Court to determine whether 'the claim of one party is positively opposed by the other'"); *Alleged Violations of Sovereign Rights and Maritime Spaces in the Caribbean Sea (Nicaragua v. Colombia), Preliminary Objections*, Judgment, *I.C.J. Reports 2016*, p. 3, at p. 26, para. 50 ("It does not matter which one of them advances a claim and which one opposes it. What matters is that 'the two sides hold clearly opposite views concerning the question of the performance or non-performance of certain' international obligations) (*Interpretation of Peace Treaties with Bulgaria, Hungary and Romania, First Phase, Advisory Opinion, I.C.J. Reports 1950*, p. 74)".

171 See John Merrills and Eric De Brabandere, *Merrills' International Dispute Settlement*, 7th ed. (Cambridge, Cambridge University Press, 2022), p. 1 ("a specific disagreement concerning a matter of fact, law or policy in which a claim or assertion of one party is met with refusal, counter-claim or denial by another").

172 Jeffrey Lehman and Shirelle Phelps (eds.), *West's Encyclopedia of American Law*, vol. 3, 2nd ed. (Farmington Hills, Thomson Gale, 2005), p. 461 ("DISPUTE: A conflict or controversy, a conflict of claims or rights; an assertion of a right, claim, or demand on one side, met by contrary claims or allegations on the other").

173 See *United States Diplomatic and Consular Staff in Tehran*, Judgment, *I.C.J. Reports 1980*, p. 3, at p. 20, para. 37 ("legal disputes between sovereign States by their very nature are likely to occur in political contexts, and often form only one element in a wider and long-standing political dispute between the States concerned").

174 See, in particular, Article 36, para. 2 (c), of the Statute of the International Court of Justice (indicating the jurisdiction of the Court in all legal disputes concerning "the existence of any fact which, if established, would constitute a breach of an international obligation").

to specific legal proceedings on the international or national level.[175] In light of the broad scope of the present draft guidelines, as explained in the commentary to draft guideline 1 above, the other parties may be other international organizations, States, *sui generis* subjects of international law or private parties, including individuals or legal persons under national law, such as companies, associations or NGOs.

Subparagraph (c)

(29) Draft guideline 2, subparagraph (*c*), is inspired by Article 33 of the Charter of the United Nations.[176] It does not define dispute settlement. Rather, it lists the available means of dispute settlement in international and national law. This is also reflected by the use of the verb "refers" instead of "means". The draft guideline's wording follows closely the provision found in the Charter of the United Nations. Its broad formulation, including the open-ended element of "other peaceful means of resolving disputes", is meant to ensure that all potential means of dispute settlement both on the international as well as on the national level are covered.

(30) Article 33 of the Charter of the United Nations captures the scope of possible settlement methods from purely *inter partes* attempts to settle a dispute, starting with negotiations, to increased involvement of non-disputing third parties, in the form of binding arbitration or adjudication.[177] As the International Court of Justice has held in its advisory opinion in *Reparation for Injuries*, these forms of dispute settlement are generally also available to international organizations.[178] Of course, especially in the case of arbitration and adjudication, the applicable jurisdictional requirements will have to be fulfilled in order to allow international organizations to sue or to be sued.

(31) In order to preserve all means referenced in Article 33, draft guideline 2, subparagraph (*c*), maintains the wording "resort to regional agencies or arrangements", although it is most likely that such resort would take the form of one of the other means of dispute settlement listed. To date, such resort appears to have been limited in practice, but it does not seem excluded that, in a specific situation, a subregional organization may be subject to dispute settlement under a regional arrangement.

(32) Draft guideline 2, subparagraph (*c*), contains only a list of available means and does not imply an order in which dispute settlement means have to be resorted to. This is also underlined by the fact that draft guideline 2, subparagraph (*c*), "refers to" these means and does not state that the parties to a dispute "shall … seek a solution by" resorting to them. Therefore, it is not necessary to keep the words "of their own choice" as contained in Article 33 of the Charter.

(33) The phrase "of their own choice" is also deliberately omitted because, in some situations, international organizations may be subject to specific dispute settlement obligations pursuant to their constituent instruments, headquarters agreements or private law contracts.[179]

---

[175] Since international organizations cannot be parties before the International Court of Justice, some treaties provide that their disputes with States be settled through requesting an advisory opinion from the Court which the parties agree to accept as binding. See *e.g.* art. VIII, sect. 30, of the Convention on the Privileges and Immunities of the United Nations.

[176] Article 33 of the Charter of the United Nations ("The parties to any dispute, the continuance of which is likely to endanger the maintenance of international peace and security, shall, first of all, seek a solution by negotiation, enquiry, mediation, conciliation, arbitration, judicial settlement, resort to regional agencies or arrangements, or other peaceful means of their own choice.").

[177] Christian Tomuschat, "Article 33", in Bruno Simma *et al.* (eds.), *The Charter of the United Nations: A Commentary*, vol. II, 3rd ed. (Oxford, Oxford University Press, 2012), p. 1076, para. 23.

[178] *Reparation for injuries suffered in the service of the United Nations* (see footnote 92 above), p. 178.

[179] See para. (8) of the commentary to draft guideline 1 above.

(34) Draft guideline 2, subparagraph (*c*), lists "means of dispute settlement" and does not refer to an obligation to seek a solution of certain disputes, as Article 33 of the Charter does. It is clear that such a provision, found in the draft guideline entitled "Use of terms", cannot be understood as such to lead to an obligation to seek a solution or to actually resolve a dispute.

Chapter VI
Prevention and repression of piracy and armed robbery at sea

A. Introduction

50. At its seventy-third session (2022), the Commission decided to include the topic "Prevention and repression of piracy and armed robbery at sea" in its programme of work and appointed Mr. Yacouba Cissé as Special Rapporteur for the topic.[180] The Commission requested the Secretariat to prepare a memorandum concerning the topic, addressing in particular: elements in the previous work of the Commission that could be particularly relevant for its future work on the topic and the views expressed by States; writings relevant to the definitions of piracy and of armed robbery at sea; and resolutions adopted by the Security Council and by the General Assembly relevant to the topic. The Commission also approved the Special Rapporteur's recommendation that the Secretariat contact States and relevant international organizations in order to obtain information and views concerning the topic.[181]

51. Subsequently, the General Assembly, in paragraph 7 of its resolution 77/103 of 7 December 2022, took note of the decision of the Commission to include the topic in its programme of work.

B. Consideration of the topic at the present session

52. At the present session, the Commission had before it the first report of the Special Rapporteur (A/CN.4/758) and the memorandum prepared by the Secretariat concerning the topic (A/CN.4/757). In his first report, the Special Rapporteur addressed the historical, socioeconomic and legal aspects of the topic, including an analysis of the international law applicable to piracy and armed robbery at sea, and the shortcomings thereof. He reviewed the national legislation and judicial practice of States concerning the definition of piracy and the implementation of conventional and customary international law. The Special Rapporteur proposed three draft articles: on the scope of the draft articles, on the definition of piracy, and on the definition of armed robbery at sea. He also discussed the future programme of work on the topic.

53. The Commission considered the first report and the memorandum at its 3619th to 3621st and 3623rd to 3625th meetings, from 5 to 16 May 2023.

54. At its 3625th meeting, on 16 May 2023, the Commission decided to refer draft articles 1, 2 and 3, as contained in the first report, to the Drafting Committee, taking into account the views expressed in the plenary debate.

55. At its 3634th meeting, on 2 June 2023, the Commission considered the report of the Drafting Committee on the topic (A/CN.4/L.984) and provisionally adopted draft articles 1, 2 and 3 (see sect. C.1 below).

56. At its 3649th and 3651st meetings, on 27 and 31 July 2023, the Commission adopted the commentaries to the draft articles provisionally adopted at the current session (see sect. C.2 below).

---

[180] At its 3582nd meeting, on 17 May 2022 (*Official Records of the General Assembly, Seventy-seventh Session, Supplement No. 10* (A/77/10), para. 239). The topic had been included in the long-term programme of work of the Commission during its seventy-first session (2019), on the basis of the proposal contained in annex C to the report of the Commission (*Official Records of the General Assembly, Seventy-fourth Session, Supplement No. 10* (A/74/10), para. 290 (b)).

[181] At its 3612th meeting, on 5 August 2022 (A/77/10, paras. 243 and 244).

C. Text of the draft articles on the prevention and repression of piracy and armed robbery at sea provisionally adopted by the Commission at its seventy-fourth session

1. Text of the draft articles

57. The text of the draft articles provisionally adopted by the Commission at its seventy-fourth session is reproduced below.

Article 1
Scope

The present draft articles apply to the prevention and repression of piracy and armed robbery at sea.

Article 2
Definition of piracy

1. Piracy consists of any of the following acts:

(*a*) any illegal acts of violence or detention, or any act of depredation, committed for private ends by the crew or the passengers of a private ship or a private aircraft, and directed:

(i) on the high seas, against another ship or aircraft, or against persons or property on board such ship or aircraft;

(ii) against a ship, aircraft, persons or property in a place outside the jurisdiction of any State;

(*b*) any act of voluntary participation in the operation of a ship or of an aircraft with knowledge of facts making it a pirate ship or aircraft;

(*c*) any act of inciting or of intentionally facilitating an act described in subparagraph (*a*) or (*b*).

2. Paragraph 1 shall be read in conjunction with the provisions of article 58, paragraph 2, of the United Nations Convention on the Law of the Sea.

Article 3
Definition of armed robbery at sea

Armed robbery at sea consists of any of the following acts:

(*a*) any illegal act of violence or detention or any act of depredation, or threat thereof, other than an act of piracy, committed for private ends and directed against a ship or against persons or property on board such a ship, within a State's internal waters, archipelagic waters and territorial sea;

(*b*) any act of inciting or of intentionally facilitating an act described in subparagraph (*a*).

2. Text of the draft articles and commentaries thereto provisionally adopted by the Commission at its seventy-fourth session

58. The text of the draft articles and commentaries thereto provisionally adopted by the Commission at its seventy-fourth session is reproduced below.

Article 1
Scope

The present draft articles apply to the prevention and repression of piracy and armed robbery at sea.

Commentary

(1) Draft article 1 defines the scope of the present draft articles, indicating that they apply to piracy and armed robbery at sea. The provision should be read together with draft articles 2 and 3, which define these two crimes and serve to delimit the scope of the topic.

(2) The present draft articles are broader in scope than the 1982 United Nations Convention on the Law of the Sea.[182] While the Convention only refers specifically to piracy, the present draft articles also include "armed robbery at sea", a crime that is not as such referred to in the Convention. For the purposes of the draft articles and commentary, reference to piracy means maritime piracy.

(3) The aim of the work on the present topic is to examine two crimes at sea: piracy and armed robbery at sea. The topic of piracy will be addressed principally within the framework of the United Nations Convention on the Law of the Sea, taking into account existing applicable international law, regional approaches, extensive State practice, and legislative and judicial practice under national legal systems, especially for armed robbery at sea, which is not addressed under the Convention. The framework of regional and subregional organizations involved in combating maritime piracy and armed robbery at sea will provide useful illustrations of the implementation of international law in this area.[183] The work on the present topic is not to duplicate existing frameworks and academic studies, but instead aims to clarify and build upon them, as well as to identify new issues of common concern.

(4) The present draft articles apply to the "prevention" and "repression" of piracy and armed robbery at sea. "Prevention" is the act of stopping something from happening or arising, while "repression" is the act of subduing or suppressing something that has arisen. The Security Council has highlighted the need to establish legal frameworks for the prevention and repression of piracy and armed robbery at sea in the Gulf of Guinea,[184] and for the repression of piracy in Somalia.[185]

(5) The term "repression" is used in article 100 of the United Nations Convention on the Law of the Sea, which requires all States to "cooperate to the fullest possible extent in the repression of piracy on the high seas or in any other place outside the jurisdiction of any State". This provision is identical to article 14 of the 1958 Convention on the High Seas,[186] which in turn was based on article 38 of the 1956 draft articles concerning the law of the sea with commentaries, adopted by the Commission at its eighth session.[187] "Repression" is broader than the term "punishment", for example as used in the draft articles on prevention and punishment of crimes against humanity, adopted by the Commission at its seventy-first

---

[182] United Nations Convention on the Law of the Sea (Montego Bay, 10 December 1982), United Nations, *Treaty Series*, vol. 1834, No. 31363, p. 3. For a commentary, see: S.N. Nandan and S. Rosenne, eds., *United Nations Convention on the Law of the Sea, 1982 A Commentary*, vol. III: *Articles 86 to 132* (Leiden, Martinus Nijhoff, 1995); A. Proelss *et al.*, eds., *United Nations Convention on the Law of the Sea: a commentary* (Munich, Oxford and Baden-Baden, C.H.N Beck/Hart/Nomos, 2017), pp. 737–744. Although old, the study published by V. Pella deserves attention : "La répression de la piraterie", *Recueil des cours de l'Académie de droit international (RCADI)*, vol. 15 (1926), pp. 145–275.

[183] Code of Conduct concerning the repression of piracy and armed robbery against ships in the Western Indian Ocean and the Gulf of Aden (Djibouti Code of Conduct) (Djibouti, 29 January 2009), Council of the International Maritime Organization, document C 102/14, annex, attachment 1, resolution 1, annex; Code of Conduct concerning the Repression of Piracy, Armed Robbery against Ships and Illicit Maritime Activity in West and Central Africa (Yaoundé Code of Conduct) (Yaoundé, 25 June 2013), available at https://au.int/sites/default/files/newsevents/workingdocuments/27463-wd-code_de_conduite.pdf; Regional Cooperation Agreement on Combating Piracy and Armed Robbery against Ships in Asia (Tokyo, 11 November 2004), available at https://www.mofa.go.jp/mofaj/gaiko/kaiyo/pdfs/kyotei_s.pdf.

[184] Security Council resolution 2039 (2012), para. 5.

[185] Security Council resolution 1838 (2008), para. 3.

[186] Convention on the High Seas (Geneva, 29 April 1958), United Nations, *Treaty Series*, vol. 450, No. 6465, p. 11.

[187] *Yearbook of the International Law Commission, 1956*, vol. II, document A/3159, pp. 256 ff, at p. 282.

session.[188] The obligation to take measures to prevent and punish is a more specific aspect of the wider concept of "repression".[189]

Article 2
Definition of piracy

1. Piracy consists of any of the following acts:

(*a*) any illegal act of violence or detention, or any act of depredation, committed for private ends by the crew or the passengers of a private ship or a private aircraft, and directed:

(i) on the high seas, against another ship or aircraft, or against persons or property on board such ship or aircraft;

(ii) against a ship, aircraft, persons or property in a place outside the jurisdiction of any State;

(*b*) any act of voluntary participation in the operation of a ship or of an aircraft with knowledge of facts making it a pirate ship or aircraft;

(*c*) any act of inciting or of intentionally facilitating an act described in subparagraph (*a*) or (*b*).

2. Paragraph 1 shall be read in conjunction with the provisions of article 58, paragraph 2, of the United Nations Convention on the Law of the Sea.

Commentary

Paragraph 1

(1) Draft article 2, paragraph 1, sets out a definition of acts of piracy for the purpose of the present draft articles. The definition in paragraph 1 is based on article 101 of the United Nations Convention on the Law of the Sea, article 15 of the 1958 Convention on the High Seas and article 39 of the draft articles concerning the law of the sea, adopted by the Commission in 1956.[190] It is regarded as reflecting customary international law and has been reproduced in several regional legal instruments.[191]

(2) The essential elements of piracy under the United Nations Convention on the Law of the Sea are that it comprises any illegal act of violence or detention, or any act of depredation, committed for private ends by the crew or the passengers of a private ship or a private aircraft,

188 See *Official Records of the General Assembly, Seventy-fourth Session, Supplement No. 10* (A/74/10), paras. 44 and 45.

189 See article 99 of the United Nations Convention on the Law of the Sea, which provides in part: "Every State shall take effective measures to prevent and punish the transport of slaves in ships authorized to fly its flag and to prevent the unlawful use of its flag for that purpose."

190 *Yearbook of the International Law Commission, 1956*, vol. II, document A/3159, pp. 256 ff, at pp. 260 and 261.

191 See Regional Cooperation Agreement on Combating Piracy and Armed Robbery against Ships in Asia, art. 1, para. 1; the CARICOM Maritime and Airspace Security Cooperation Agreement (3 July 2008), available from *Law of the Sea Bulletin*, No. 68 (2008), arts. 1, para. 2 (*b*), and 2, para. 2 (*g*); the Djibouti Code of Conduct, art. 1, para. 1; Revised Code of Conduct concerning the Repression of Piracy, Armed Robbery against Ships, and Illicit Maritime Activities in the Western Indian Ocean and Gulf of Aden Area (Jeddah, 12 January 2017), available from https://wwwcdn.imo.org/localresources/en/OurWork/Security/Documents/A2%20Revised%20Code%20Of%20Conduct%20Concerning%20The%20Repression%20Of%20Piracy%20Armed%20Robbery%20Against%20Ships%20Secretariat.pdf, art. 1, para. 1; the Memorandum of Understanding on the Establishment of a Sub-Regional Integrated Coast Guard Function Network in West and Central African, July 2008, available from https://www.imo.org/en/OurWork/Security/Pages/Code-of-Conduct-against-illicit-maritime-activity.aspx, art. 1; the Yaoundé Code of Conduct, art. 1(310); the African Charter on Maritime Security, Safety and Development in Africa (Lomé Charter) (Lomé, 15 October 2017), available at https://au.int/sites/default/files/treaties/37286-treaty-african_charter_on_maritime_security.pdf, art. 1.

and directed on the high seas or a place outside the jurisdiction of any State, against another ship or aircraft, or against persons or property on board such ship or aircraft.

(3) The Commission felt that the integrity of the definition of piracy contained in article 101 of the United Nations Convention on the Law of the Sea should be preserved. This is in line with the objective of the topic, which is not to seek to alter any of the rules set forth in existing treaties, including the Convention.[192]

(4) The Commission acknowledged that there were certain elements of the definition of piracy contained in article 101 of the United Nations Convention on the Law of the Sea that posed questions of interpretation and application, especially in view of the evolving nature of modern piracy. The Commission found it advisable to explain in the commentaries certain terms in article 101, which are set out below.

"[A]ny illegal act of violence or detention, or any act of depredation"

(5) Drawing on its earlier work in 1956, the Commission has adopted a definition of illegal acts of violence where the intention to rob (*animus furandi*) is not required.[193] The Commission also considered that the term "violence" included intimidation, as well as violence of different kinds, including physical and psychological violence. Material acts that constitute piracy result from any "illegal act of violence" exercised against persons on board a ship or aircraft, the deprivation of liberty of persons on board, or acts of depredation against property. "Depredation" implies the looting of property on board a ship or aircraft, accompanied by destruction.

"[C]ommitted for private ends"

(6) It was recognized that the expression "committed for private ends" in paragraph 1 (*a*) primarily refers to the pursuit of profit or private gain, most often including ransom demands and theft of property on board private ships or ships belonging to a State. This could also include acts against a State ship for private ends. It was further recognized that the pursuit of private ends can coexist with political or ideological objectives, sometimes making it difficult to distinguish between piracy committed for purely private ends and maritime crimes other than piracy, which can be committed for political or other ends. There is an ongoing debate as to whether "private ends" can be assimilated to ideological or political ends. Some scholars have contended that any maritime violence lacking public authority can be regarded as violence "for private ends".[194]

"[O]n the high seas"

(7) The definition of piracy specifies that it is committed "on the high seas" or "in a place outside the jurisdiction of any State". The regime applicable to piracy under international law is an exception to the exclusive jurisdiction of the flag State which applies on the high seas.[195] This regime does not apply to acts committed within the territorial jurisdiction of a State. The Commission decided to retain this geographical limitation of piracy as set out in the United

---

[192] *Official Records of the General Assembly, Seventy-fourth Session, Supplement No. 10* (A/74/10), annex C, Prevention and repression of piracy and armed robbery at sea, para. 11.

[193] *Yearbook of the International Law Commission, 1956*, vol. II, document A/3159, p. 282. The Commission in 1956 also considered that: "Acts of piracy may be prompted by feelings of hatred or revenge, and not merely by the desire for gain."

[194] R. Churchill, V. Lowe and A. Sander, *The Law of the Sea*, 4th ed. (Manchester, Manchester University Press, 2022), pp. 385–386. See also Belgian Court of Cassation, *Castle John and Nederlandse Stichting Sirius v. NV Nabeco and NV Parfin*, 19 December 1986, *International Law Reports*, vol. 77, p. 537, at p. 540 (1986); Supreme Court of Seychelles, *The Republic v. Mohamed Ahmed Dahir & 10 others*, Case No. 51 of 2009, Judgment, 25 July 2010, para. 37; Supreme Court of Seychelles, *The Republic v. Abdukar Ahmed & 5 others*, Case No. 21 of 2011, 14 July 2011, para. 21; United States Court of Appeals for the Ninth Circuit, *The Institute of Cetacean Research v. Sea Shepherd Conservation Society*, 25 February 2013, *International Law Reports*, vol. 156 (2014), pp. 718–763, 756 (US CA 2nd Cir, 2013); D. Guilfoyle, *Shipping Interdiction and the Law of the Sea* (Cambridge, Cambridge University Press, 2009), pp. 32–42; R. O'Keefe, *International Criminal Law* (Cambridge, Cambridge University Press, 2015), p. 20; United Nations Office on Drugs and Crime, *Maritime Crime: A Manual for Criminal Justice Practitioners*, 3rd ed. (Colombo, 2020), para. 9.3.

[195] This extends to the exclusive economic zone; see para. 2 of draft article 2.

Nations Convention on the Law of the Sea and to provide a definition of "armed robbery at sea" to cover other geographical areas at sea where acts, which can be assimilated to piracy, may occur.

"[A]gainst another ship or aircraft"

(8) The definition of piracy in the United Nations Convention on the Law of the Sea is based on acts committed by the crew or the passengers of a private ship or aircraft against another ship or aircraft. The requirement for piracy to involve acts of violence by one ship directed towards another ship is based on the historical antecedents of the provision. When illegal or violent conduct on the high seas involves only one ship, the 1988 Convention for the Suppression of Unlawful Acts against the Safety of Maritime Navigation[196] is likely to be implicated for its parties. Regarding "aircraft", it is important to note that the Convention on International Civil Aviation[197] declares that "aircraft used in military, customs and police services shall be deemed to be State aircraft". As a result, according to article 2, paragraph 1 (*a*), of the present draft articles – which repeats article 101 (*a*) of the United Nations Convention on the Law of the Sea – piracy entails acts against "private aircraft" not "State aircraft".

(9) The Commission noted that, according to the legislative practice of some States, "piracy" is also considered to include piratical acts against offshore oil platforms.[198] Such State practice is, however, at best *de lege ferenda* as a matter of international law as oil platforms do not qualify as either a "ship or aircraft" or as "property in a place outside the jurisdiction of any State". Furthermore, the arbitral tribunal in *The Arctic Sunrise* award on the merits concluded that the conduct in question was not piracy because "[t]he *Prirazlomnaya* is not a ship. It is an offshore ice-resistant fixed platform".[199]

(10) The legal instruments referred to in paragraph (1) of the present commentary have recognized, on the basis of the debates that took place in the Commission in 1954, that piracy can be committed by an aircraft against a ship. In reality, modern piracy is no longer committed using only ships and aircraft as they were understood when the definition of piracy was developed. The use of drones, UAV (unmanned aerial vehicles) or MAV (maritime autonomous vehicles) in the commission of acts of piracy or armed robbery at sea is a new phenomenon. So too is the use of other devices for carrying out cyberattacks at sea. It is recognized that such actions are within the scope of the definition of piracy in draft article 2, paragraph 1.

(11) Acts of piracy under the definition in paragraph 1 of draft article 2 involve acts from a private ship or aircraft. However, article 102 of the United Nations Convention on the Law of the Sea specifically provides that "acts of piracy … committed by a warship, government ship or government aircraft whose crew has mutinied and taken control of the ship or aircraft are assimilated to acts committed by a private ship or aircraft".[200]

(12) The definition of piracy in paragraph 1 of draft article 2 is limited to acts involving two ships, two aircraft or a ship and an aircraft. It does not extend to situations of unlawful violence or detention or acts of depredation by the crew or the passengers of a ship or aircraft against that same ship or aircraft. A view was expressed that piracy should not always be

---

196 Convention for the Suppression of Unlawful Acts against the Safety of Maritime Navigation, (Rome, 10 March 1988), United Nations, *Treaty Series*, vol. 1678, No. 29004, p. 201.

197 Convention on International Civil Aviation (Chicago, 7 December 1944), United Nations, *Treaty Series*, vol. 15, No. 102, p. 295.

198 Some national laws distinguish between piracy targeting ships and "maritime offences" targeting fixed or floating platforms: see Suppression of Piracy and other Maritime Offences Act, 2019, of Nigeria, available at: https://placbillstrack.org/8th/upload/Suppression%20of%20Piracy%20and%20Other%20Maritime%20Offences%20Act%202019.pdf.

199 Permanent Court of Arbitration, *The Arctic Sunrise Arbitration (Netherlands v Russia)*, Case No. 2014-02, Award on the Merits, 14 August 2015, *Reports of International Arbitral Awards*, vol. XXXII (2019), p. 205, at para. 238, also para. 240.

200 United Nations Convention on the Law of the Sea, art. 102.

considered as involving two ships, but may involve action by a crew on a ship against that ship.

(13) Piracy may also be conducted from land against ships, but the Commission decided to avoid specifically referring to "land" as the place where preparations are made to commit acts of piracy. Some members considered that acts of piracy could also be conducted from offshore platforms.

(14) The Commission gave consideration to whether to include a definition of "ship" to assist in clarifying the definition in draft article 2, paragraph 1. Although the International Maritime Organization has defined "vessels and aircraft" in some of the conventions concluded under its auspices,[201] the United Nations Convention on the Law of the Sea does not define "ship" or "vessel". The Commission did not consider it productive to include a definition of ship in the present draft articles.

"[A]ny act of inciting or of intentionally facilitating" such an act

(15) The definition of piracy includes conduct that is ancillary to piracy, such as incitement, financing or intentional facilitation of piracy. The Security Council has seen the need to address this element of acts of piracy in its resolutions concerning the situation in Somalia and the Gulf of Guinea. In its resolution 1976 (2011) on Somalia, the Council emphasized the importance of all States criminalizing under their domestic law "incitement, facilitation, conspiracy and attempts to commit acts of piracy".[202] In its subsequent resolution 2020 (2011), the Security Council inserted text to cover not only pirates apprehended off the coast of Somalia, but also "their facilitators and financiers ashore".[203] A similar approach was adopted most recently by the Security Council with regard to the Gulf of Guinea[204]. Consistent with the approach of the Security Council, the Commission considered that the expression "any act of inciting or of intentionally facilitating" a piratical act is sufficiently broad to include, in particular, the financing of acts of piracy.[205] Arming a vessel intended for piracy, or leasing a vessel in the knowledge that it will be used for the same purpose, constitutes an act of complicity. It should also be noted that preparatory acts, assistance given to pirates or an unsuccessful attempt to commit an act of piracy are punishable under national laws.[206]

Paragraph 2

(16) Paragraph 1 of draft article 2 refers to acts of piracy committed "on the high seas". Nevertheless, article 58, paragraph 2, of the United Nations Convention on the Law of the Sea, regarding the rights and obligations of States in the exclusive economic zone, provides: "Articles 88 to 115 and other pertinent rules of international law apply to the exclusive economic zone in so far as they are not incompatible with this Part". It follows that article 101

---

201 See, for example: Convention on the Prevention of Marine Pollution by Dumping of Wastes and Other Matter (London, Mexico City, Moscow and Washington, 29 December 1972), United Nations, *Treaty Series*, vol. 1046, No. 15749, p. 120, at art. III, para. 2: "'Vessels and aircraft' means waterborne or airborne craft of any type whatsoever. This expression includes air-cushioned craft and floating craft, whether self-propelled or not."

202 Security Council resolution 1976 (2011), para. 13.

203 Security Council resolution 2020 (2011), para. 15.

204 Security Council resolution 2634 (2022), para. 3, which "Calls upon Member States in the region to criminalize piracy and armed robbery at sea under their domestic laws, and to investigate, and to prosecute or extradite, in accordance with applicable international law, including international human rights law, perpetrators of piracy and armed robbery at sea, as well as those who incite, finance or intentionally facilitate such crimes, including key figures of criminal networks involved in piracy and armed robbery at sea who plan, organize, facilitate, finance or profit from such attacks".

205 United States Court of Appeals, District of Colombia Circuit, *United States v. Ali*, 21 August 2013, 718 F.3d 929.

206 British Empire, Judicial Committee of the Privy Council, *In re Piracy Jure Gentium*, 26 July 1934 (available at https://vlex.co.uk/vid/re-piracy-jure-gentium-805016117), cited in *Dahir* (see footnote 194 above), para. 57: "As was held in *Re Piracy Jure Gentium* (1934) A.G. 586, 'an actual robbery is not an essential element of the crime. A frustrated attempt to commit a piratical robbery will constitute piracy *jure gentium*'". Cyprus, Criminal Code, art. 69; Republic of Korea, Act concerning Punishment of Unlawful Acts against Ships and Maritime Navigational Facilities, art. 5; India, Maritime Anti-Piracy Act, 2022, No. 3 of 2023, sect. 3.

of the United Nations Convention on the Law of the Sea and related provisions thereof regarding piracy apply to the exclusive economic zone. This is confirmed by the arbitral tribunal in *The "Enrica Lexie" Incident*, which observed that article 58, paragraph 2, of the United Nations Convention on the Law of the Sea "extends specific rights and duties of States as regards the repression of piracy to the exclusive economic zone".[207]

(17) The Commission considered whether an explicit reference should be made to the exclusive economic zone, but decided to include a reference to the provisions of article 58, paragraph 2, of the United Nations Convention on the Law of the Sea to indicate that piracy can also be committed in the exclusive economic zone.[208] The paragraph was drafted in a neutral manner so as not to prejudice the position of non-parties to the United Nations Convention on the Law of the Sea.

(18) The separation between the two paragraphs recognizes that the exclusive economic zone and the high seas are two distinct maritime spaces in which different rights and obligations apply.

National legislative practices

(19) The Commission noted that the evolution of States' legislative practice has given rise to a variety of definitions of piracy.[209] It examined whether a definition of piracy based on definitions in national law might supplement the definition under international law. It considered, however, that any such definition risked encompassing all kinds of illegal acts at sea not defined in article 101 (*a*) and (*b*) of the United Nations Convention on the Law of the Sea. Such an expansion would undermine the integrity of the definition of piracy under the United Nations Convention on the Law of the Sea. Nevertheless, the Commission noted that national anti-piracy laws may help shed light on State practice, and common elements should be examined to promote harmonization of national laws.

Subsequent developments

(20) The Commission recognized that the current definition of piracy may not encapsulate technological developments in maritime security, which may lead to subsequent efforts by the international community to update it. It nonetheless considered it unnecessary to introduce a "without prejudice" clause to accommodate possible further developments.

Article 3
Definition of armed robbery at sea

Armed robbery at sea consists of any of the following acts:

(*a*) any illegal act of violence or detention or any act of depredation, or threat thereof, other than an act of piracy, committed for private ends and directed against a ship or against persons or property on board such a ship, within a State's internal waters, archipelagic waters and territorial sea;

(*b*) any act of inciting or of intentionally facilitating an act described in subparagraph (*a*).

Commentary

(1) Draft article 3 concerns the definition of armed robbery at sea. The definition is drawn from the one adopted by the Assembly of the International Maritime Organization (IMO) in its Code of Practice for the Investigation of Crimes of Piracy and Armed Robbery against Ships.[210] Subparagraphs (a) and (b) of draft article 3 correspond to subparagraphs 1 and 2 respectively of paragraph 2.2 of the Code.

---

207 Permanent Court of Arbitration, *The "Enrica Lexie" Incident (Italy v India)*, Case 2015-28, Award, 21 May 2020, para. 979.

208 International Court of Justice, *Alleged Violations of Sovereign Rights and Maritime Spaces in the Caribbean Sea (Nicaragua v. Colombia)*, Judgment, 21 April 2022, para. 62.

209 See first report by the Special Rapporteur, A/CN.4/758.

210 IMO resolution A.1025(26) of 2 December 2009, annex.

(2) There is not necessarily any substantive difference between piracy and armed robbery at sea as far as the conduct itself is concerned. The main difference between piracy and armed robbery at sea is the location of the act: the high seas and exclusive economic zone on one hand, and waters subject to the jurisdiction of the coastal State on the other. This has consequences for the applicable jurisdiction in respect of the two crimes. In the case of piracy, it is acknowledged that universal jurisdiction applies such that any State has the right to prosecute the crime of piracy committed on the high seas. With respect to armed robbery at sea, the coastal State has the exclusive competence to exercise prescriptive and enforcement jurisdiction over such acts.

(3) The difference between the definition in draft article 3 and the IMO Assembly's definition is that, in the chapeau of the draft article, the Commission used the term "armed robbery at sea", instead of "armed robbery against ships" as in the IMO Assembly's definition. A recent Security Council resolution on maritime piracy in the Gulf of Guinea in particular has used the phrase "armed robbery at sea", instead of "armed robbery against ships".[211] In view of the practice of the Security Council, and to avoid unduly restricting the definition, the Commission considered that it was unnecessary to replicate the IMO definition verbatim.

(4) Unlike piracy, to which universal jurisdiction applies, IMO Resolution A.1025(26) states that armed robbery is punishable under coastal State's jurisdiction, as examined in some national legislation and regional conventions as described above. In addition, it has to be noted that armed robbery at sea does not necessarily involve two ships.

(5) "Armed robbery at sea" applies within a State's internal waters, archipelagic waters and territorial sea. Although a number of acts of armed robbery at sea occur in straits used in international navigation, such straits may include areas that are within the maritime zones of a coastal State as well as high seas. For example, the Strait of Korea/Tsushima includes areas of high seas. It was therefore considered not necessary, and indeed confusing, to include a specific reference to straits used for international navigation within the definition.

---

211 Security Council resolution 2634 (2022). See also statement by the President of the Security Council S/PRST/2021/15 of 9 August 2021.

Chapter VII
Subsidiary means for the determination of rules of international law

A. Introduction

59. The Commission, at its seventy-third session (2022), decided to include the topic "Subsidiary means for the determination of rules of international law" in its programme of work and appointed Mr. Charles Chernor Jalloh as Special Rapporteur.[212] Also at its seventy-third session,[213] the Commission requested the Secretariat to prepare a memorandum identifying elements in the previous work of the Commission that could be particularly relevant for its future work on the topic, to be submitted for the seventy-fourth session (2023); and a memorandum surveying the case law of international courts and tribunals, and other bodies, which would be particularly relevant for its future work on the topic, to be submitted for the seventy-fifth session (2024).

60. The General Assembly, in paragraph 26 of its resolution 77/103 of 7 December 2022, subsequently took note of the decision of the Commission to include the topic in its programme of work.

B. Consideration of the topic at the present session

61. At the present session, the Commission had before it the first report of the Special Rapporteur (A/CN.4/760), as well as the memorandum prepared by the Secretariat, identifying elements in the previous work of the Commission that could be particularly relevant to the topic (A/CN.4/759), which were considered at its 3625th to 3632nd meetings, from 16 to 25 May 2023.

62. In his first report, the Special Rapporteur addressed the scope of the topic and the main issues to be addressed in the course of the work of the Commission. The report also considered: the views of States on the topic; questions of methodology, which is to be grounded in State and international tribunal practice; the previous work of the Commission on the topic; the nature and function of sources of international law and their relationship to the subsidiary means; and the drafting history of Article 38, paragraph 1 (*d*), of the Statute of the International Court of Justice and its status under customary international law. It also provided an initial assessment of certain aspects of the topic, including judicial decisions, teachings of the most highly qualified publicists of the various nations and possible additional subsidiary means used in the practice of States and international tribunals to determine rules of international law, such as unilateral acts, resolutions and decisions of international organizations and the works of expert bodies. The Special Rapporteur addressed the outcome of the work and, consistent with the related prior work of the Commission, proposed draft conclusions as the final form of output, with the main object of clarifying the law based on current practice. He proposed five draft conclusions and also made suggestions for the future programme of work on the topic.

63. At its 3633rd meeting, on 26 May 2023, the Commission decided to refer draft conclusions 1 to 5, as contained in the Special Rapporteur's first report, to the Drafting Committee, taking into account the views expressed in the plenary debate.[214]

---

[212] At its 3583rd meeting, on 17 May 2022. The topic had been included in the long-term programme of work of the Commission during its seventy-second session (2021), on the basis of the proposal contained in an annex to the report of the Commission to that session (*Official Records of the General Assembly, Seventy-sixth Session, Supplement No. 10* (A/76/10), annex).

[213] At its 3612th meeting, on 5 August 2022.

[214] The draft conclusions proposed by the Special Rapporteur in his first report read as follows:

64. At its 3635th meeting, on 3 July 2023, the Commission considered the report of the Drafting Committee (A/CN.4/L.985) on the topic and provisionally adopted draft conclusions 1 to 3 (see sect. C.1 below). At its 3651st to 3657th meetings, from 31 July to 4 August 2023, the Commission adopted the commentaries to draft conclusions 1 to 3, as provisionally adopted at the current session (see sect. C.2 below).

65. At its 3642nd meeting, on 21 July 2023, the Commission considered an additional report of the Drafting Committee containing draft conclusions 4 and 5 provisionally adopted by the Drafting Committee (A/CN.4/L.985/Add.1), as orally revised, and took note of the

---

"**Draft conclusion 1**
Scope

The present draft conclusions concern the way in which subsidiary means are used to determine the existence and content of rules of international law.

Draft conclusion 2
Categories of subsidiary means for the determination of rules of law

Subsidiary means for the determination of rules of international law include:

(a) Decisions of national and international courts and tribunals;

(b) Teachings of the most highly qualified publicists of the various nations;

(c) Any other means derived from the practices of States or international organizations.

Draft conclusion 3
Criteria for the assessment of subsidiary means for the determination of rules of law

Subsidiary means used to determine a rule of international law are assessed on the basis of the quality of the evidence presented, the expertise of those involved, conformity with an official mandate, the level of agreement among those involved and the reception by States and others.

Draft conclusion 4
Decisions of courts and tribunals

(a) Decisions of international courts and tribunals on questions of international law are particularly authoritative means for the identification or determination of the existence and content of rules of international law;

(b) For the purposes of paragraph (a), particular regard shall be had to the decisions of the International Court of Justice;

(c) Decisions of national courts may be used, in certain circumstances, as subsidiary means for the identification or determination of the existence and content of rules of international law.

Draft conclusion 5
Teachings

Teachings of the most highly qualified publicists of the various nations, especially those reflecting the coinciding views of scholars, may serve as subsidiary means for the identification or determination of the existence and content of rules of international law."

report.[215] The commentaries to these two draft conclusions are expected to be adopted during the next session.[216]

1. Introduction by the Special Rapporteur of the first report

66. The Special Rapporteur introduced his report by making some general observations and discussing the structure and organization of the 10 chapters contained in the report. He noted, as a starting point, that subsidiary means were an important component of the international legal system, for which reason the Commission considered that they could be usefully clarified long after their inclusion in Article 38 of the Statute of the International Court of Justice. He explained that, as indicated in chapter I of the report, the main purpose thereof was to provide a solid foundation for the Commission's work on the topic and to obtain the views of members of the Commission and States. He indicated that, in principle, Article 38 of the Statute of the International Court of Justice, which was the basis for the topic, was an applicable law provision directed at the judges of the Court, and was widely recognized by States, practitioners and scholars as the most authoritative statement of the sources of international law. He recalled that the consideration of the topic served as a final addition to the work of the Commission on the sources enumerated in Article 38 of the Statute of the International Court of Justice. The fact that this provision was considered a settled part of customary international law and was used widely in national and international practice indicated that, by adopting a cautious and rigorous approach, rooted in the actual manner in which subsidiary means were employed to determine the rules of international law, the Commission could provide useful guidance to States, international organizations, courts and tribunals, and all those called upon to use subsidiary means to assist in the determination of rules of international law.

67. In relation to chapter II, the Special Rapporteur noted that the reactions by Member States in the Sixth Committee to the inclusion of the topic in the programme of work of the Commission had been generally positive. He pointed out the views of 24 delegations in the Sixth Committee that had supported the consideration of the topic to complement and complete the prior work of the Commission on the sources of international law and that had suggested that its consideration could help to avoid certain negative consequences of the fragmentation of international law. He observed that, even the few delegations that initially seemed hesitant during the General Assembly debate in 2021, appeared to embrace the Commission's decision by 2022. The only exception was the delegation that had suggested in 2021 that the Commission may find it challenging to garner interest and input on the topic from States. The Special Rapporteur also noted the Commission's interest in receiving information from States on how they, including their national courts, used subsidiary means to determine rules of international law. He expressed appreciation to the two States that had submitted written comments and the hope that additional States from all geographic regions

---

[215] The report and the corresponding statement of the Chair of the Drafting Committee are available in the Analytical Guide to the Work of the International Law Commission: https://legal.un.org/ilc/guide/1_16.shtml. The draft conclusions 4 and 5, provisionally adopted by the Drafting Committee, read as follows:

> "**Draft conclusion 4**
> **Decisions of courts and tribunals**
>
> 1. Decisions of international courts and tribunals, in particular of the International Court of Justice, are a subsidiary means for the determination of the existence and content of rules of international law.
>
> 2. Decisions of national courts may be used, in certain circumstances, as a subsidiary means for the determination of the existence and content of rules of international law.
>
> **Draft conclusion 5**
> **Teachings**
>
> Teachings, especially those generally reflecting the coinciding views of persons with competence in international law from the various legal systems and regions of the world, are a subsidiary means for the determination of the existence and content of rules of international law. In assessing the representativeness of teachings, due regard should also be had to, *inter alia*, gender and linguistic diversity."

[216] See infra paras. 84–108 for the summary of the plenary debate on these two draft conclusions.

would share their practice with the Commission, as that could help to strengthen the practical relevance and utility of its work on the topic.

68. The Special Rapporteur then referred to chapter III, which proposed three topics for the consideration of the Commission. First, the origins, nature and scope of subsidiary means: that part of the report discussed the nature and functions of sources in the international legal system, focusing on mostly theoretical issues and on how different ways of thinking about the sources of international law and their interaction with the subsidiary means could affect the practical work of the Commission on the topic. A key question linked to that discussion concerned how narrow or broad the universe of subsidiary means was; in other words, whether, in addition to judicial decisions (and clarifying their scope) and teachings (and clarifying their scope), the work should reflect the decades of practice whereby international lawyers – including courts and tribunals – used a range of additional subsidiary means and materials to determine rules of international law. The report analysed in detail the drafting history of Article 38, paragraph 1 (*d*), of the Statute of the International Court of Justice. He noted that the report then carried out a systematic textual analysis of the various elements of Article 38, paragraph 1 (*d*), and explored the possibility of addressing additional subsidiary means for the determination of rules of international law.

69. A second component of the topic concerned the function and relationship between subsidiary means and the sources of international law, namely, treaties, customary international law and general principles of law. The Special Rapporteur stressed that some of the questions that needed to be addressed included the weight and value given to the decisions of international courts and tribunals, and the relationship between Articles 38 and 59 of the Statute of the International Court of Justice, *inter alia*, whether there existed a system of *de facto* precedent. He explained that the notion that the findings of judicial bodies could serve as a basis to identify obligations when interpreting and applying treaties, customary international law and general principles would also need to be examined.

70. A third component of the topic concerned the opportunity to clarify additional subsidiary means. The Special Rapporteur suggested that the Commission could explore the evolution of subsidiary means to establish the existence of obligations of States, with examples such as unilateral acts and declarations of States, and resolutions of international organizations, as well as the works of expert bodies, in particular those created and mandated by States and international organizations to carry out certain functions. He considered that the Commission should proceed with caution and rigour in its choice of specific subsidiary means to study, without hampering the development of international law as manifested in the practices of States and international organizations.

71. The Special Rapporteur indicated that the question of coherence and unity of international law, sometimes referred to as the problem of fragmentation, could affect the scope and utility of the topic. He noted that, at the time of the preparation of the syllabus for the topic, in 2021, he had considered that the issue of conflicting judicial decisions on the same legal question could fall outside the scope of the project. However, given its relevance to the consideration of judicial decisions and the fact that the Commission had not addressed the substance of the question to date, he asked other members to comment on whether the issue of fragmentation should be kept outside the scope of the present topic or not. He also indicated that, while it would be for the Commission, in the exercise of its independent mandate conferred on it by States, to decide on the matter based on a scientific evaluation, it would be useful for the Commission to do so after taking into account the views of States in the Sixth Committee.

72. The Special Rapporteur further referred to the form of the possible outcome of the work. He considered that it would be best in the form of draft conclusions accompanied by commentaries, consistent with the practice of the Commission in relation to the other topics dealing with the sources of international law, which had been supported by States at the Sixth Committee.

73. In chapter IV of the report, the Special Rapporteur considered the question of methodology, and observed that the study of the topic would require a comprehensive examination of a wide variety of primary and secondary materials and legal scholarship on the subject. He referred to the emphasis in decisions of national and international courts on

questions of international law and the extent to which courts and States applied a similar methodology to that of the International Court of Justice. He underlined that the analysis should rely on materials from all States, regions and legal systems of the world that were as representative as possible. The Special Rapporteur proposed that, as part of the work on the topic, the Commission could include a multilingual bibliography, as had been the practice with topics concluded recently. He stressed the need for such a bibliography to be representative of the various regions and legal systems of the world and invited members of the Commission and States to propose items for inclusion, especially in all the official languages of the United Nations.

74. The Special Rapporteur had then analysed the use of subsidiary means by the Commission on its prior work in chapter V of the report and referred to the memorandum prepared by the Secretariat surveying the previous work of the Commission related to subsidiary means. He noted that: (*a*) judicial decisions and teachings were prevalent in the work of the Commission, but that the nature and extent of their use, as with other materials, varied and depended on the topic under consideration; (*b*) the use of judicial decisions was prevalent in the Commission and suggested that such decisions could be perceived as being akin to primary sources of international law; (*c*) the Commission relied on judicial decisions more than teachings; and (*d*) the Commission in some cases had relied on teachings to identify the practice of States, and that it had attached different weight to the work of individual scholars than to that of expert groups.

75. Chapter VI of the report addressed the nature and function of sources in the international legal system. The Special Rapporteur indicated that he had intended to situate subsidiary means in the broader context of the sources of international law and sought to address some theoretical debates, including the reference to formal and material sources of international law. He emphasized the relevance of Article 38 of the Statute of the International Court of Justice and observed that certain questions of hierarchy arose from that provision. Those included whether the sources were listed in a particular sequence and thereby suggested a hierarchy, what was the role and status of subsidiary means, and whether there existed a distinction between primary and secondary sources.

76. Chapter VII focused on the drafting history of Article 38 of the Statute of the International Court of Justice, in particular the debate and common ground among the drafters of the provision concerning the appropriate role of subsidiary means in the determination of rules of international law. He recalled that Article 38 had been included in both the Statute of the Permanent Court of International Justice and the Statute of the International Court of Justice.

77. The Special Rapporteur presented four observations with respect to the drafting of the Statute of the Permanent Court of International Justice. First, he observed that the drafting history confirmed that there had been diverse views at the time of the drafting of Article 38 concerning the role of judicial decisions and teachings. For some, judges could only apply the law, while others considered that international judges also had a function to develop the law owing to the existence of gaps in international law and the slow formation process of customary international law. Second, he observed that the members of the Advisory Committee of Jurists established pursuant to the mandate in Article 14 of the Covenant of the League of Nations[217] (Advisory Committee) had considered that the role of teachings was to assist with objectively determining the existence of rules agreed to by States that could be applied in a specific case. Third, the debate in the Advisory Committee had revealed that the majority of members considered that, in principle, both judicial decisions and teachings were important in the process of the identification of rules of international law. He observed that both served to help resolve practical legal problems. Fourth, the Advisory Committee had debated whether the sources in Article 38 should be used in successive order as a guide to the judicial task: some members of the Advisory Committee had considered that to be the case, while others had been of the view that the list only implied that the sources should be addressed systematically.

[217] Covenant of the League of Nations (Versailles, 28 April 1919), League of Nations, *Official Journal*, No. 1, February 1920, p. 3.

78. Chapter VIII of the report analysed the elements of Article 38, considering its ordinary meaning and then its elements. The Special Rapporteur had presented two tentative observations: first, that subsidiary means were not sources in the formal sense as the first three listed in Article 38, but documentary or auxiliary sources indicating where a court could find evidence of the existence of rules, even if courts, including the International Court of Justice, did rely, for reasons of legal security and legal stability, on their prior judicial decisions – a practice that also is found among States – more than on scholarly writings; and second, that, in principle, teachings and judicial decisions were placed on the same footing, performing complementary roles without any hierarchy between them.

79. In chapter IX, the Special Rapporteur had analysed other materials that could be considered as subsidiary means for the determination of rules of international law. The chapter considered the non-exhaustive nature of Article 38, paragraph 1 (*d*), of the Statute of the International Court of Justice, the potential subsidiary means found in practice, and how to distinguish between subsidiary means and the evidence of the existence of rules of international law, and tentatively addressed issues of the weight to be accorded to the materials.

80. The Special Rapporteur indicated that Article 38 of the Statute of the International Court of Justice was merely a directive to the Court and not necessarily intended as an exhaustive enumeration of the sources of international law. That said, it was widely considered an authoritative, if sometimes incomplete, statement of the sources of international law. He added that, against that backdrop, the Commission could add value by clarifying the role of subsidiary means and attempting to identify materials as candidates for subsidiary means. He further cited some of the main examples found in legal scholarship, including unilateral acts or declarations of States, resolutions or decisions of international organizations, agreements between States and multinational enterprises, religious law, equity and soft law.

81. The Special Rapporteur observed that unilateral acts could be considered as being binding or non-binding depending on the context, and that resolutions of international organizations or intergovernmental conferences could also be binding or non-binding. He added that subsidiary means would have varying levels of weight and authority, which would depend on, *inter alia*, the legal context, the way in which they were drafted and the expertise of the individuals involved in the drafting. Additional factors to consider when assessing the weight of a particular source included the mandate of the institution that produced the material, as well as the level of agreement within and beyond the relevant body.

82. The Special Rapporteur recalled that he had tentatively favoured the inclusion of resolutions and decisions of international organizations and the work of expert bodies as relevant subsidiary means. He had, however, considered that unilateral acts and religious law should not be addressed for a variety of reasons, including the lack of certainty whether some were not formal sources of international law as opposed to subsidiary means for determining rules of international law.

83. Finally, in chapter X, the Special Rapporteur had presented five draft conclusions and a tentative programme of work. The Special Rapporteur had further proposed that the second report would address the function of subsidiary means and study judicial decisions, while the third report would be dedicated to teachings and, as appropriate, other subsidiary means, including the study of the role of individuals and private expert bodies, as well as those established by States. He had suggested that, if the proposed timetable was maintained, the Commission could adopt on first reading the entire set of draft conclusions in 2025.

2. Summary of the plenary debate

(a) General comments

84. Members welcomed the first report of the Special Rapporteur. Members also agreed on the practical importance and relevance of the work on the topic, for its own intrinsic merit, but also taking into account the need for the completion of the Commission's work on that last remaining aspect of Article 38 of the Statute of the International Court of Justice, which concerned the subsidiary means for the determination of rules of international law. They

agreed with the Special Rapporteur that subsidiary means were not sources of international law, as opposed to those mentioned in Article 38, paragraph 1 (*a*) to (*c*), of the Statute of the International Court of Justice.

85. Members also emphasized that the function of subsidiary means was to assist in the determination of rules of international law. As such, it was important for the Commission to elaborate the functions of subsidiary means and to define what "determination" of rules meant.

86. With respect to the terminology, some members expressed the view that it would be important to recall that the term used in Article 38, paragraph 1 (*d*), of the Statute of the International Court of Justice in French and Spanish expressly referred to the auxiliary function of such materials, which confirmed that they were not sources of international law. This was not, however, to suggest that subsidiary means were not important in practice; only that they played an auxiliary role in the process of determining the rules of international law.

87. There was consensus among the members on the need, where possible, for consistency with the prior work of the Commission on other topics relating to the sources of international law, including that recently concluded on the identification of customary international law, the identification and legal consequences of peremptory norms of general international law (*jus cogens*) and the ongoing work on general principles of law. That was to be without prejudice to the particular needs of the present topic.

88. Members generally agreed that the category of subsidiary means for the determination of rules of international law was not necessarily exhaustive. Several proposals were made for additional means that could be examined in the present topic. In that connection, some members favoured further analysis of the work of expert bodies and resolutions of international organizations. Other members also gave the opinion that the Commission should study certain types of unilateral acts capable of producing legal obligations as part of additional subsidiary means that could be used to determine rules of international law. Yet other members cautioned against an undue expansion of the category of subsidiary means, suggesting instead the expansion of existing categories of subsidiary means to encompass new subsidiary means, which could be dealt with separately.

89. Some members referred to the principle of *iura novit curia* and the possible relation it would have to subsidiary means. Accordingly, in their view, the role of the judge was to know the law. The suggestion was made that the Commission consider how that could affect, if at all, its approach to the present topic. Others referred to the function of counsel representing the parties to disputes, who typically sought to espouse a particular interpretation or understanding of the content of the law, thereby indicating that the ascertainment of norms was not a task exclusive to judges. That reinforced the practical relevance of the study of the present topic.

90. Members generally expressed support for the study of the weight to be given to subsidiary means. Some members expressed the view that Article 38 paragraph 1 (*d*), of the Statute of the International Court of Justice did not distinguish between judicial decisions and teachings. Other members were of the view that, in practice, judicial decisions carried greater weight. Several members suggested that additional criteria should be provided for resorting to the decisions of national courts as subsidiary means, and that the resolutions and decisions of international organizations and bodies should be addressed.

(*i*) *Scope and outcome of the topic*

91. Members generally agreed with the issues set forth for consideration by the Commission in the Special Rapporteur's first report, namely: (*a*) the origins, nature and scope of subsidiary means; (*b*) the function of subsidiary means and their relationship to the sources of international law; and (*c*) additional subsidiary means for the determination of rules of international law. Members broadly agreed that the subsidiary means mentioned in Article 38, paragraph 1 (*d*), of the Statute of the International Court of Justice were not exhaustive and that the Commission should elaborate on possible additional subsidiary means for the determination of rules of international law other than those included in such category. Some members agreed with the Special Rapporteur that unilateral acts of States capable of creating legal obligations should not be considered as subsidiary means. Several members agreed that

there were other subsidiary means that warranted further consideration by the Commission, including unilateral acts. Frequently mentioned were certain resolutions and decisions of international organizations and bodies, as well as the works of private expert bodies and treaty bodies, all of which could assist in the determination of rules of international law. Some members, however, expressed doubts about the use of resolutions of international organizations as subsidiary means because they pertain rather to the process of interpretation or formation of international law.

92. Members agreed that the main function of subsidiary means was to assist in the determination of rules. A proposal was made to include a draft conclusion concerning the functions, which could also refer to the use of subsidiary means to interpret other sources or to determine the effects and legal consequences of certain rules. Another suggestion was to include a draft conclusion addressing the relationship between subsidiary means and sources of international law.

93. It was suggested that the Commission consider the distinction between the formation, interpretation and identification of rules of international law. It was also proposed that the Commission's consideration could elaborate on the distinction between the supplementary means of interpretation provided in the Vienna Convention on the Law of Treaties[218] and the subsidiary means for the determination of rules of international law.

94. Support was also expressed for focusing on the practical aspects of the use of subsidiary means. The view was expressed that the Commission should avoid excessively theoretical discussions and rather concentrate on existing law and practice. Some members considered that the analysis of conflicting decisions of international courts and tribunals fell naturally within the scope of the topic. They considered that clarification of the matter by the Commission could be useful as guidance for practitioners. Other members suggested that the fragmentation of international law had proved to be a more theoretical than practical problem and, consequently, that the question of fragmentation should thus not be considered. Other members indicated that it was important to refer to the proliferation of international tribunals and the phenomenon of cross-fertilization and harmonization of international law.

95. Support was expressed for referring to the degree of representativeness in the context of the draft conclusions and when assessing subsidiary means. Such representativeness should cover several aspects, including considerations of regional distribution, legal traditions and gender.

96. As to the outcome of the topic, members generally agreed that there was no need to depart from the previous decision of the Commission to have draft conclusions as an appropriate form of output for the topic, since that was consistent with the approach in prior related topics. A view was expressed that draft guidelines could also be an appropriate outcome. Several members expressed support and appreciation for the Special Rapporteur's proposal to prepare a multilingual bibliography as part of the work of the Commission on the topic.

(ii) Methodology

97. Members generally agreed with the methodology proposed by the Special Rapporteur, which included a careful examination of practice and literature. Some indicated that, while the practice of States and the jurisprudence of international courts and tribunals were a good starting point, the jurisprudence of national courts, the output of international organizations and academic literature would also be relevant. Members further referred to a need for more diverse sources and references in more languages and from the various regions of the world and legal traditions to be used in the consideration of the topic, which would help to strengthen the utility and legitimacy of the Commission's work on the topic.

98. Some members expressed the view that there could be some methodological difficulty in the consideration of the practice of tribunals, since some subsidiary means, especially teachings, were often consulted but not always cited formally in court decisions. A number

[218] Vienna Convention on the Law of Treaties (Vienna, 23 May 1969), United Nations, *Treaty Series*, vol. 1155, No. 18232, p. 443.

of members also stressed the importance of keeping in mind the applicable law clauses of each tribunal when analysing their use of subsidiary means.

(b) Draft conclusions 1 to 3

99. Draft conclusions 1 to 3 were provisionally adopted by the Commission with commentaries at the present session (see sect. C below). Accordingly, following the practice of the Commission, the summary of the plenary debate on these draft conclusions is not included in the present report.

(c) Draft conclusion 4

100. With respect to draft conclusion 4 (decisions of courts and tribunals),[219] several members noted that the draft conclusion overlapped with and further developed draft conclusion 2 on the decisions of courts and tribunals. Some members referred to the need to consider what was meant by the decisions of international courts and tribunals being particularly authoritative for the determination of rules of international law.

101. While it was agreed that, in general, no system of judicial precedent existed in international law, there was nonetheless value in consistency and predictability. A consistent approach to the draft conclusions was called for and it was noted that, while draft conclusions 1 to 3 proposed by the Special Rapporteur in his first report referred to the determination of rules of international law, the proposed draft conclusions 4 and 5 referred to the identification or determination of the existence and content of rules of international law.

102. Some members were of the view that the authority of the decisions of the International Court of Justice should be taken in context and that, in certain cases, the decisions of other international courts and tribunals could be more relevant due to their expertise in a particular subject. Other members agreed with a general reference to the importance of the decisions of the International Court of Justice. Some of them highlighted that such special regard had already been accorded to such decisions in previous conclusions on completed topics of Commission.

103. Members generally stressed the need for additional criteria specifically applicable to the decisions of national courts. Other members supported the Special Rapporteur's formulations, including the need to proceed with caution with some national court decisions. In the view of other members, only the decisions of national courts applying international law could be considered as constituting subsidiary means for purposes of the determination of rules of international law.

(d) Draft conclusion 5

104. With respect to draft conclusion 5 (teachings),[220] members supported the reference to highly qualified publicists of the various nations and underlined that writings should be representative of the principal legal systems and regions of the world. Members also stressed that teachings may influence international law beyond Article 38 of the Statute of the International Court of Justice.

105. Members were also of the view that the cogency and quality of the reasoning should be a more important criterion than the eminence of the writer. It was questioned why the "coinciding" of views should be a criterion and wondered how such factor could be related to those included in draft conclusion 3. It was suggested that the commentary should address the issue of the coinciding views of scholars. Some members considered that the coinciding views of scholars should not be included, as it could imply a requirement of consensus. Other criteria suggested for the consideration of teachings included the quality of the material, the reputation of the writers and an analysis of whether their positions had been accepted or challenged by peers.

---

[219] See above footnote 214 for the initial proposal of the Special Rapporteur and footnote 215 for the text provisionally adopted by the Drafting Committee after the plenary debate.

[220] See above footnote 214 for the initial proposal of the Special Rapporteur and footnote 215 for the text provisionally adopted by the Drafting Committee after the plenary debate.

106. It was noted that the lack of diversity in teachings used should be addressed. It was further suggested that the criterion of representativeness, including considerations of regional distribution, legal traditions, gender and racial diversity, should be included in draft conclusion 5 or in a separate draft conclusion.

107. It was also suggested that the Commission could elaborate in the commentary on the status of the work of certain bodies, such as the International Committee of the Red Cross, or the possible value of other materials that would not fall within the category of teachings, such as individual and joint separate opinions of judges.

(e) Future programme of work

108. Members generally supported the proposal by the Special Rapporteur to address the origins, nature and function of subsidiary means and to focus on judicial decisions and their relationship to the sources of international law. They considered that analysis of that issue in his next report could be complemented by the memorandum requested from the Secretariat surveying the case law of international courts and tribunals, and other bodies. While most members agreed with the proposed timeline in the tentative programme of work suggested by the Special Rapporteur, some members advised caution. It was recalled that more time had been needed to complete the consideration of certain other topics relating to the sources.

3. Concluding remarks of the Special Rapporteur

109. In his summary of the debate, the Special Rapporteur welcomed the interest that the topic had received from the members of the Commission. He noted that the extensive participation of members during the plenary debate had demonstrated the importance and practical relevance of the topic to States and practitioners of international law. He underlined that, while individual members might place their emphasis differently or hold differently nuanced views, there was consensus on the substantive issues raised for discussion in what had proved to be a rich and intellectually stimulating debate. Importantly, he recalled that there had been strong support for his approach, including for the proposed scope and outcome of the topic discussed in his first report. The three prongs of the topic had found consensus. In that regard, there had been unanimous support for the consideration of the two specific categories of subsidiary means expressly mentioned in Article 38, paragraph 1 (*d*), of the Statute of the International Court of Justice, namely judicial decisions and teachings.

110. He also recalled that members had also reached consensus that Article 38 was not exhaustive and, therefore, would only be a starting point and not the end point for the Commission's consideration of the topic if the topic was to prove practically useful to international lawyers. In his view, there had been general consensus that there were additional subsidiary means used for the determination of rules of international law, which were prevalent in the practice of States and international organizations, and therefore properly fell within the scope of the present topic. Without prejudice to his addressing other issues in future reports, based on what the research actually demonstrated and taking into account State input, the Commission should, in his view, at a minimum, address during the present topic the works of expert bodies and resolutions and decisions of international organizations in order to clarify their role as subsidiary means for the determination of rules of international law.

111. The Special Rapporteur noted the general support for the final outcome of the Commission's work, which should take the form of draft conclusions accompanied by commentaries, since the purpose of the topic was to clarify various aspects of subsidiary means for the determination of rules of international law and that such outcome was consistent with previous work of the Commission. He also noted that the use of that form of output in the present topic – reflecting primarily codification – would not preclude the Commission, consistent with its settled practice dating back to 1949, from engaging in progressive development if needed.

112. As to the methodology regarding the use of subsidiary means, he recalled that support had been expressed for following the practice of the Commission and that of States and, as appropriate, of international organizations and others. The Special Rapporteur also noted that members had broadly agreed with the proposed scope of the topic and the centrality of a

careful analysis of Article 38, paragraph 1 (*d*), of the Statute of the International Court of Justice as a starting point, but not necessarily a limit on the work of the Commission. In particular, he underlined the customary international law nature of the provision and the existence of nearly a century of practice confirming the extensive use of additional subsidiary means.

113. The Special Rapporteur stated that the concerns raised by some members related to the linguistic versions of the text of Article 38 of the Statute of the International Court of Justice which refer to "*moyens auxiliaires*", "*medios auxiliaries*", in French and Spanish, respectively. He emphasized the importance of multilingualism and recalled that the practice of drafting in English, French and Spanish would assist in ensuring that the same meaning is conveyed across the official languages.

114. The Special Rapporteur recalled that the syllabus for the topic had noted three issues relating to judicial decisions and teachings, and the scope of such categories. He observed that several members had addressed some of those issues, and that members largely upheld that the category of judicial decisions should be understood in a broad sense and include advisory opinions, in line with the previous work of the Commission.

115. The Special Rapporteur further noted the support of members for referring to the decisions of the International Court of Justice, which was also consistent with the recent work of the Commission. He mentioned that, while those decisions had particular relevance, especially on questions of general international law, reference thereto should not be understood as suggesting a hierarchy among courts or decisions. He also recalled that the first report had referred to the importance of the work of specialized tribunals, which may issue decisions and rulings that were quite authoritative in their respective areas of competence. In any event, in a decentralized system such as international law, each court had its own statute and the quality of the decisions and their compliance with norms in their respective areas would be quite important.

116. The Special Rapporteur observed that some members had raised questions on whether to include in the work on the topic decisions of certain bodies, for example, arbitral panels, conciliation commissions, the dispute settlement system of the World Trade Organization, commissions of inquiry and other mechanisms without judicial character. He also noted that, when referring to arbitral tribunals, certain peculiarities should be taken into account and that investor-State tribunals could fall within the scope of the topic. The Special Rapporteur also noted the broad support for including the decisions of international human rights treaty bodies. He recalled that members had discussed whether the appropriate way to include them was as judicial decisions or under a separate category. He explained that many of the suggestions made were already intended for examination in his future reports.

117. The Special Rapporteur observed that there had been general consensus that references to the decisions of national courts on questions of international law could be particularly relevant, while other members had emphasized the need for caution when examining such materials. He added that it was possible that a decision of a national court could serve as subsidiary means when carrying out a comparative survey of a well-accepted rule of international law. He also stressed that, as stated by the Commission in its recent work, national court decisions played a dual role as evidence of State practice and as a form of subsidiary means for the identification of the existence and content of a rule of international law. Furthermore, the Special Rapporteur also noted that members had referred to the importance of ensuring diversity in the consideration of jurisdictions, legal traditions and regions of the world.

118. In relation to the second category of subsidiary means (teachings), the Special Rapporteur observed that the majority of members had referred to the individual and collective work of scholars. Other members had called for a distinction between teachings, whether individual or collective, and works produced by expert bodies that could be considered as additional subsidiary means. The Special Rapporteur observed that it was his intention, in line with the analysis contained in his first report, to propose a set of stand-alone draft conclusions addressing the contemporary role of private and public or State-empowered bodies, and the differences between them. The Special Rapporteur noted that he would take

into account the suggestions of some members to address further functions of subsidiary means in future reports.

119. The Special Rapporteur observed that many members had referred to the question of diversity of the publicists and the over-reliance by some courts and tribunals on materials from the Anglo-American tradition and limiting to a few languages and legal traditions, and that proposals had been presented advocating for gender diversity as well. He recalled that he had raised various questions of diversity that might affect the perception of the universality of international law in his first report, including in relation to aspects that had not even been debated by members, such as the imbalance in the nationality of counsel appearing before the International Court of Justice. In any case, he welcomed that members of the Commission had expressed an openness and even support for ensuring representativeness in the work, especially in the present topic.

120. In the context of judicial decisions, he noted that members had supported his intention to carry out a more detailed study of the relationship between Articles 38 and 59 of the Statute of the International Court of Justice and the notion of precedent (*stare decisis*), or lack thereof, under international law, as well as its link to the rights of third parties. The Special Rapporteur noted that members had broadly agreed that there existed no formal system of precedent (*stare decisis*) in general international law, while recognizing that following the methodology of legal reasoning adopted in previous cases was not the same as being bound by past decisions. He added that, while not mandatory, there existed extensive practice by parties to international disputes and judges in international courts and tribunals of relying on their own prior decisions for reasons of legal security and predictability. He added that reference had been made to certain cases where tribunals had departed from their consistent practice, and that the commentary to the relevant draft conclusion could clarify that the authority of judicial decisions as subsidiary means was also dependent on contextual elements.

121. In relation to a third category of other subsidiary means, the Special Rapporteur recalled that several members had agreed with his proposed exclusion of unilateral acts of States capable of creating legal obligations. He added that many members had supported the inclusion of the resolutions of international organizations as additional subsidiary means. He noted that other members were of the view that the resolutions of international organizations could only serve as evidence of the elements of certain sources like customary international law, but were not subsidiary means themselves. However, he indicated that, in practice, much as was the case with decisions of national courts, there was no reason why resolutions could not play a dual function as elements that could be considered either in the determination of rules of law derived from the established sources or as subsidiary means for the determination of such rules. The Special Rapporteur recalled that additional subsidiary means proposed had included non-binding resolutions, equity, arbitral awards, religious law and certain types of decisions from regulatory organizations. He did not consider some of the candidates mentioned in literature as potential subsidiary means as meriting further examination by the Commission. Some of them, such as unilateral acts of States and religious law, did not, in his view, even fall within the category of subsidiary means for the determination of rules of international law. In any event, some of those same candidates, such as unilateral acts, had previously been examined by the Commission. He saw no need to revisit them or to examine politically sensitive topics such as religious law.

122. As regards the question of whether the unity and coherence of international law should be examined, at least in terms of the possible conflict between judicial decisions issued by different courts and tribunals, the Special Rapporteur noted that some members had argued that the fragmentation of international law had already been studied by the Commission and expressed the view that it did not create difficulties in practice and as such was best left out of the consideration of the topic. Others considered that the issue of fragmentation, especially with the risk of conflicting judicial decisions arising from the proliferation of international courts and tribunals, was quite important and that the present topic was the opportunity to clarify it. Other members suggested that the matter could be referred to in the commentary or dealt with by way of a without prejudice clause. The Special Rapporteur, for his part, agreed that the issue of conflicting decisions was important, if sometimes complex, and could well be an area for the Commission to seek to add practical value. He explained that the

Commission, in its 2006 report of the Study Group on the fragmentation of international law,[221] had only indicated that the topic of conflicting jurisprudence concerned the institutional competencies and hierarchical relations between tribunals *inter se*, which was better left to them to address. Thus, the Commission had not substantively addressed the issue. In any case, he was of the firm view that, given its potential implications for the scope of the topic and, although it should be for the independent Commission to ultimately decide based on a scientific assessment, it would be especially important to invite and to take into careful account the views of States and others expressed in the Sixth Committee. He therefore underlined the need to invite State input on that and other issues raised in his first report since, after all, it was hoped that States would be the primary beneficiaries of the Commission's work. He expressed intention to return to the matter in the future.

123. In relation to the proposal to include a multilingual bibliography, the Special Rapporteur noted that several members had provided scholarly works and State practice from various jurisdictions. He observed that the intention to request contributions from members and States was aimed at addressing the problem of unequal representation in the consideration of subsidiary means and to ensure more diversity and bring more legitimacy to the work of the Commission.

124. The Special Rapporteur noted the general support for the proposed programme of work. He also indicated that his proposed timeline for future work, as indicated in his first report, was tentative and could be adjusted in order to properly address the substance. He was committed to scientific rigour and did not believe in speed in the consideration of the topic coming at the expense of the substance and rigour of the work.

125. In terms of substance for the future work, the Special Rapporteur indicated his intention, in his next report, to address the decisions of courts and tribunals and how they used the subsidiary means to determine rules of international law.[222] He was confident that the memorandum from the Secretariat surveying the decisions of international courts and tribunals, and other bodies – showing how they employ subsidiary means – would contribute to the Commission's debate next year.

C. Text of the draft conclusions on subsidiary means for the determination of rules of international law provisionally adopted by the Commission at its seventy-fourth session

1. Text of the draft conclusions

126. The text of the draft conclusions provisionally adopted by the Commission at its seventy-fourth session is reproduced below.

Conclusion 1
Scope

The present draft conclusions concern the use of subsidiary means for the determination of rules of international law.

Conclusion 2
Categories of subsidiary means for the determination of rules of international law

Subsidiary means for the determination of rules of international law include:

(*a*) decisions of courts and tribunals;

(*b*) teachings;

(*c*) any other means generally used to assist in determining rules of international law.

---

[221] *Yearbook ... 2006*, vol. II (Part Two) (Addendum 2), document A/CN.4/L.682 and Add.1.

[222] See chap. X below.

Conclusion 3
General criteria for the assessment of subsidiary means for the determination of rules of international law

When assessing the weight of subsidiary means for the determination of rules of international law, regard should be had to, *inter alia*:

(*a*) their degree of representativeness;

(*b*) the quality of the reasoning;

(*c*) the expertise of those involved;

(*d*) the level of agreement among those involved;

(*e*) the reception by States and other entities;

(*f*) where applicable, the mandate conferred on the body.

2. Text of the draft conclusions and commentaries thereto

127. The text of the draft conclusions, together with commentaries provisionally adopted by the Commission at its seventy-fourth session, is reproduced below.

Subsidiary means for the determination of rules of international law

General commentary

(1) As always with the Commission's output, the draft conclusions are to be read together with the commentaries.

(2) The present draft conclusions seek to contribute greater clarity on the use of subsidiary means and their relationship with the sources of international law in two principal ways. First, they aim to identify and elucidate the roles of subsidiary means for the determination of rules of international law, consistent with the letter and spirit of Article 38, paragraph 1, of the Statute of the International Court of Justice.[223]

(3) Second, the present draft conclusions offer a consistent methodological approach when using subsidiary means for determining the existence and content[224] of rules of international law. Such determination relates to two main aspects. Firstly, in some cases, there may be a question whether, using subsidiary means, a rule of international law can be identified or determined to exist based on one of the established sources of international law, such as a treaty, customary international law or a general principle of law. Secondly, in other cases, it may be determined that a certain rule exists, but debate could remain about its content and scope. In either scenario, the subsidiary means, for instance a judicial decision, could be used as an auxiliary means to make that determination. The interaction between subsidiary means and the sources of international law, as well as the potentially far-reaching implications of the possible expansion of the category of subsidiary means, indicates that it is vital that the use of any subsidiary means to elucidate the sources of rules of international law be carried out using a coherent and systematic methodology.[225] Such a methodology

---

[223] Statute of the International Court of Justice, Article 38, available at http://www.icj-cij.org/en/statute.

[224] The Commission also addressed the question of the existence and content of rules in its topic on identification of customary international law (see conclusions on identification of customary international law and commentaries thereto, *Yearbook ... 2018*, vol. II (Part Two), paras. 65–66). The same logic applies here, even though the discussion in the present context is about subsidiary means instead of a source of international law. See the first report of the Special Rapporteur on the present topic (A/CN.4/760).

[225] The Commission, in various projects, has already determined that a methodology is needed to clarify the sources of international law. It should build, as appropriate, on its previous conclusions on subsidiary means that may be used for the determination of the existence and content of rules of international law, which have already found general support among States, whether those rules are of a customary international law nature (conclusion 13, para. 1: "[d]ecisions of international courts and tribunals, in particular of the International Court of Justice, concerning the existence and content of rules of customary international law are a subsidiary means for the determination of such rules";

should contribute to enhancing the consistency, predictability and stability of international law.

(4) Article 38 of the Statute of the International Court of Justice, which is regarded as the authoritative statement of the sources of international law, is the point of departure for the current draft conclusions. Paragraph 1 of Article 38 directs that the Court, whose primary function is to decide in accordance with international law the disputes submitted to it by States, shall apply: (*a*) treaties, whether general or particular, establishing rules expressly recognized by the contesting States; (*b*) international custom, as evidence of a general practice accepted as law; (*c*) the general principles of law recognized by the "community of nations";[226] and (*d*) as subsidiary means for the determination of rules of law, "judicial decisions" and "the teachings of the most highly qualified publicists of the various nations".

(5) Article 38 is the applicable law provision of the Statute of the International Court of Justice. However, its significance stems not only from its inclusion in the Statute of the principal judicial organ of the United Nations[227] and the only universal court with general jurisdiction, but also from the broader acceptance and reliance on Article 38 by States and tribunals, as well as legal scholars, as an authoritative statement of the sources of international law under customary international law. There is no suggestion from the practice of States and international organizations or established literature that Article 38 is an exhaustive enumeration of the sources of international law or the subsidiary means for the determination of rules of international law. Thus, in addition to judicial decisions and teachings, which may be thought of as the traditional subsidiary means, the present draft conclusions will also address additional subsidiary means prevalent in the practice of States and international organizations, which will be elaborated in later draft conclusions. The view was expressed, however, that the list of subsidiary means found in Article 38, paragraph 1 (*d*), can be read broadly to address contemporary developments.

(6) The Commission has selected "draft conclusions" as the final form of output for its work on this topic. This is consistent with, and complements, the Commission's recent output on four topics addressing the sources and related issues of international law, namely, identification of customary international law,[228] general principles of law,[229] identification and

conclusion 14: "[t]eachings of the most highly qualified publicists of the various nations may serve as a subsidiary means for the determination of rules of customary international law", *Yearbook ... 2018*, vol. II (Part Two), para. 65), general principles of law (draft conclusion 8, para. 1: "[d]ecisions of international courts and tribunals, in particular of the International Court of Justice, concerning the existence and content of general principles of law are a subsidiary means for the determination of such principles"; draft conclusion 9: "[t]eachings of the most highly qualified publicists of the various nations may serve as a subsidiary means for the determination of general principles of law", contained in chap. IV of the present report) or even peremptory norms of general international law (*jus cogens*) (draft conclusion 9, para. 1: [d]ecisions of international courts and tribunals, in particular of the international court of justice, are a subsidiary means for determining the peremptory character of norms of general international law"; draft conclusion 9, para. 2: "[t]he works of expert bodies established by States or international organizations and the teachings of the most highly qualified publicists of the various nations may also serve as subsidiary means for determining the peremptory character of norms of general international law", *Official Records of the General Assembly, Seventy-seventh Session, Supplement No. 10* (A/77/10), para. 43).

226 Article 38, paragraph 1 (*c*), of the Statute of the International Court of Justice refers to "civilized nations". The Commission has, in the context of its topic "General principles of law", rightly dispensed with that outdated term in favour of the more inclusive term "community of nations". The latter term will therefore also be used in this topic. See draft conclusion 2 on general principles of law, contained in chap. IV of the present report.

227 Charter of the United Nations, Article 92: "The International Court of Justice shall be the principal judicial organ of the United Nations. It shall function in accordance with the annexed Statute, which is based upon the Statute of the Permanent Court of International Justice and forms an integral part of the present Charter."

228 *Yearbook ... 2018*, vol. II (Part Two), chap. V, pp. 89–113, paras. 53–66.

229 Contained in chap. IV of the present report.

legal consequences of peremptory norms of general international law (*jus cogens*)[230] and subsequent agreements and subsequent practice in relation to the interpretation of treaties.[231]

(7) Regarding the normative value of "draft conclusions", the Commission has, to date, not adopted a one-size fits all definition of draft conclusions, since it must examine the specific needs of each topic on its own terms. That said, because States and other users of the Commission's work may be more familiar with "draft articles" as a final form of output, draft conclusions as used here should be understood as the outcome of a process of reasoned deliberation and, more specifically, a statement of the rules derived from the practice found on subsidiary means in the determination of rules of international law. Their essential characteristic is to clarify the law based on the current practice. Thus, the content of the present draft conclusions, in line with the statute of the Commission and the general practice on the related topics mentioned above, reflects primarily codification and possibly elements of progressive development of international law.

(8) Taking the above considerations into account, and given its mandate to assist States with the codification and progressive development of international law consistent with article 1 of its statute, the Commission expects that the present draft conclusions may facilitate the work of all those who may be called upon to address subsidiary means for the determination of rules of international law. Nonetheless, as the present draft conclusions do not address all possible subsidiary means, it is the process of applying the established subsidiary means to determine rules of international law and of determining the scope of new subsidiary means that may emerge in the future which would benefit from the application of the criteria contained in the present draft conclusions. Ultimately, when the text and the accompanying commentaries are read together, the draft conclusions should provide useful guidance to States, international organizations, international and national courts and tribunals and all those, including legal scholars and practitioners of international law, who may have reason to address subsidiary means for the determination of the rules of international law.

Conclusion 1
Scope

The present draft conclusions concern the use of subsidiary means for the determination of rules of international law.

Commentary

(1) Draft conclusion 1 is introductory in nature. It provides, in a general way, that the present draft conclusions concern the use of subsidiary means for the determination of rules of international law. The use of the term "present draft conclusions" makes clear that the objective is to set out the scope of the entire set of draft conclusions. The term "concern", instead of "apply" (which is typically used in outcomes that would be recommended to States as bases for future conventions), relates to the object of the work. It also reflects the practice of the Commission in the work on similar topics that result in "draft conclusions" or "draft guidelines" rather than "draft articles".

(2) The term "the use of" was selected after a consideration of two main options. First, like the scope provision on the topic of identification of customary international law,[232] the formula "the way in which subsidiary means are used" was proposed in order to underline the methodological nature of this topic. Second, during the Commission's discussions, consideration was given to an alternative formulation that would have provided that subsidiary means "are to be used". The Statute of the International Court of Justice directs the Court to apply judicial decisions and teachings, as subsidiary means, but at the same time indicates that the judges may use them as a means for the determination of the rules of

[230] *Official Records of the General Assembly, Seventy-seventh Session, Supplement No. 10* (A/77/10), chap. IV, paras. 43–44.

[231] *Yearbook ... 2018*, vol. II (Part Two), chap. IV, pp. 23–88, paras. 39–52.

[232] The scope provision, in conclusion 1, stated: "[t]he present draft conclusions concern the way in which the existence and content of rules of customary international law are to be determined." See conclusion 1 of the conclusions on identification of customary international law, *Yearbook ... 2018*, vol. II (Part Two), para. 65.

international law. That said, in practice, while the judges could and do refer to the subsidiary means when they deem it necessary, Article 38, paragraph 1 (*d*), of the Statute does not actually obligate the Court to apply the subsidiary means. The Commission settled on the formulation that the draft conclusions concern "the use of" subsidiary means, which was seen as less imperative than the phrase "are to be used". In addition, the formulation employed was preferred because it was more neutral.

(3) For the purposes of the present commentaries, and with the view to enhancing clarity, terminological explanations are important. First, while the reference to "subsidiary means for the determination of rules of international law" is derived from Article 38, paragraph 1 (*d*), of the Statute of the Court, it is not identical to the wording in that provision which speaks of the determination of "rules of law". The term "subsidiary means for the determination of rules of international law" will be frequently used in this topic and the commentaries but the broader term "rules of law" contained in the Statute will sometimes be substituted with the term "rules of international law." The latter formula ensures consistency with the title of the present topic, the choice of which was intended to emphasize that the principal thrust of the project is the determination of the rules of international law, as opposed to the rules of law more generally. Importantly, the fact that the term "rules of law" is broader than the term "rules of international law" does not operate as a limitation on the substantive scope of the present draft conclusions. Nor does it change the analytical approach that is required. At the same time, the reference to rules of international law should be understood as not being an *a priori* exclusion of other rules of law that could provide assistance in the determination of rules of international law.

(4) Second, an analysis of the ordinary meaning of the term "subsidiary" under Article 38, paragraph 1 (*d*), of the Statute, in the various authentic language versions,[233] indicates that they are auxiliary in character.

(5) The term as expressed in English was derived from the Latin "*subsidiarius*" and refers to something that provides assistance, that is "subordinate", "supplementary" or "secondary"; "something which provides additional support or assistance; an auxiliary, an aid".[234] The second term "means" is a reference to an "intermediary agent or instrument"; "something interposed or intervening".[235]

(6) Third, and more substantively, the Commission's study of the French (*moyens auxiliaires*), Spanish (*medios auxiliares*) and other equally authentic language versions of Article 38, paragraph 1 (*d*), found that they more precisely underline the ancillary or auxiliary nature of the subsidiary means.[236] The other authentic language versions also set forth a relatively narrower understanding of the term subsidiary than a broader ordinary understanding which also became associated with the English term. They further confirm that both judicial decisions and teachings differ in their nature from the sources of law, expressly enumerated in Article 38, paragraph 1 (*a*) to (*c*), of the Statute: treaties, international custom and general principles of law. In other words, judicial decisions and teachings are subsidiary simply because they are not sources of law that may apply in and of themselves. Rather, they are used to assist or to aid in determining whether or not rules of international law exist and, if so, the content of such rules. This is not to suggest that the

[233] See, in this regard, Vienna Convention on the Law of Treaties, art. 33. Furthermore, pursuant to Article 111 of the Charter of the United Nations, the Chinese, French, Russian, English, and Spanish texts are equally authentic. In accordance with Article 92 of the Charter, the annexed Statute of the Court forms an integral part of the Charter. The Charter has therefore been authenticated in the above five languages. Pursuant to resolution 3190 (XXVIII) of the General Assembly of 18 December 1973, Arabic was included among the official and the working languages of the General Assembly and its Main Committees.

[234] "Subsidiary", *Oxford English Dictionary* (Clarendon, 3d ed., 2013). Available at www.oed.com.

[235] "Means", *ibid.*

[236] The same understanding is reflected in the Chinese and Russian versions. The Arabic version of the Charter and of the annexed Statute is not covered by Article 111 of the Charter, and different translations exist. The Arabic-speaking members of the Commission therefore engaged in a useful linguistic exchange in a meeting with the United Nations translators and interpreters, leading to an assessment that the better translation of "subsidiary means" would be: وسائل احتياطية.

subsidiary means are not important. On the contrary, they remain so, albeit only as auxiliary means for the identification and determination of rules of international law.

(7) On the preceding point, the Commission has already determined in its 2022 draft conclusions on identification and legal consequences of peremptory norms of general international law (*jus cogens*) that some subsidiary means, specifically decisions of international courts and tribunals, are even "a subsidiary means for determining the peremptory character of norms of general international law".[237] Before reaching that conclusion, the Commission had also concluded – in its work on two other topics that are particularly relevant because they concern the sources in Article 38 of the Statute – that subsidiary means may be used for the identification or determination of rules of customary international law (Article 38, para. 1 (*b*)) and for general principles of law (Article 38, para. 1 (*c*)).

(8) That the sources of law are distinct from the subsidiary means, but at the same time interact with some of the latter, such as prior judicial decisions, is confirmed by the approach of the International Court of Justice to the application of Article 38 in several cases. For instance, in *Military Activities in and against Nicaragua (Nicaragua v. United States of America)*, in resolving the question of the law applicable to that case, the Court cited its prior judgment in the *North Sea Continental Shelf* cases for the rule that it was required to apply the various "sources of law enumerated in Article 38 of the Statute",[238] which would include both multilateral treaties, customary law and general international law, even where they overlap. In the *Continental Shelf (Tunisia/Libya)* case, the Court recalled that "[w]hile the Court is, of course, bound to have regard to all the legal sources specified in Article 38, paragraph 1, of the Statute of the Court in determining the relevant principles and rules applicable to the delimitation, it is also bound, in accordance with paragraph 1 (*a*), of that Article, to apply the provisions of the Special Agreement" and that, referring to the *North Sea Continental Shelf* judgment, international law required delimitation be effected "in accordance with equitable principles, and taking account of all the relevant circumstances".[239]

(9) Similarly, in the *Gulf of Maine* case, a Chamber of the Court determined that

> the Court, in its reasoning on the matter, must obviously begin by referring to Article 38, paragraph 1, of the Statute of the Court. For the purpose of the Chamber at the present stage of its reasoning, which is to ascertain the principles and rules of international law which in general govern the subject of maritime delimitation, reference will be made to conventions (Art. 38, para. 1 (*a*)) and international custom (para. 1 (*b*)), *to the definition of which the judicial decisions (para. 1 (d)) either of the Court or of arbitration tribunals have already made a substantial contribution*.[240] [Emphasis added].

In *Maritime Delimitation in the Area between Greenland and Jan Mayen (Denmark v. Norway)*, the Court examined "the sources listed in Article 38 of the Statute of the Court", which it found that it "must consider" in relation to "the law applicable to the fishery zone"

237 See, in this regard, draft conclusion 9, para. 1, entitled "Subsidiary means for the determination of the peremptory character of norms of general international law" and paras. (1) to (4) of the commentary thereto, *Official Records of the General Assembly, Seventy-seventh Session, Supplement No. 10* (A/77/10), para. 44, at pp. 43–45. See also para. (2) of the commentary to conclusion 13 of the conclusions on identification of customary international law, *Yearbook ... 2018*, vol. II (Part Two), para. 66, at p. 109 ("The term 'subsidiary means' denotes the ancillary role of such decisions in elucidating the law, rather than being themselves a source of international law (as are treaties, customary international law and general principles of law). The use of the term 'subsidiary means' does not, and is not intended to, suggest that such decisions are not important for the identification of customary international law").

238 *Military and Paramilitary Activities in and against Nicaragua (Nicaragua v. United States of America), Merits, Judgment, I.C.J. Reports 1986*, p. 14, at p. 82–85.

239 *Continental Shelf (Tunisia/ Libyan Arab Jamahiriya), Judgment, I.C.J. Reports 1982*, p. 18. at p. 37, para. 23.

240 *Delimitation of the Maritime Boundary in the Gulf of Maine Area, Judgment, I.C.J. Reports 1984*, p. 246, at p. 290–291, para. 83.

including its "material" prior decisions in the *Gulf of Maine* case.[241] Finally, in *Frontier Dispute (Burkina Faso/Niger)*, the Court interpreted Article 38, paragraph 1, in the context of the object of the Special Agreement between the parties and found that it "clearly indicates that the rules and principles mentioned in that provision of the Statute must be applied to any question that it might be necessary for the Court to resolve in order to rule on the dispute".[242] Among those rules the Court found applicable to that case was the principle of the intangibility of boundaries inherited from decolonization (*uti possidetis juris*), for which the Court referred to prior judgments in *Frontier Dispute (Burkina Faso/Republic of Mali)* and *Frontier Dispute (Benin/Niger)*.[243]

(10) As regards the phrase "for the determination of rules of international law", the term "determination" comes from Article 38, paragraph 1 (*d*), of the Statute. In the view of the Commission, the term could be understood in at least two ways. First, "determination" has one meaning when considered in its noun form "determination" and another as a verb "determine". As a noun it can mean "ascertainment" (a means of ascertaining what the rule is, a piece of evidence), whereas the word "determine" as a verb can also mean to "decide" (as will be explained in paragraph (13)). Under the first meaning, "determination" is "limited to a determination in the sense of finding out what is the existing law".[244] Such determination would encompass several operations, which may include, depending on the factual context, the identification of a rule or the determination of whether a certain rule exists; and, if it does exist, the content of the rule and its possible application to a specific case.

(11) For example, the determination process could involve analysis of a particular type of subsidiary means, *e.g.* a decision of an international court, establishing that an international legal rule exists on a given point in issue. The rule may be assessed to exist (or not) as any of the sources of international law contained in Article 38, paragraph 1 (*a*) to (*c*), namely international conventions or treaties, international custom and general principles of law. To take the example of treaties, the existence of a given rule may be relatively easy to establish, but the scope of the rule may be contested. This is where both the source of the rule and the subsidiary means may interact to help solve a practical problem. For example, a prior judicial decision, being used as a subsidiary means, might be cited by the parties and the court, since the decision might have already referred to and provided an interpretation of a rule stated in a treaty, such as the principle of the sovereign equality of all States in Article 2, paragraph 1, of the Charter of the United Nations. Both the treaty rule, in the example from the Charter, and the prior decision explaining it could then be relevant to resolving the dispute between the parties.

(12) In other instances, when it comes to the sources of law other than treaties, i.e. customary international law or general principles of law, more analysis will be required of the interaction between the subsidiary means and the source. This is because both proof of customary international law and proof of general principles of law each require certain additional legal tests to be fulfilled before the existence and content of the legal rule can be identified. Irrespective of the source consulted, reference to the prior judicial decision as a subsidiary means does not mean that the latter is the source of the law; rather, the decision itself may provide evidence of the existence and content of a rule of international law that could then apply. The binding effect of the rule, if and when it is applied, would stem from the treaty, custom or general principle and not the prior judicial decision, since there is no doctrine of judicial precedent (*stare decisis*) in general international law (as confirmed by Article 59 of the Statute of the International Court of Justice).

(13) But, in addition to the meaning given in paragraph (10) above, the word "determine" as a verb can also mean to state the law. In some cases, and although as a formal matter Article 59 will continue to apply, the Court simply refers to the rule whose content it determined in previous decisions. In most cases, it may do so without engaging in further

---

241 *Maritime Delimitation in the Area between Greenland and Jan Mayen, Judgment, I.C.J. Reports 1993*, p. 38, at p. 61, para. 52.

242 *Frontier Dispute (Burkina Faso/Niger), Judgment, I.C.J. Reports 2013*, pp. 44, at p. 73, para. 62.

243 *Ibid.*, paras. 63 and 66.

244 M. Shahabuddeen, *Precedent in the World Court* (Cambridge, Cambridge University Press, 1996), p. 76.

analysis to establish whether the rule exists or not, since that could at a later stage be taken as a given, following the prior decision to that effect. For, after all, in practice, judges – as well as States and their legal representatives for that matter – do not start with a clean slate when they have to resolve a new dispute raising factual and legal issues similar to those already considered. Indeed, prior decisions are "frequently used to identify or elucidate a rule of the law, not to make such a rule, i.e. not so much in the quality of binding precedents as having persuasive influence".[245] For reasons of legal security,[246] not only does the Court itself refer to its own prior decisions, it often seeks to explain a prior position that is based on previous decisions or to justify a departure from a prior decision.[247]

Conclusion 2
Categories of subsidiary means for the determination of rules of international law

Subsidiary means for the determination of rules of international law include:

(*a*) decisions of courts and tribunals;

(*b*) teachings;

(*c*) any other means generally used to assist in determining rules of international law.

Commentary

(1) Draft conclusion 2 sets out three main categories of subsidiary means for the determination of rules of international law. These are: the decisions of courts and tribunals; the teachings, in the sense of by those of scholars from the various nations, regions and legal systems of the world; and any other means generally used to assist in determining rules of international law. The first two categories are rooted in and largely track the language of Article 38, paragraph 1 (*d*), of the Statute of the International Court of Justice, with the adjustments discussed below. The third category addresses the fact that there are other means used generally in practice to assist in the determination of the rules of international law. Below, the present commentary explains each of these categories in turn, but starts with the *chapeau*.

Chapeau *of draft conclusion 2*

(2) The *chapeau* of draft conclusion 2 simply states that "subsidiary means for the determination of rules of international law include". In formulating the current *chapeau*, consideration was given to using the alternative term "including but not limited to," or to

245 Rosenne, *The Law and Practice of the International Court, 1920–2005*, p. 1553.

246 See *Application of the Convention on the Prevention and Punishment of the Crime of Genocide (Bosnia and Herzegovina v. Serbia and Montenegro), Judgment, I.C.J. Reports 2007*, p. 43, at pp. 90–92 and 101, paras. 116, 120 and 139 ("116. Two purposes, one general, the other specific, underlie the principle of *res judicata*, internationally as nationally. First, the stability of legal relations requires that litigation come to an end. The Court's function, according to Article 38 of its Statute, is to 'decide', that is, to bring to an end, 'such disputes as are submitted to it'. Secondly, it is in the interest of each party that an issue which has already been adjudicated in favour of that party be not argued again. Article 60 of the Statute articulates this finality of judgments. Depriving a litigant of the benefit of a judgment it has already obtained must in general be seen as a breach of the principles governing the legal settlement of disputes.").

247 See, for instance, *Jurisdictional Immunities of the State (Germany v. Italy: Greece intervening), Judgment, I.C.J. Reports 2012*, p. 99, at p. 122, where the Court determined that it must "determine, in accordance with Article 38 (1) (*b*) of its Statute, the existence of 'international custom, as evidence of a general practice accepted as law' conferring immunity on States and, if so, what is the scope and extent of that immunity. To do so, *it must apply the criteria which it has repeatedly laid down* for identifying a rule of customary international law. In particular, *as the Court made clear* in the *North Sea Continental Shelf* cases, the existence of a rule of customary international law requires that there be 'a settled practice' together with *opinio juris* (*North Sea Continental Shelf (Federal Republic of Germany/Denmark; Federal Republic of Germany/Netherlands), Judgment, I.C.J. Reports 1969*, p. 44, para. 77)" (emphasis added).

replacing "include" with "can take the form of", all of which were aimed at confirming the non-exhaustive nature of the categories of subsidiary means mentioned in the draft conclusion. In the end, the Commission decided to use simply the term "include", at the end of the sentence, as it was sufficiently clear and general. Substantively, as already indicated earlier, the point of departure for the *chapeau* is that the list of subsidiary means contained in Article 38, paragraph 1 (*d*), of the Statute is not exhaustive and those means have broader relevance because they are part and parcel of customary international law.

(3) The first two categories, set out in draft conclusion 2, subparagraphs (*a*) and (*b*), are rooted in Article 38, paragraph 1 (*d*), of the Statute of the Court, which refers to "judicial decisions" and the "teachings of the most highly qualified publicists of the various nations" as subsidiary means for the determination of rules of law. Those formulations were shortened to refer to "decisions of courts and tribunals" and then "teachings". Then there is the third category of "any other means". The latter encompasses other subsidiary means that are not expressly mentioned in Article 38, but that have emerged in practice to also perform an auxiliary or assistive role in the determination of the rules of international law. That there is a third category of means described as subsidiary is captured in two senses: first, by the use of the term "include" at the end of the *chapeau* and, second and more substantively, by the inclusion of a paragraph (*c*) which anticipates the existence of a more open-ended category of any other subsidiary means.

*Subparagraph (*a*) – decisions of courts and tribunals*

(4) Subparagraph (*a*) recognizes the first category of subsidiary means as being comprised of "decisions of courts and tribunals". Consistent with its prior work addressing the subsidiary means,[248] the Commission decided to delete the qualifying word "judicial" in favour of the much broader formulation "decisions of courts and tribunals". This was intended to ensure that a wider set of decisions from a variety of bodies could be covered by the present draft conclusions. The view was expressed, however, that the much narrower formulation "judicial decisions", which mirrors the exact term in Article 38, paragraph 1 (*d*), of the Statute of the International Court of Justice, was preferable to the broader formulation "decisions of courts and tribunals" that was adopted.

(5) Article 38, paragraph 1 (*d*), of the Statute of the International Court of Justice expressly mentions "judicial decisions" as being among the subsidiary means for the determination of rules of international law. It is not immediately apparent from an examination of the Charter of the United Nations (Chapter XIV), the Statute, the secondary documents of the Court (for example, the Rules of Court or the Practice Directions) or the jurisprudence of the Court that they contain any explicit definitions of the term "judicial decisions". Questions have arisen in practice and in the present topic concerning the meaning and scope of the term "judicial decisions". That is why the Commission ultimately settled on the broader term "decisions of courts and tribunals" here, as it has done in other prior topics.

(6) The term "decisions" refers to a judgment, decision or determination by a court of law or a body of persons or institution, as part of a process of adjudication with a view to bringing to an end a controversy or settling a matter. While normally such a decision, especially a judicial one, would be issued by a court of law, such as the International Court of Justice or other international or national courts, it may also be issued by another type of appropriate adjudicative body. Relatedly, as regards the decisions of the International Court of Justice or other international courts, it should be clarified that decisions would include not just final judgments rendered by a court, but also advisory opinions and any orders issued as part of incidental or interlocutory proceedings.[249] The latter would include orders on provisional

[248] For example, as was the case in the title of conclusion 13 in the topic identification of customary international law: "Decisions of courts and tribunals". *Yearbook ... 2018*, vol. II (Part Two), para. 65.

[249] The above reading is consistent with the Commission's view in identification of customary international law, where, in the commentary to conclusion 13 addressing subsidiary means, it explained that "the term 'decisions' includes judgments and advisory opinions, as well as orders on procedural and interlocutory matters": para. (5) of the commentary to conclusion 13, *Yearbook ... 2018*, vol. II (Part Two), para. 66, at p. 109.

measures issued by international courts and tribunals.[250] The term "decisions", understood in a broad sense, includes those taken under individual complaints procedures of State-created treaty bodies, such as the Human Rights Committee. Thus, instead of the term "judicial decisions", which is found in Article 38, paragraph 1 (*d*), of the Statute, the Commission, consistent with its prior work, selected the broader term "decisions", the merit of which is to encompass decisions issued by a wider range of bodies.

(7) The term "courts and tribunals" should generally be understood broadly. It encompasses both international courts and tribunals and national courts or, as they are sometimes referred to, municipal courts. The broad meaning captures, for example, the International Court of Justice, the International Tribunal for the Law of the Sea, the ad hoc International Criminal Tribunals for the former Yugoslavia and Rwanda, the Special Court for Sierra Leone, the Special Tribunal for Lebanon and the dispute settlement bodies of the World Trade Organization as well as investment tribunals. Reference to courts and tribunals would also encompass regional judicial bodies, such as the African Court on Human and Peoples' Rights, the Court of Justice of the European Union, the Economic Community of West African States (ECOWAS) Court of Justice, the European Court of Human Rights and the Inter-American Court of Human Rights.

(8) For reasons of clarity, although this point will be elaborated in later draft conclusions, national courts means the courts or tribunals that may operate within a domestic legal system. They usually operate on the basis of national law: this includes some, but not all, of the so-called "hybrid" courts with mixed subject-matter jurisdiction and composition.[251] Here, it can be noted that national court decisions perform a dual function in the sense that, in addition to serving as subsidiary means, they can be also indications of State practice and a basis for finding *opinio juris* or to determine the existence of a principle common to the various legal systems. In the conclusions on identification of customary international law, for example, the Commission observed that State practice consisted of the conduct of the State, whether in the exercise of its executive, legislative, judicial or other functions.[252] Importantly, they could also, as already indicated above, be a form of subsidiary means. Their findings, especially on questions relating to international law, may prove to be valuable.

(9) The extensive practice of using decisions of international and national courts and tribunals as subsidiary means for the determination of rules of international law will be further elaborated upon in future draft conclusions, starting with draft conclusion 4.

*Subparagraph (*b*) – teachings*

(10) Article 38, paragraph 1 (*d*), of the Statute directs the Court to apply "the teachings of the most highly qualified publicists of the various nations, as subsidiary means for the determination of rules of law". Like the category of "decisions of courts and tribunals", which forms subparagraph (*a*) of draft conclusion 2, neither the Charter of the United Nations (Chapter XIV), the Statute nor the secondary documents of the Court (in particular the Rules of Court or the Practice Directions), contain any definition of the term "teachings". Neither the Court nor the Permanent Court of International Justice have defined the term "teachings" as a category in their practice. It would therefore seem useful to briefly examine the ordinary meaning of the term.

(11) In the present draft conclusions, and as will be further explained in draft conclusion 5, the Commission decided to use the term "teachings" to describe the second well-established category of subsidiary means. The Commission debated the possibility of using

---

[250] Para. (5) of the commentary to conclusion 13 of the conclusions on identification of customary international law, *Yearbook...2018*, vol. II (Part Two), para. 66, at pp. 109–110.

[251] The Commission, in the context of the topic of identification of customary international law, has offered working definitions of the terms "international courts and tribunals" and "hybrid" courts which is a convenient albeit starting point for our purposes: para. (6) of the commentary to draft conclusion 13 of the conclusions on identification of customary international law, *Yearbook ... 2018*, vol. II (Part Two), pp. 109–110.

[252] *Ibid.*, para. 65, conclusion 5 of the conclusions on identification of customary international law. Further discussion of "hybrid courts", and their output, will follow in later draft conclusions on the present topic.

the "most highly qualified publicists" reference contained in Article 38, paragraph 1 (*d*). The formulation was found to be a historically and geographically charged notion that could be considered elitist. It was also felt that it focused too heavily on the status of the individual as an author as opposed to the scientific quality of the individual's work, which ought to be the primary consideration. The view was, however, expressed that the formulation "the teachings of the most highly qualified publicists of the various nations", which mirrors the exact phrase used in Article 38, paragraph 1 (*d*), of the Statute of the Court, was preferable to the succinct formulation "teachings".

(12) In draft conclusion 2, the reference to teachings is not just to any teachings, but those that may be considered as originating from either individual or groups of scholars that are eminent in the sense of being among the most highly qualified publicists of the various nations. Special attention should be given to the works of those considered prominent in their fields. That said, as indicated above, while the reputation of the author of the work may provide a useful indication of quality, it should also be stressed that it is ultimately the quality of the particular writing that is more important.

(13) The term "teachings," both in its ordinary meaning and in the form of its synonyms, is evidently a broad category. Its meaning encompasses written works as well as lectures. This meaning may be the immediate one that comes to mind, when one hears a reference to teachings, but the term need not be understood so narrowly. In fact, it is best understood more broadly given the possibilities that technological advancements may offer. Indeed, in its prior work, the Commission has determined that both "teachings" or "writings" are "to be understood in a broad sense".[253] The Commission also considered that the category would include "teachings in non-written form, such as lectures and audiovisual materials".[254] Thus, it can be concluded that teachings are comprised of writings or doctrine, as well as recorded lectures and audiovisual materials and, for that matter, materials in any other format for dissemination, including those which might be developed in the future.

(14) As in the case of subparagraph (*a*), which addresses decisions of courts and tribunals and is further elaborated upon in draft conclusion 4, the nature of and the need for representativeness of teachings in terms of the various legal systems and regions of the world will be elaborated upon in future draft conclusions, starting with draft conclusion 5.[255] That draft conclusion makes clear that teachings would include the works of individual scholars, especially – as the drafting history of Article 38, paragraph 1 (*d*), confirms – the coinciding views of such scholars or doctrine. The coinciding views of scholars is not a requirement that there be scholarly consensus, assuming that were even possible. However, where there appears to be a general trend evident from a review of a diverse and representative body of scholarly works, such trend would likely be a reliable indication, on balance, that those views are more likely to be accurate. This is particularly the case where the general views follow objective individual assessments by the authors concerned. They would also include the works of private expert bodies such as the Institute of International Law and the International Law Association. Texts produced by State-empowered bodies, such as the Commission, may be considered separate from the "teachings of publicists". Their texts are produced under the auspices of official institutions and may reflect the involvement of States and or their representatives in the work. This makes them different from the "teachings of publicists". The Commission will elaborate on this matter in future draft conclusions.

[253] Para. (1) of the commentary to conclusion 14 of the conclusions on identification of customary international law, *Yearbook ... 2018*, vol. II (Part Two), para. 66, at p. 110; and the memorandum by the Secretariat on ways and means for making the evidence of customary international law more readily available (A/CN.4/710/Rev.1).

[254] *Ibid.* See also third report on identification of customary international law, by Sir Michael Wood, Special Rapporteur (A/CN.4/682), chap. V, and statement of the Chair of the Drafting Committee on identification of customary international law, p. 15, available from https://legal.un.org/ilc/guide/1_13.shtml#dcommrep.

[255] The commentary to draft conclusion 5 will be considered by the Commission at its next session.

*Subparagraph (*c*) – any other means generally used to assist in determining rules of international law*

(15) Subparagraph (*c*) of draft conclusion 2 provides for the third category of subsidiary means when it states that subsidiary means for the determination of rules of international law include "any other means generally used to assist in determining rules of international law". While various candidates that could be included in the "any other means" category emerge from practice and the literature, the key ones may include the works of expert bodies and resolutions/decisions of international organizations, as explained elsewhere.[256] The view was expressed that this subparagraph is best understood in the light of future work on the question of additional subsidiary means.

(16) Alternatives for subparagraph (*c*) were considered, ranging from formulating an illustrative list of subsidiary means to simply leaving a placeholder as an indication that text would be included in the future. Regarding the illustrative list of additional subsidiary means, express mention was made to the works of expert bodies and the resolutions or decisions of international organizations. After a thorough deliberation, taking into account the various positions, the Commission settled on referring in general terms to "any other means generally used to assist in determining rules of international law". That formulation was thought sufficiently broad to allow for further elaboration of its contents in future draft conclusions and the commentaries thereto. Express mention was made of the need to have separate and additional draft conclusions addressing the works of expert bodies especially those created by States, which found broad support for inclusion. The categories mentioned would also accord with the prior work of the Commission in several topics completed since 2018.

(17) The role of the works of expert bodies and other entities has been examined by the Commission in its recent work on other topics: "Identification of customary international law" (specifically conclusions 13 on decisions of courts and tribunals and 14 on teachings), "Subsequent agreements and subsequent practice in relation to the interpretation of treaties" (conclusion 13 on pronouncements of expert treaty bodies), "General principles of law" (draft conclusions 8 on decisions of courts and tribunals and 9 on teachings)[257] and "Peremptory norms of general international law (*jus cogens*)" (draft conclusion 9 on subsidiary means for the determination of the peremptory character of norms of general international law – addressing both judicial decisions, teachings and the works of expert bodies).[258] However, there is a need to further assess to what extent they can specifically contribute as subsidiary means for the determination of rules of international law in the context of the present draft conclusions.

(18) The Commission has left the third category open in order not to foreclose the possibility of other subsidiary means, which may not be in widespread use now or that are in use but left out of the work on the present topic, from being covered by the present draft conclusions as the work develops. Still, it did consider it prudent to add the qualifier "generally", to indicate that a degree of qualification or usage in practice was needed. The goal is to make clear that not just any subsidiary means would qualify. It is those that are generally used, including by courts and tribunals. Specifically, the use of the term "generally" conveys that a particular material used on a single occasion as a subsidiary means by one specific court or tribunal would not automatically become a subsidiary means more generally.

(19) Finally, subparagraph (*c*) alluded to the role of subsidiary means, namely "to assist" in determining the rules of international law. This may raise the question of the function of the traditional and additional subsidiary means, which will be the subject of a future draft conclusion, much as was the case in the topic "General principles of law".[259] At this stage, the formulation "to assist" was introduced to foreshadow some of the elements that could be

---

[256] See, in this regard, the detailed discussion of additional subsidiary means in A/CN.4/760, chap. IX.

[257] Contained in chap. IV of the present report.

[258] *Official Records of the General Assembly, Seventy-seventh Session, Supplement No. 10* (A/77/10), para. 43.

[259] Draft conclusion 9, contained in chap. IV of the present report.

helpful in both identifying possible candidates for other subsidiary means and emphasizing their auxiliary function.

Conclusion 3
General criteria for the assessment of subsidiary means for the determination of rules of international law

When assessing the weight of subsidiary means for the determination of rules of international law, regard should be had to, *inter alia*:

(*a*) their degree of representativeness;

(*b*) the quality of the reasoning;

(*c*) the expertise of those involved;

(*d*) the level of agreement among those involved;

(*e*) the reception by States and other entities;

(*f*) where applicable, the mandate conferred on the body.

Commentary

(1) Draft conclusion 3, which concerns the general criteria for assessing subsidiary means for the determination of rules of international law, seeks to provide guidance to assess the weight to be given to those means.

Chapeau *of draft conclusion 3*

(2) The *chapeau* of draft conclusion 3 provides that reference should be made to various factors when assessing the weight of subsidiary means as part of the determination of rules of international law. Different subsidiary means will have varying levels of "weight". These may also vary between fields of international law, in the sense that one subsidiary means may have different weight in different contexts. For example, decisions by one international court or tribunal usually have great significance to that court or tribunal itself, but they may be considered less important by another, which may instead give priority to its own decisions.

(3) The six criteria are to be used as general factors for determining the relative weight to be given to materials that are already considered subsidiary means under one of the categories identified in draft conclusion 2. They are not intended for determining whether a particular material is to be considered a subsidiary means within the meaning of the draft conclusions as a whole. This point is made explicit in the *chapeau*. The factors listed in the draft conclusion, which have been explained in previous works of the Commission, are therefore possible elements contributing to assessing the weight to be given to subsidiary means, and the use of those elements would be dependent on the circumstances under which they are being used. The provision sets out the criteria in subparagraphs to enhance readability and help clarify that not all factors would be applicable to all the categories of subsidiary means. Instead, which factors would be relevant, and to what extent, would depend on the specific subsidiary means in question and the prevailing circumstances. The view was nonetheless expressed that there may be insufficient practice supporting these criteria at this stage of the topic or that listing the factors risks being seen as a theoretical exercise.

(4) The applicability of the rule is confirmed by the phrase stating that "regard should be had to, *inter alia*" in the *chapeau* of draft conclusion 3. Two elements are worth stressing. First, the use of the term "should" indicates that reference to the criteria is not mandatory, although in many cases, it would plainly be desirable. The idea is to signal that what follows is not meant to be a prescriptive statement or to establish an obligation to use a particular subsidiary means. Second, the use of the term "*inter alia*", was also intended to convey that the list of criteria encompassed those that would likely be the most frequently encountered and could serve as a useful guide, but were illustrative instead of exhaustive.

Subparagraph (a) – their degree of representativeness

(5) Subparagraph (*a*) refers to the degree of representativeness of the materials being used as subsidiary means. This criterion entails, *inter alia*, that in assessing subsidiary means, recourse should be had to the decisions of courts and tribunals, teachings and any other subsidiary means from various regions or legal systems. This criterion should be applied flexibly if the rules of international law under consideration are bilateral or regional in nature. In such cases, the focus would instead be on the content and degree of specialization of the subsidiary means used to aid in the determination of the rules in question. This is an example of a flexible application of the criteria identified in draft conclusion 3.

Subparagraph (b) – the quality of the reasoning

(6) Subparagraph (*b*) refers to the quality of the reasoning. The Commission considered that such criterion should prevail over the renown of the author in the case of teachings. At the same time, the criterion is subjective and not necessarily applicable to all subsidiary means. For example, on the one hand, the quality of the reasoning of a judicial decision or the pronouncement of an expert body may usefully be assessed. On the other hand, it might be less relevant when examining certain other materials.

Subparagraph (c) – the expertise of those involved

(7) Subparagraph (*c*) refers to the level of expertise of those involved. The Commission was of the view that, similarly to subparagraph (*b*), this criterion referred to the background and the qualifications of those involved in relation to the topic, which should demonstrate expertise on the subject matter in a number of ways, rather than focusing exclusively on the renown or academic titles of the particular author or actors. The expertise of the individuals involved in drafting a text is also mentioned by the Commission in the conclusions on identification of customary international law as a factor influencing the "value" of "the output of international bodies engaged in the codification and development of international law".[260] This too is suggested by the Commission in its previous work and is considered by individual judges of the International Court of Justice when applying the teachings of publicists.

Subparagraph (d) – the level of agreement among those involved

(8) Subparagraph (*d*) lists the level of agreement of those involved. This criterion is meant to refer to the internal consensus when a decision was made or among the authors of a text. Once again, such criterion would need to be applied flexibly. Accordingly, evaluating the level of agreement could be most appropriate when considering teachings, where the level of convergence among scholars in relation to a specific point of law would be of significance.

(9) The level of agreement may reflect in the coinciding views of individual scholars, which is not a requirement that there be scholarly consensus, assuming that were even possible. However, where there appears to be a general trend evident from a review of a diverse and representative body of scholarly works, such trend would likely be a reliable indication, on balance, that those views are more likely to be correct. This is particularly the case where the general views follow objective individual assessments by the authors concerned.

(10) The Commission has previously noted "support ... within the body" as a factor influencing the "value" of "[t]he output of international bodies engaged in the codification and development of international law" in its conclusions on identification of customary international law.[261] A high level of agreement may be particularly significant if the concurring persons represent different geographical regions or legal systems.

[260] Para. (5) of the commentary to conclusion 14 of the conclusions on identification of customary international law, *Yearbook ... 2018*, vol. II (Part Two), para. 66, at p. 110.

[261] *Ibid.*

Subparagraph (e) – the reception by States and other entities

(11) An external component is addressed in subparagraph (*e*): the reception by States and other entities. It should be noted that, even when there is a measure of consensus among those who participated in producing a particular work or decision, the outcome can be subject to external criticism. The reactions and views of others in the field are also indications of how well received, or not, a particular subsidiary means might be. In other words, the external component is the reaction after the decision was made: "[t]he reception of the output by States and others", i.e. the level of agreement *outside* the relevant body (this was also mentioned by the Commission in the conclusions on identification of customary international law).[262] The Commission has suggested that its own output "merits special consideration" in part due to its "close relationship with the General Assembly and States", but that its value depends "above all upon States' reception of its output".[263]

Subparagraph (f) – where applicable, mandate conferred on the body

(12) Finally, subparagraph (*f*) refers to the significance of the mandate conferred on the body that took the decision being assessed. The opening qualifier "where applicable" was included to make it clear that what is being referred to are those situations where the subsidiary means being assessed were produced by a body operating under an official or intergovernmental mandate, such as human rights treaty bodies, or certain expert bodies, like the International Law Commission. In its previous work on the identification and legal consequences of peremptory norms of general international law (*jus cogens*), the Commission described such entities as being "established by States or international organizations" and further clarified that they would encompass both the organs created by such entities and their subsidiary organs.[264]

(13) This criterion is useful in assessing whether particular regard should be had to decisions of a particular court and, if so, whether to give it greater weight: for example, because it is a specialist tribunal with particular competence, such as the International Tribunal for the Law of the Sea in relation to the law of the sea; the International Criminal Court in relation to matters of international criminal law; or the Dispute Settlement Body of the World Trade Organization in relation to matters of international trade law. In any event, the criterion in question is not necessarily meant to apply to the works of purely private expert bodies, such as the Institute of International Law or the International Law Association. This is not, however, to imply that the "works of expert bodies without an intergovernmental mandate are irrelevant".[265] It is only to indicate that those works are necessarily going to be treated differently from those created by States or international organizations.

(14) "Mandate" is mentioned by the Commission in its previous work as a factor influencing the "value" of "[t]he output of international bodies engaged in the codification and development of international law".[266] The works of universal and regional codification bodies would here be relevant to the extent that such bodies were created by and interact with States. In the same previous work, the Commission suggested that its own output "merits special consideration" in part owing to its "unique mandate".[267] Subsidiary means are often produced by organizations that have been given a mandate by States. Particular regard may be given to subsidiary means that fall squarely within such a mandate than those that fall outside it. Some institutions have a general mandate, such as the Commission, which is empowered to develop and codify "international law" whether public or private.[268] The

[262] Para. (5) of the commentary to conclusion 14 of the conclusions on identification of customary international law, *Yearbook ... 2018*, vol. II (Part Two), para. 66, at p. 110.

[263] Para. (2) of the commentary to Part Five, *ibid.*, at pp. 104–105.

[264] See draft conclusion 9, para. 2, and para. (8) of the commentary thereto of the draft conclusions on identification and legal consequences of peremptory norms of general international law (*jus cogens*), *Official Records of the General Assembly, Seventy-seventh Session, Supplement No. 10* (A/77/10), para. 44, at p. 46.

[265] Para. (8), *ibid.*

[266] Para. (5) of the commentary to conclusion 14 of the conclusions on identification of customary international law, *Yearbook ... 2018*, vol. II (Part Two), para. 66, at p. 110.

[267] Para. (2) of the commentary to Part Five, *ibid.*, pp. 104–105.

[268] Statute of the International Law Commission, 1947, art. 1, para. 1.

United Nations Commission on International Trade Law (UNCITRAL) also has a special mandate in relation to matters of private international law. Other institutions may have a more specialized mandate. That the International Court of Justice in *Diallo* believed "that it should ascribe great weight to the interpretation adopted by" the Human Rights Committee,[269] which was within the Committee's mandate, supports this view. In the *Committee on the Elimination of Racial Discrimination* case, the Court, in its reasoning, "carefully considered the position taken by the … Committee" but did not follow it.[270] Such bodies will need to be considered separately. Their work, and other subsidiary means found in practice, will be subject to further analysis and specific draft conclusions in the future work in the present topic.

[269] The Court explained that "[a]lthough the Court is in no way obliged, in the exercise of its judicial functions, to model its own interpretation of the Covenant on that of the Committee, it believes that it should ascribe great weight to the interpretation adopted by this independent body that was established specifically to supervise the application of that treaty. The point here is to achieve the necessary clarity and the essential consistency of international law, as well as legal security, to which both the individuals with guaranteed rights and the States obliged to comply with treaty obligations are entitled." In the same case, the Court referred to the interpretations of certain regional human rights provisions in various treaties by the African Commission on Human and Peoples' Rights, the European Court of Human Rights and the Inter-American Court of Human Rights. In relation to issues of compensation for human rights violations, it also took into careful account the practice of various international courts, tribunals and commissions. See *Ahmadou Sadio Diallo (Republic of Guinea v. Democratic Republic of the Congo), Compensation, Judgment, I.C.J. Reports 2012*, p. 324, at pp. 331, 334, 339 and 342, paras. 13, 24, 40 and 49.

[270] *Application of the International Convention on the Elimination of All Forms of Racial Discrimination (Qatar v. United Arab Emirates), Preliminary Objections, Judgment, I.C.J. Reports 2021*, p. 71, at p. 104, para. 101; see also para. 100.

Chapter VIII
Sea-level rise in relation to international law

A. Introduction

128. At its seventy-first session (2019), the International Law Commission decided to include the topic "Sea-level rise in relation to international law" in its programme of work. The Commission also decided to establish an open-ended Study Group on the topic, to be co-chaired, on a rotating basis, by Mr. Bogdan Aurescu, Mr. Yacouba Cissé, Ms. Patrícia Galvão Teles, Ms. Nilüfer Oral and Mr. Juan José Ruda Santolaria. The Study Group discussed its composition, its proposed calendar and programme of work, and its methods of work. At its 3480th meeting, on 15 July 2019, the Commission took note of the joint oral report of the Co-Chairs of the Study Group.[271]

129. At its seventy-second session (2021), the Commission reconstituted the Study Group, and considered the first issues paper on the topic, related to the law of the sea,[272] which had been issued together with a preliminary bibliography.[273] At its 3550th meeting, on 27th July 2021, the Commission took note of the joint oral report of the Co-Chairs of the Study Group.[274]

130. At its seventy-third session (2022), the Commission reconstituted the Study Group, and considered the second issues paper on the topic, related to statehood and the protection of persons affected by sea-level rise,[275] which had been issued together with a preliminary bibliography.[276] At its 3612th meeting, on 5 August 2022, the Commission considered and adopted the report of the Study Group.[277]

B. Consideration of the topic at the present session

131. At the present session, the Commission reconstituted the Study Group on sea-level rise in relation to international law, chaired by the two Co-Chairs on issues related to the law of the sea, namely Mr. Aurescu and Ms. Oral.

132. In accordance with the agreed programme of work and methods of work, the Study Group had before it the additional paper (A/CN.4/761) to the first issues paper on thc topic, prepared by Mr. Aurescu and Ms. Oral, and issued on 20 April 2023. A selected bibliography, prepared in consultation with members of the Study Group, was issued on 9 June 2023 as an addendum to the additional paper (A/CN.4/761/Add.1).

133. The Study Group, which at the current session comprised 32 members, held 12 meetings, from 26 April to 4 May and from 3 to 5 July 2023.

134. At its 3655th meeting, on 3 August 2023, the Commission considered and adopted the report of the Study Group on its work at the present session, as reproduced below.

---

[271] *Official Records of the General Assembly, Seventy-fourth Session, Supplement No. 10* (A/74/10), paras. 265–273.

[272] A/CN.4/740 and Corr.1.

[273] A/CN.4/740/Add.1.

[274] *Official Records of the General Assembly, Seventy-sixth Session, Supplement No. 10* (A/76/10), paras. 247–296.

[275] A/CN.4/752.

[276] A/CN.4/752/Add.1.

[277] *Official Records of the General Assembly, Seventy-seventh Session, Supplement No. 10* (A/77/10), paras. 153–237.

1. Introduction of the additional paper (A/CN.4/761 and Add.1) to the first issues paper by the Co-Chairs

(a) General introduction of the topic

135. At the first meeting of the Study Group, held on 26 April 2023, four of the Co-Chairs (Mr. Aurescu and Ms. Oral, and Ms. Galvão Teles and Mr. Ruda Santolaria) noted that the topic had generated great and increased interest among members of the Commission and Member States, including, but not exclusively, those particularly affected by sea-level rise. The Co-Chairs briefly recalled the manner in which the topic had been placed on the programme of work of the Commission, underlining the progress that had been achieved so far on all three subtopics under consideration through robust discussions within the framework of the Study Group and the Commission and further enriched by Member States' comments conveyed either in the Sixth Committee or in response to questions raised by the Commission. Within a few years, the topic had become cross-regional and global in nature, and of immediate relevance to Member States, which required global solutions of varying kinds. Some regions, including those most affected by the phenomenon, had been particularly active in shedding light on the urgency of addressing the multiple challenges ahead and in identifying potential legal solutions. In that regard, three of the Co-Chairs (Ms. Galvão Teles, Ms. Oral and Mr. Ruda Santolaria) indicated that they had participated in a regional conference on preserving statehood and protecting persons in the context of sea-level rise, organized by the Pacific Islands Forum and held in Nadi, Fiji, from 27 to 30 March 2023, and they stressed the importance of the work of such regional organizations. In addition to the Commission, the Security Council and various United Nations bodies had addressed the topic of sea-level rise, and the topic had been included in requests for advisory opinions addressed first to the International Tribunal for the Law of the Sea[278] and then to the International Court of Justice.[279]

(b) Procedure followed by the Study Group

136. Also at the first meeting of the Study Group, Mr. Aurescu and Ms. Oral, in their capacity as Co-Chairs addressing issues related to the law of the sea, indicated that the purpose of the meetings scheduled in the first part of the session was to allow for an exchange of views on the additional paper. The content of the additional paper had been guided by the outcome of the meetings of the Study Group held during the seventy-second (2021) session of the Commission,[280] and by the specific issues flagged by Member States in comments conveyed either in the Sixth Committee or in response to questions raised by the Commission. As such, the additional paper addressed a number of principles and issues on which the Study Group had specifically requested further study in 2021. In that regard, the Co-Chairs explained that, owing to word-count limitations, they had addressed a selection of these principles and issues only, giving priority to those on which Member States' had commented. The additional paper was structured in such a way as to including preliminary observations on each principle or issue addressed, with the expectation that the members of the Study Group would then reach conclusions and define practical solutions. The Co-Chairs invited members to engage in a structured and interactive debate, drawing upon the contents of the additional paper, and to provide input on a draft bibliography on the subtopic, to be issued as an addendum to the additional paper. As had been the case for the topic during the two preceding sessions of the Commission, the outcome of the first part of the session would be an interim report of the Study Group, to be considered and complemented during the second part of the session so as to reflect a further interactive discussion on the future programme of work. The report would then be agreed upon in the Study Group and

[278] International Tribunal for the Law of the Sea, Request for Advisory Opinion submitted by the Commission of Small Island States on Climate Change and International Law, Order of 16 December 2022, *ITLOS Reports 2022–2023*, to be published.

[279] International Court of Justice, Request for an advisory opinion of the International Court of Justice on the obligations of States in respect of climate change, General Assembly resolution 77/276 of 29 March 2023.

[280] *Official Records of the General Assembly, Seventy-sixth Session, Supplement No. 10* (A/76/10), paras. 247–296.

subsequently presented by the Co-Chairs to the Commission, with a view to being included in the annual report of the Commission. That procedure, agreed upon by the Study Group, was based on the 2019 report of the Commission.[281]

137. The Co-Chairs also recalled that, as outlined in chapter XIII of the additional paper, which addressed the future programme of work of the Study Group, in the present quinquennium, the Study Group would revert to each of the subtopics – the law of the sea, statehood and the protection of persons affected by sea-level rise – and would then seek to prepare a substantive report on the topic as a whole by consolidating the results of the work undertaken since 2019, expected to be issued in 2025.

2. Summary of the exchange of views

138. Members of the Study Group underscored the importance of the topic for the international community, noting that sea-level rise would have a large impact on people in a broad range of areas and that it was of direct relevance to the question of peace and security. In that regard, they recalled that the Security Council had held a meeting on 14 February 2023 on the subject of "Sea-level rise: implications for international peace and security", under the agenda item "Threats to international peace and security", at which Mr. Aurescu, in his capacity as Co-Chair, had delivered a briefing on the progress of the Commission's work.[282] Furthermore, the Inter-American Juridical Committee had recently appointed a rapporteur on the topic of legal implications of sea-level rise in the inter-American regional context, Mr. Julio José Rojas Báez. Among other initiatives, a special meeting of the Committee on Juridical and Political Affairs of the Organization of American States was held on 4 May 2023 on the consequences of sea-level rise and its legal implications. In that regard, the Study Group should exercise caution when interpreting the silence of some affected States, which does not necessarily reflect a position on the interpretation of the United Nations Convention on the Law of the Sea.[283] Sea-level rise had led to the emergence of new concepts, such as "climate displacement", "climate refugees" and "climate statelessness", that were undefined in international law, and the term "specially affected State" ought to be used with caution, given its multiple implications since it did not reflect the fact that a large number of States were affected, in particular developing countries.

139. Members welcomed the work of the Co-Chairs and the methodological, detailed and comprehensive nature of the additional paper, underlining that it was well researched and constituted a sound basis for the Commission to meaningfully discharge its mandate.

(a) Issue of "legal stability" in relation to sea-level rise, with a focus on baselines and maritime zones

(i) Introduction by the Co-Chair

140. At its first and second meetings, held on 26 and 27 April 2023, the Study Group had an exchange on chapter II of the additional paper, on the issue of "legal stability" in relation to sea-level rise, with a focus on baselines and maritime zones. The Co-Chair (Mr. Aurescu) recalled that the preliminary observations in paragraphs 82 to 95 of the additional paper were based on numerous views expressed over the period from 2021 to 2022 on the meaning of the terms "legal stability", "certainty" and "predictability", including in the Sixth Committee, where some Member States had requested further exploration of those terms. The Co-Chair noted that Member States had adopted a pragmatic approach, referring to legal stability as inherently linked to the preservation of maritime zones, and that no States, even those with national legislation providing for ambulatory baselines, had contested that approach or the preliminary observations in paragraph 104 of the first issues paper, which supported the solution of fixed baselines.

141. The Co-Chair observed that Member States had underlined the need to interpret the United Nations Convention on the Law of the Sea in such a way as to effectively address

[281] *Ibid., Seventy-fourth Session, Supplement No. 10* (A/74/10), paras. 270–271.

[282] See S/PV.9260 and S/PV.9260 (Resumption 1).

[283] United Nations Convention on the Law of the Sea (Montego Bay, 10 December 1982), United Nations, *Treaty Series*, vol. 1833, No. 31363, p. 3.

sea-level rise in order to provide practical guidance to affected States. Although, in the past, before the Commission had embarked on the topic of sea-level rise, the doctrine had interpreted the Convention to the effect that the baselines and outer limits of the territorial sea, contiguous zone and exclusive economic zone were ambulatory, Member States had, in ever-increasing numbers, expressed the contrary view, pointing to an interpretation of the Convention in the sense that it did not forbid or exclude the option of fixing baselines. In doing so, they had stressed the importance of interpreting the Convention with a view to preserving maritime zones, and had noted that the Convention did not prohibit the freezing of baselines.

142. The Co-Chair noted that few Member States had made references to customary international law, and that those States had considered that there was no obvious evidence of *opinio juris* concerning the existence of a custom regarding the fixing of baselines.

(ii) Concept of legal stability

143. Members of the Study Group noted that the concept of legal stability was encapsulated in the United Nations Convention on the Law of the Sea. In addition, it contributed to the maintenance of international peace and security. Although a general view was expressed emphasizing the importance of that legal concept, it was also pointed out that there was a need to exercise caution when approaching it, as it could not be considered in a vacuum and was difficult to separate from other concepts, such as the principle of the immutability of boundaries. It was also noted that the loss of land territory, which could result from failure to respect the concept of legal stability, would lead to catastrophic consequences for the most vulnerable States.

144. It was further stated that the concept of legal stability was not necessarily linked only to the safety of navigation: the concepts of legal stability and respect for existing boundaries reflected customary international law, and as such could also be applied to maritime boundaries. A view was expressed that the freezing of baselines, and the consequent lack of an obligation to report on updated baselines, could pose hazards to the safety of navigation and could potentially be in contravention of the relevant instruments concerning the safety of navigation.

(iii) Ways in which the concept of legal stability is reflected in the context of sea-level rise

a. Interpretation of the United Nations Convention on the Law of Sea

145. Members of the Study Group broadly supported the preliminary observations of the Co-Chairs in favour of fixed baselines, considering, *inter alia*, that the United Nations Convention on the Law of the Sea did not prohibit the option of fixed baselines, and that it was critical that the final outcome of the Commission's work on the topic should guarantee the sovereign rights that States were claiming over their maritime spaces. Caveats and doubts relating to the interpretation of the Convention were expressed, including in relation to the manner in which to achieve that objective.

146. A view was expressed that the United Nations Convention on the Law of the Sea did not equate the declaration and publication of the baselines with the acquisition of sovereignty or sovereign rights over the spaces affected by those baselines; otherwise, it could be concluded that the Convention allowed a State to decide unilaterally on its maritime spaces.

147. Differing views were expressed as to the applicability to sea-level rise of the concept of the legal stability of baselines under article 7, paragraph 2, of the United Nations Convention on the Law of the Sea and of the outer limits of the continental shelf under article 76, which had been raised in the first issues paper and by some States.

148. Another suggested option to ensure legal stability was to amend the United Nations Convention on the Law of the Sea, which was deemed difficult. A meeting of States parties to the Convention might be considered with a view to interpreting that instrument, including a close examination of the text, context, and object and purpose of its relevant provisions.

b. Emergence of rules of customary international law

149. Some members considered that a further option with a view to ensuring legal stability would be the emergence of a rule of customary international law. Reference was made to the prima facie indication of the formation of a new rule of customary international law providing for fixed baselines. However, it was opined that it was too early to draw any related conclusions as to the existence of widespread practice and *opinio juris* in favour of fixed baselines and the preservation of maritime zones, whether on the regional or the international plane. Emphasis was nonetheless placed on the new trend of practices and views of States based on a good-faith interpretation of the United Nations Convention on the Law of the Sea. It was further stressed that the Commission should be clear in stating that the existence of practice could justify not only a rule of customary international law, but a certain interpretation of the Convention. A view was expressed that determining whether a rule of customary international law existed was beyond the mandate of the Commission.

150. On the issue of fixed baselines, and recalling the 2021 declarations by the Pacific Islands Forum and the Alliance of Small Island States,[284] members stressed that there was no explicit provision in the United Nations Convention on the Law of the Sea requiring State parties to update their baselines and outer limits of maritime zones in response to changes in coastlines as a result of sea-level rise. In that regard, it was observed that there was a difference between legally freezing the territorial sea baselines and not updating published baselines, since the latter was simply an administrative matter, while the former could possibly involve the creation of a new rule of law and should be done with great caution. It was nonetheless noted that if there was an obligation to update baselines, it should have been expressly mentioned in the Convention. At the same time, it was also stated that the Commission should not take a one-sided position, as both the permanent and ambulatory approaches were legal and viable, and should instead consider favouring practical solutions.

c. Subsequent agreements and subsequent practice

151. It was suggested that subsequent agreements, as provided for in article 31 of the Vienna Convention on the Law of Treaties,[285] might be useful as an authentic means of interpretation of the United Nations Convention on the Law of the Sea. Such interpretation could take the form of a resolution of a meeting of States parties to the Convention, as referred to in paragraph 148 above. It was underlined that subsequent practice as a means of interpretation of the United Nations Convention on the Law of the Sea might also be a useful way forward in lieu of the emergence of a rule of customary international law. Some members expressed the view that consideration would then also need to be given to how subsequent practice satisfied the relevant legal benchmarks, as developed by the Commission.[286]

152. It was further emphasized that the current practice was insufficient to justify the existence of either a regional or a general rule of customary international law. It could nonetheless be used to support a particular interpretation of the United Nations Convention on the Law of the Sea.

(iv) Sui generis *regimes*

153. On the topic of *sui generis* regimes, questions were raised as to how the international community could address the problems encountered by States who faced a loss of territory

[284] Pacific Islands Forum Leaders' Declaration on Preserving Maritime Zones in the Face of Climate Change-related Sea-level Rise, 6 August 2021 (available at https://www.forumsec.org/2021/08/11/declaration-on-preserving-maritime-zones-in-the-face-of-climate-change-related-sea-level-rise/); and Alliance of Small Island States Leaders' Declaration, 22 September 2021 (available at https://www.aosis.org/launch-of-the-alliance-of-small-island-states-leaders-declaration/).

[285] Vienna Convention on the Law of Treaties (Vienna, 23 May 1969), United Nations, *Treaty Series*, vol. 1155, No. 18232, p. 331.

[286] See conclusions on subsequent agreements and subsequent practice in relation to the interpretation of treaties, *Official Records of the General Assembly, Seventy-third Session, Supplement No. 10* (A/73/10), para. 51.

owing to sea-level rise. It was suggested that the Study Group should consider *sui generis* status for territories submerged owing to sea-level rise, in particular because sea-level rise was not a natural phenomenon, but was human-caused. While support was expressed for adopting a flexible approach to baselines – ambulatory baselines for certain scenarios and fixed baselines for others – a call was made for reflection and deliberation on the merits of *sui generis* regimes.

(v) Concluding remarks by the Co-Chairs

154. In his concluding remarks, the Co-Chair (Mr. Aurescu) thanked the members of the Study Group for their valuable contribution and welcomed their focus on the question of the interpretation of the United Nations Convention on the Law of the Sea, which was an important subject for Member States, as reflected in the additional paper.

155. As concerns had been expressed that the additional paper did not provide a clear direction for the Study Group's future work, he recalled that it was the Co-Chairs' duty to present their analysis, including preliminary observations, to enable the Study Group to collectively reflect on the issues addressed and reach conclusions.

156. The Co-Chair stressed the importance of further exploring the issue of submerged territories, which had not been raised in 2021. Given that the issue was related to the law of the sea and to statehood, he suggested that it be addressed in the Study Group's consolidated final report, expected to be issued in 2025.

157. The Co-Chair recalled that interest had been expressed in determining the moment of reference from which it could be considered that baselines were fixed, which could be done in consultation with scientists on sea-level rise.

158. With regard to the suggestion to amend the United Nations Convention on the Law of the Sea, he recalled that the Commission had agreed, in the syllabus prepared in 2018,[287] to limit the Study Group's mandate so that it would not propose any amendments to the Convention, as also reflected in the positions expressed by Member States in the light of the delicate balance between the rights and obligations under the Convention. Nonetheless, consideration could be given to interpreting the Convention.

159. Noting the suggestion that the Study Group could prepare practical guidance for States, the Co-Chair expressed the view that consideration ought to be given to providing practical legal solutions in line with the requests conveyed by Member States, so as to ensure legal stability as an outcome of the various measures that they could take.

160. The Co-Chair welcomed the view that the term "specially affected State" should be used with caution, given that two thirds of Member States were currently or could in the future be affected in some way by sea-level rise.

161. The Co-Chair noted that it was difficult to evaluate State practice within the context of sea-level rise, as it appeared to be the decision of certain States or groups of States not to update coordinates or charts deposited with the Secretary-General. As such, practice in those cases was in fact inaction, absent the visibility usually relied upon to determine the content of such practice.

162. The Co-Chair (Ms. Oral) noted that the mandate of the Study Group was a mapping exercise of the legal questions raised by sea-level rise and its interrelated issues, and that the additional paper had been based on the requests made by members of the Study Group further to the debate in 2021, except for the issue of nautical charts.

(b) Immutability and intangibility of boundaries

(i) Introduction by the Co-Chair

163. At the third meeting of the Study Group, held on 1 May 2023, the Co-Chair (Ms. Oral) recalled that chapter III of the additional paper related to the existing definitions and functions of boundaries, and contained an examination of relevant international case law and

[287] *Ibid.*, annex B.

preliminary observations in paragraph 111. The chapter further addressed the principle of *uti possidetis juris* and its applicability to existing maritime boundaries. The Co-Chair observed that the intention had not been to conclude that *uti possidetis juris* should apply to maritime delimitations within the context of sea-level rise, but rather to emphasize the importance accorded to ensuring the continuity of pre-existing boundaries in the interests of legal stability and the prevention of conflict.

(ii) *General comments*

164. Several members generally agreed with the Co-Chairs' preliminary observations. It was also emphasized that the question of immutability and intangibility of boundaries should be addressed from the perspective of the principle of legal stability.

165. Some members noted that the intangibility of boundaries was a fundamental principle of international law, and called upon the Study Group to place more emphasis on it. At the same time, a view was expressed that the legal stability of boundaries had limited application in the field of the law of the sea. According to another view, application of the principle of the immutability of boundaries to maritime delimitations should have some degree of flexibility, as maritime entitlements were always based on geographic features and there was no settled case law with regard to the effect of physical land changes on maritime boundaries.

(iii) *Application of the principle of* uti possidetis juris

166. Several members called for caution in applying the principle of *uti possidetis juris*, which in their view was predominantly or exclusively applied in the context of succession of States. It was also recalled that the principle had been crystallized in the context of decolonization. Several members disagreed with the view expressed in the additional paper that *uti possidetis juris* was considered a general principle of law. Some members emphasized that the principle was applicable to pre-existing titles only. A view was expressed that introducing *uti possidetis juris* to maritime delimitations could affect the integrity of the United Nations Convention on the Law of the Sea, which did not include that principle.

167. It was noted that the principle of *uti possidetis juris* was not helpful or relevant within the context of the topic. It was argued that *uti possidetis juris* implied a different dynamic, where factual realities were not affected by the change in the broader legal framework, while the present topic sought to ensure consistency of the legal framework despite radical factual changes. Furthermore, some members emphasized that the application of *uti possidetis juris* required a critical date. According to one view, such a date was difficult to determine for a gradual process such as sea-level rise. Several members observed that the principle was not applicable to maritime boundaries. Nonetheless, for certain members application of *uti possidetis juris* to maritime delimitations should not be excluded.

168. It was observed that the principle of *uti possidetis juris*, which was linked to the issues of legal stability and security, was intended to prevent a legal vacuum and avoid conflicts between States. In that regard, some members proposed that *uti possidetis juris*, if not directly applicable, could be used as a source of inspiration, as the Study Group had similar objectives. It was emphasized that the principle supported the continuity of pre-existing boundaries.

169. The Co-Chairs were requested to clarify the meaning of paragraph 111 (*b*) of the additional paper, according to which the principle of the intangibility of boundaries, as developed under the principle of *uti possidetis juris*, was considered a general principle of law beyond application to the traditional decolonization process and was a rule of customary international law. It was argued that those observations were not supported by international case law. The Co-Chair (Ms. Oral) responded that the point was not the applicability of the principle of *uti possidetis juris* to maritime boundaries in the context of sea-level rise, but the example of the preservation of existing boundaries under international law for the purposes of legal stability and the prevention of conflict.

(iv) *Self-determination*

170. The importance of the principle of self-determination was recalled in the present context. It was noted that self-determination was closely linked to sovereignty over natural

resources and the territorial integrity of States. With regard to the latter, it was observed that the principle of self-determination implied that States should not lose their right to territorial integrity as a result of sea-level rise. The Co-Chairs (Ms. Galvão Teles and Mr. Ruda Santolaria) observed that the principle of self-determination was relevant to all three subtopics under consideration and that it would be addressed by the Study Group during the next session of the Commission, to be held in 2024.

(c) Fundamental change of circumstances (*rebus sic stantibus*)

171. At the third meeting of the Study Group, held on 1 May 2023, the Co-Chair (Ms. Oral) introduced chapter IV of the additional paper, on fundamental change of circumstances (*rebus sic stantibus*). She recalled that the question as to whether sea-level rise would constitute an unforeseen change of circumstances within the meaning of article 62, paragraph 2, of the Vienna Convention on the Law of Treaties had been addressed in the first issues paper,[288] and in the presentation on the practice of African States given by the Co-Chair (Mr. Cissé) during the Commission's seventy-second session (2021).[289] Both had reflected the view that the cited provision could not be applied in the context of sea-level rise. In the course of their discussion in 2021, members of the Study Group had nonetheless concluded that additional study should be undertaken on the issue. Furthermore, a number of delegations in the Sixth Committee had shared the view expressed by the Co-Chairs in the first issues paper, underlining the need for legal stability, and no delegations had conveyed that they were in favour of the application of article 62, paragraph 2, of the Vienna Convention on the Law of Treaties in the context of sea-level rise, although one delegation had indicated that it was still considering the matter. The Co-Chair also recalled that article 62, paragraph 1, of that Convention established a high threshold for invoking fundamental change of circumstances, and that it was thus noted in the preliminary observations, in paragraph 125 (*d*) of the additional paper, that the objective of preserving the stability of boundaries and peaceful relations under article 62 would equally apply to maritime boundaries, as underlined by the International Court of Justice and arbitral tribunals in three cases addressing the issue.[290]

172. Members of the Study Group generally expressed support for the Co-Chairs' preliminary observations, considering that the principle of fundamental change of circumstances was not applicable to maritime boundaries because the latter involved the same element of legal stability and permanence as land boundaries and were thus subject to the exclusion foreseen in article 62, paragraph 2 (*a*), of the Vienna Convention on the Law of Treaties. It was noted that the principles of legal stability and certainty of treaties would accordingly support an argument against the use of the principle *rebus sic stantibus* to upset the maritime boundary treaties resulting from the rise in sea levels. It was further noted that the principle was difficult to invoke successfully in practice.

173. The following additional points were raised by individual members:

(a) It would be useful to clarify what should be considered as a cut-off date on which baselines and outer limits of maritime zones had been fixed, as it was unrealistic to decide on uniform dates for all States. In paragraph 104 (*e*) and (*f*) of the first issues paper, reference was made to the moment of deposit of coordinates or charts with the Secretary-General, which would, however, disadvantage those States that had not made such deposits;

(b) There was a difference in international case law between the delimitation and the delineation of maritime zones. Delimitation applied where States with adjacent or

---

288 A/CN.4/740 and Corr.1, paras. 113–141. See also *Official Records of the General Assembly, Seventy-sixth Session, Supplement No. 10* (A/76/10), para. 281.

289 *Official Records of the General Assembly, Seventy-sixth Session, Supplement No. 10* (A/76/10), para. 261 (*b*).

290 *Aegean Sea Continental Shelf, Judgment, I.C.J. Reports 1978*, p. 3, at pp. 35–36, para. 85; *Bay of Bengal Maritime Boundary Arbitration (Bangladesh v. India)*, Case No. 2010-16, Permanent Court of Arbitration, Award, 7 July 2014, p. 63, paras. 216–217 (available from www.pca-cpa.org/en/cases/18); and *Maritime Delimitation in the Indian Ocean (Somalia v. Kenya), Judgment, I.C.J. Reports 2021*, p. 206, at p. 263, para. 158.

opposite coasts had overlapping maritime claims, and, unlike delineation, was covered by an agreement. As such, delimitation agreements were governed by the law of treaties;

(c) There was a need to study a number – albeit limited – of specific cases that might constitute a fundamental change of circumstances, such as when two States merge into a single State or when a decision is taken to reduce the maritime space of a State applying ambulatory baselines;

(d) Similarly, it might be helpful to consider whether and to what extent article 62 of the Vienna Convention on the Law of Treaties might apply in the case of treaties establishing provisional boundaries, as opposed to permanent boundaries, or treaties simultaneously establishing maritime boundaries and regimes for the shared exploitation of resources;

(e) Further study could be conducted on the requirements to be fulfilled in order to invoke fundamental change of circumstances as grounds for terminating or withdrawing from a treaty where such a possibility had not been foreseen, and on the extent to which the impossibility of performance might be invoked within the context of sea-level rise.

(d) Effects of the potential situation whereby overlapping areas of the exclusive economic zones of opposite coastal States, delimited by bilateral agreement, no longer overlap, and the issue of objective regimes; effects of the situation whereby an agreed land boundary terminus ends up being located out at sea; judgment of the International Court of Justice in the *Maritime Delimitation in the Caribbean Sea and the Pacific Ocean (Costa Rica v. Nicaragua)* case

174. At the fourth meeting of the Study Group, held on 2 May 2023, the Co-Chair (Mr. Aurescu) introduced chapter V of the additional paper, including preliminary observations in paragraph 147, on the following: effects of the potential situation whereby overlapping areas of the exclusive economic zones of opposite coastal States, delimited by bilateral agreement, no longer overlapped, and the issue of objective regimes; effects of the situation whereby an agreed land boundary terminus ended up being located out at sea; and the judgment of the International Court of Justice in the *Maritime Delimitation in the Caribbean Sea and the Pacific Ocean (Costa Rica v. Nicaragua)* case.[291] He emphasized that the issues addressed in the chapter had been selected on the basis of suggestions made by members of the Study Group in 2021. The Co-Chairs had explored, *inter alia*, the supervening impossibility of performance, obsolescence, objective regimes, and situations of submerged land boundaries, and had described relevant State practice and case law on those issues.

175. Some members agreed with the Co-Chairs' preliminary observations in paragraph 147 of the additional paper.

176. A view was expressed that maritime delimitation treaties took varying approaches to respond to potential physical changes in the basepoints and baselines used. While some treaties contained a mechanism to readjust the boundary, most were silent on that and the broader issue of legal stability and did not include amendment provisions. Moreover, there had been revisions of baselines without any readjustment of the boundary.

177. In line with the findings of the additional paper, some members were doubtful as to the relevance and applicability of the supervening impossibility of performing a treaty, as enshrined in article 61 of the Vienna Convention on the Law of Treaties, to the sea-level rise context. It was noted, as also mentioned in the additional paper, that article 61 was not automatically applied, and that sea-level rise could not have an effect on the performance of a maritime delimitation treaty. An abstract examination of that rule was seen as not helpful to the work of the Study Group. According to one view, the only practical scenario in which the impossibility of performance could arise was where a treaty established additional legal

[291] *Maritime Delimitation in the Caribbean Sea and the Pacific Ocean (Costa Rica v. Nicaragua)* and *Land Boundary in the Northern Part of Isla Portillos (Costa Rica v. Nicaragua), Judgment, I.C.J. Reports 2018*, p. 139.

regimes together with maritime delimitation. However, even in that case, article 62 of the Convention would be more appropriate.

178. A question was raised as to whether legal regimes could be regarded "an object indispensable for the execution of the treaty", as referred to in article 61 of the Vienna Convention on the Law of Treaties. Members expressed diverging views on that question. It was recalled that the International Court of Justice had avoided pronouncing on the question in the *Gabčíkovo-Nagymaros Project (Hungary/Slovakia)* case.[292] At the same time, it was noted that article 61 of the Vienna Convention on the Law of Treaties between States and International Organizations or between International Organizations could be construed as allowing for a legal regime to be considered an object indispensable for the execution of the treaty.[293] Given the lack of clarity in international law in that respect, it was proposed that the Study Group should not focus its work on the question of the applicability of article 61 of the Vienna Convention on the Law of Treaties.

179. With respect to cases in which an agreed land boundary terminus ended up being located out at sea, it was observed that two legal options existed: to recognize, as a legal fiction, that the land boundary remained; or to conclude that it had become a maritime boundary. With respect to the latter case, it was recalled that article 15 of the United Nations Convention on the Law of the Sea provided that the delimitation of the territorial sea between States with opposite or adjacent coasts should be done on the basis of the median line. However, the submerged land boundary would not always coincide with the median line, and such a case would require an interpretation of article 15 to allow a special circumstance to be taken into account. It was also noted that the method of using fixed points at sea could be applied in such cases for maritime delimitation between States with adjacent coasts.

180. With respect to the issue of objective regimes, it was noted that maritime delimitation agreements should not be considered as imposing any objective regime *vis-à-vis* third States. It was proposed that the issue be approached from the perspective of the legal effects of acquiescence. It was also noted that articles 11 and 12 of the 1978 Vienna Convention on the Succession of States in respect of Treaties, as referred to in paragraph 141 of the additional paper, were not applicable in the context of sea-level rise.[294]

181. In line with the additional paper, the question of obsolescence, or desuetude, of treaties was seen as highly controversial and hardly helpful in the context of sea-level rise. It was proposed that the Study Group should not focus on it.

182. Some members agreed on the relevance of the *Maritime Delimitation in the Caribbean Sea and the Pacific Ocean (Costa Rica v. Nicaragua)* case of the International Court of Justice in the sea-level rise context.[295] However, it was noted that the conclusions reached by the Court in that case could not be generally applied in all situations. It was also emphasized that the Court had never held that baselines should be fixed. A view was expressed that the statement of Costa Rica, cited in paragraph 146 of the additional paper, in which that State noted that legal stability did not necessarily require a fixed delimitation line and could also be achieved with a moving delimitation line, introduced too much complexity and should be taken with caution.

---

[292] *Gabčíkovo-Nagymaros Project (Hungary/Slovakia), Judgment, I.C.J. Reports 1997*, p. 7, at p. 63, para. 103.

[293] Vienna Convention on the Law of Treaties between States and International Organizations or between International Organizations (Vienna, 21 March 1986, not yet in force), *Official Records of the United Nations Conference on the Law of Treaties between States and International Organizations or between International Organizations (Documents of the Conference)*, vol. II, document A/CONF.129/15 (reproduced in A/CONF.129/16/Add.1 (Vol. II)).

[294] Vienna Convention on Succession of States in respect of Treaties (Vienna, 23 August 1978), United Nations, Treaty Series, vol. 1946, No. 33356, p. 3.

[295] *Maritime Delimitation in the Caribbean Sea and in the Pacific Ocean (Costa Rica v. Nicaragua)* and *Land Boundary in the Northern Part of Isla Portillos (Costa Rica v. Nicaragua)* (see footnote 291 above).

(e) Principle that "the land dominates the sea"

183. At the fourth meeting of the Study Group, held on 2 May 2023, the Co-Chair (Ms. Oral) introduced chapter VI of the additional paper, including preliminary observations in paragraph 155, on the principle that "the land dominates the sea". She explained that it had been the Co-Chairs' intention not to reconsider the principle, but rather to highlight the fact that it was a judicially established principle that was broadly applied, and to examine it in the context of sea-level rise further to a mapping exercise of the relevant practice and case law. She stressed that the Co-Chairs had specifically aimed to consider whether the principle was an absolute rule, and whether it could be applicable in cases where portions of land had become submerged. She presented the principle of natural prolongation, a codified rule that, for practical reasons, had fallen into disuse by the International Court of Justice and arbitral tribunals, and the principle of the permanency of the outer boundaries of the continental shelf, under article 76 of the United Nations Convention on the Law of the Sea. Both of those principles had been cited by the Co-Chairs as examples of exceptions to the application of the rule that "the land dominates the sea".

184. In the course of their exchange, members expressed diverging views on the nature and status of the concept in international law. Some members of the Study Group noted that "the land dominates the sea" was neither a principle nor a rule of customary international law. Another view was expressed that it was a question not of contemplating exceptions to the principle that "the land dominates the sea", but of establishing solid support for the preliminary observations in favour of preservation and permanency of baselines and maritime boundaries.

185. Some members considered that "the land dominates the sea" was rather a legal maxim developed in international case law and that, while rights over maritime spaces depended on the sovereignty over the coastline, "the land dominates the sea" was not a rule that could be used in practice to determine maritime zones. A view was expressed that, with the exception of historic title and rights, every privilege enjoyed by States in the form of maritime spaces under their jurisdiction was based on their sovereignty over the coastline. There was, however, no overarching principle that made it possible for States to determine, in accordance with the traditional sources of international law, another rationale for the granting of privileges over the sea. Rather, maritime entitlements were determined on the basis of the baselines rule, on which, it was thus suggested, the Study Group should therefore focus. It was also recalled that the outer limits of the continental shelf remained fixed despite the landward shift of baselines, which showed that the principle that "the land dominates the sea" was not universal.

186. According to another view, the principle that "the land dominates the sea" was a long-existing principle of international law, stemming from the cannon-shot rule, and was used in practice for maritime delimitation. It was also noted that the principle was a rule of customary international law and was reflected in various international instruments, including the United Nations Convention on the Law of the Sea. At the same time, the necessity for consistent treatment of changes in coastlines and changes in maritime features was stressed.

187. It was emphasized that maritime spaces existed in direct relation to the land and that it would be helpful to reconsider the matter in the context of the subtopic on statehood.

188. It was suggested that the Study Group explore further the issue of basepoints, which were also used for maritime delimitation, to consider, in particular, whether basepoints could be fixed, similarly to baselines. In that regard, a call was made for States, in particular those facing the threat of sea-level rise, to publish their basepoints.

(f) Historic waters, title and rights

189. At the fifth meeting of the Study Group, held on 3 May 2023, the Co-Chair (Ms. Oral) introduced chapter VII of the additional paper, including preliminary observations in paragraphs 168 and 169, on historic waters, title and rights. She noted that the chapter explored the history of the development of the principle, its application by States and international courts and tribunals, and its possible applicability in the context of sea-level rise for the purposes of preserving existing rights in maritime areas.

190. Some members noted the exceptional nature of the principle of historic waters, title and rights. Several members called for caution in examining the applicability of the principle in the context of sea-level rise. A view was expressed that the content of the principle was ambiguous. It was also emphasized that international law did not provide for a single regime for historic waters, title or rights, but provided only for a particular regime for each individual case. Furthermore, it was recalled that the International Court of Justice, in the *Territorial and Maritime Dispute (Nicaragua v. Colombia)* case in 2012, had pronounced that historic considerations did not create legal rights *per se*, but had primarily evidentiary value in confirming that the disputed territory belonged to a specific State.[296]

191. It was recalled that the establishment of a historic regime was conditioned on several requirements, including the need to exercise effective authority over a region. The requirement of effective authority, beyond mere legal pronouncements, was seen as potentially problematic for small island and archipelagic States, as it required considerable financial and technical resources.

192. It was noted that the principle of historic waters, title and rights would be relevant if an ambulatory baselines approach were adopted. Some members expressed reservations as to the applicability of the principle in the context of sea-level rise. In particular, a concern was expressed that the universal nature of sea-level rise would render all existing maritime titles historic. At the same time, it was noted that the principle could be useful in situations of submerged land boundaries.

193. A view was expressed that the Co-Chairs should refrain from citing the *South China Sea Arbitration* award as it exceeded the scope of the United Nations Convention on the Law of the Sea and the award had been criticized.[297] A contrary view was expressed, recalling that the South China Sea was a sensitive area.

194. The Co-Chair (Ms. Oral) noted that the principle of historic waters, title and rights had led to an exceptional regime of limited application, which, by its nature, would be considered on a case-by-case basis rather than as a general rule applicable to sea-level rise, and was relevant only if baselines were accepted as ambulatory. Moreover, she stressed that, in her opinion, the principle was relevant to the present study as it provided an example of the preservation of existing rights in maritime areas that would otherwise not be in accordance with international law.

(g) Equity

195. At the fifth meeting of the Study Group, held on 3 May 2023, the Co-Chair (Ms. Oral) introduced chapter VIII of the additional paper, including preliminary observations in paragraph 183, on the question of equity. She noted that the request for the Study Group to examine the issue of equity had been made by several States, including small island and small island developing States. While equity was a broad concept of international law, the Co-Chairs had focused in the chapter on the issue of equity first in general and then in the context of the law of the sea and sea-level rise. She recalled that certain examples of case law and State practice had been reflected in the chapter.

196. It was noted that equity was an important principle that was enshrined in various international conventions and instruments, including the United Nations Convention on the Law of the Sea. It was recalled that those who stood to suffer the most from human-induced sea-level rise had contributed the least to the problem, and the preservation of baselines and maritime entitlements gave expression not only to the foundational principles of equity and legal stability, but also to notions of climate justice that were deeply rooted in human rights and general principles of international law. The link between the principle of equity and the principle of common but differentiated responsibilities was also mentioned by several members. It was noted that the latter principle, established in international law, was relevant to the obligations of all States to address climate change and its effects, including sea-level rise, and could prove useful in addressing the impact of sea-level rise through mitigation and

---

296 *Territorial and Maritime Dispute (Nicaragua v. Colombia), Judgment, I.C.J. Reports 2012*, p. 624.

297 *South China Sea Arbitration between the Philippines and the People's Republic of China*, Case No. 2013-19, Permanent Court of Arbitration, Award, 12 July 2016.

adaptation measures, especially in developing States. Furthermore, it was noted that legal stability and equity should be the guiding principles of the Study Group's work on rising sea levels, given that equity was at the heart of the object and purpose of the United Nations Convention on the Law of the Sea itself. A view was expressed that equity required that the special needs and interests of developing States, especially those vulnerable to climate change, be fully taken into account. A view was also expressed that the Study Group should conduct further research into the legal question of the application of the principle of equity to sea-level rise in the context of climate change.

197. A question was raised as to whether equity could be considered a rule of customary international law or a general principle of law. It was noted that equity as a source had been specifically excluded from article 38 of the Statute of the Permanent Court of International Justice, which had been transposed *verbatim* to the Statute of the International Court of Justice. Furthermore, since there was no single position among States on the legal character of equity, it was considered premature at the present stage to pronounce on whether equity was a source of international law within the meaning of Article 38 of the Statute of the International Court of Justice. According to another view, equity could be considered a general principle of law. It was recalled that the principle of equity had been referred to by the Commission in some of its previous work and had been reflected in international instruments. A question was also raised as to whether equity could be considered part of subsidiary means for the determination of rules of international law.

198. Some members recalled that equity was a broad concept, and stressed that particular care was needed in its application to the context of sea-level rise. It was noted that equity was a complex legal concept with various permutations, and that the interpretation of equity by the International Court of Justice in maritime delimitation cases was different from the concept of equity in general that was being discussed by the Study Group. Relatedly, one view was that the additional paper seemed to conflate the distinction between equity as a substantive rule and as a procedural ability of the Court in deciding specific cases. It was recalled that the Court had never resolved a case *ex aequo et bono* and suggested that the Study Group should likewise avoid that concept. A proposal was made for the Study Group to adopt a definition of equity for the purposes of its work on the topic. Some members disagreed with the idea that equity allowed a deviation from positive law.

199. A view was expressed that the concept of equity introduced a teleological dimension to the choice and implementation of applicable rules. It was noted that the notion of equitable results was universally present in the United Nations Convention on the Law of the Sea and that it was possible to consider equity as a legitimizing factor that would support, for example, the notion of fixed baselines. It was recalled that the Convention exempted developing States from certain obligations on account of equity. At the same time, it was emphasized that the notion of equitable results could not be used for all areas of international law. It was suggested that equity should be seen as the ultimate goal to be achieved, rather than a principle to be relied upon. It was also noted that the concept of equity in the context of sea-level rise meant that any solution to address the impact of sea-level rise on maritime entitlements ought to apply to all States, including the most vulnerable ones.

200. A view was expressed that the methodology for maritime delimitation, and in particular the role of equity in it, as described in the additional paper, was not necessarily up to date with international case law. The need for clarity with regard to the rules of maritime delimitation was therefore emphasized.

201. Some support was voiced for the Co-Chairs' preliminary observation that equity, as a method under international law for achieving justice, should be applied in favour of the preservation of existing maritime entitlements. In particular, a view was expressed that the legal stability principle invoked by States as a justification for the fixed baselines approach was supported by the application of equity. According to another view, while equity might strengthen the legal argument in favour of the solution of fixing baselines, the legal vagueness of the concept of equity meant that the fixed baselines approach should not at the present stage be seen as the only possible or preferable solution. It was emphasized that equity in some cases could contribute to legal instability.

202. Some members expressed reservations about the applicability of equity in the context of sea-level rise. It was noted that the preliminary observations contained the assumption that any loss of maritime entitlement would be inherently inequitable. A question was raised as to whether that would always be the case. In particular, doubt was expressed as to whether the landward shift of exclusive economic zones without change to their size could be considered inequitable. In that regard, it was noted that equity could work against the objective of the Study Group, namely that of ensuring the legal stability of the system in the light of the changing realities resulting from sea-level rise.

203. The Co-Chairs (Mr. Aurescu and Ms. Oral) recalled that the intention of the chapter was to map various issues related to equity and explore the applicability of the concept to the context of sea-level rise. The Co-Chairs expressed concern that the views of the Study Group could be interpreted as being against equity, and emphasized the need to reach a conclusion on how equity could be helpful in the context of sea-level rise.

(h) Permanent sovereignty over natural resources

204. At the sixth meeting of the Study Group, held on 4 May 2023, the Co-Chair (Ms. Oral) introduced chapter IX of the additional paper, including preliminary observations in paragraphs 192 to 194, on the principle of permanent sovereignty over natural resources. She recalled that members had raised the need for the Study Group to address the principle in greater detail. The chapter explored the development and scope of the principle of permanent sovereignty over natural resources, as reflected in relevant international instruments and the doctrine, and its application to marine resources. The Co-Chair also observed that the principle was widely recognized as a principle of customary international law.

205. Some members considered the principle of permanent sovereignty over natural resources to be relevant to the topic under consideration. Members agreed that it was a principle of customary international law, as outlined in the additional paper. It was recalled that, on 11 December 1970, the General Assembly had adopted resolution 2692 (XXV), entitled "Permanent sovereignty over natural resources of developing countries and expansion of domestic sources of accumulation for economic development", whereby it recognized that the principle of permanent sovereignty over natural resources was applicable to marine natural resources. A doubt was expressed as to whether the loss by a State of its maritime entitlements outside of its own volition could be considered a violation of the inalienable rights, as recognized by other States, that were inherent in its sovereignty.

206. A view was expressed that a distinction should be drawn between natural resources in the seabed and subsoil and those in the water column. It was also noted that the principle of permanent sovereignty over natural resources had a special historical meaning and that the question of its applicability outside the colonial context was not yet settled.

207. Several members underlined the link between the principle of permanent sovereignty over natural resources and the right of peoples to self-determination. In that regard, it was recalled that examination of the principle of permanent sovereignty over natural resources could continue the following year, when the Study Group would return to the subtopics of statehood and the protection of persons affected by sea-level rise. The link between the principle of permanent sovereignty over natural resources and the presumption of continuity of statehood, as addressed in the subtopic of statehood, was also noted.

208. Support was expressed for the preliminary observations in paragraph 194 of the additional paper. At the same time, several members expressed doubt that the principle of permanent sovereignty over natural resources necessarily supported the observations in paragraph 194 (b), concerning the loss of marine natural resources. A view was expressed that the principle would not in itself be sufficient to override the change of maritime entitlements caused by changes to the coast. Another view was expressed that the principle of permanent sovereignty over natural resources was agnostic about the existence and spatial scope of sovereign rights and jurisdiction over maritime spaces, and instead identified the manner in which they could be exercised.

209. The Co-Chair (Ms. Oral) welcomed the rich discussion between the members of the Study Group on chapter IX of the additional paper. She emphasized that while the principle of permanent sovereignty over natural resources was linked to the decolonization process, it

continued to play an important part in economic development for many developing States. The Co-Chair noted that the principle was relevant in the context of sea-level rise, as it provided for additional layers of support for the concept of the preservation of maritime entitlements.

(i) Possible loss or gain by third States

210. At the sixth meeting of the Study Group, held on 4 May 2023, the Co-Chair (Ms. Oral) introduced chapter X of the additional paper, including preliminary observations in paragraph 214, on possible loss or gain by third States. She noted that the question of the possible legal effects of sea-level rise on the exercise of sovereign rights and jurisdiction of coastal States and third States had been addressed in the first issues paper.[298] She recalled that, during the seventy-second session (2021) of the Commission, the Study Group had decided that there was a need to explore the question further, in particular from the perspective of third States, which prompted the inclusion of the matter in the additional paper. The chapter thus explored different scenarios, triggered by baselines shifting landward, and their effect on the possible benefits and losses to third States, concluding that the preservation of existing baselines and maritime boundaries would not result in any loss to either party.

211. The Co-Chairs were commended for the clear and analytical discussion of possible loss or gain by third States. A view was expressed that the legal issues arising from scenarios addressed in the additional paper could occur only where there was no prior maritime delimitation agreement between States, and the question of practical relevance, given the limited number of scenarios in which the legal issues could occur, was therefore raised. It was further noted that the legal consequences of sea-level rise for existing delimitation treaties were of particular importance, in terms of their influence on third States specifically. In that regard, a proposal was made for the Study Group to explore available options for third States that could have an interest in the termination, owing to the effects of sea-level rise, of existing delimitation treaties to which they were not parties.

212. A view was expressed that sea-level rise, in the context of ambulatory baselines, would not disturb the balance established by the United Nations Convention on the Law of the Sea, as maritime zones would move landward, but their size would remain unchanged and loss by States would be limited to land territory. It was nonetheless observed that the fixed baselines approach, if adopted, would undoubtedly affect the rights of third States, and would also lead to significant changes in the rules governing the law of the sea. A concern was raised that the increase in portions of waters under the sovereignty of coastal States would have a considerable effect on the right of innocent passage for third States. At the same time, it was noted that the fixed baselines approach was indispensable to maintaining the predictability of maritime entitlements and preserving the balance of rights and obligations established by the Convention. A view was also expressed that, in addition to fixing baselines, the existing defined outer limits of maritime zones must be preserved in order to maintain the *status quo* of maritime entitlements as established in accordance with international law.

213. With regard to paragraph 199 of the additional paper, a point was made suggesting that there were different positions in international law as to whether the right of innocent passage applied to both merchant and military vessels.

214. The Co-Chair (Ms. Oral) emphasized the link between the matter under consideration and the principle of equity, discussed in chapter VIII of the additional paper.

(j) Nautical charts and their relationship to baselines, maritime boundaries and the safety of navigation

215. At the sixth meeting of the Study Group, held on 4 May 2023, the Co-Chair (Ms. Oral) recalled that the issue of navigational charts had been raised during the Study Group discussions during the seventy-second session (2021) of the Commission.[299] She noted that

[298] A/CN.4/740 and Corr.1, paras. 172–190.

[299] *Official Records of the General Assembly, Seventy-sixth Session, Supplement No. 10* (A/76/10), paras. 247–296.

the purpose of chapter XI of the additional paper was to examine in greater detail the various functions of navigational charts under international law and to determine whether States had an obligation to update such charts periodically under the United Nations Convention on the Law of the Sea. She also brought to the attention of the Study Group that the Co-Chairs had prepared the chapter on the basis, *inter alia*, of information from States and international organizations, in particular the International Hydrographic Organization, the International Maritime Organization and the Division for Ocean Affairs and the Law of the Sea of the United Nations Office of Legal Affairs.

216. Referring to the preliminary conclusions in paragraphs 245–249 of the additional paper, the Co-Chair emphasized that nautical charts were principally used for the purposes of the safety of navigation, and that the depiction of baselines or maritime zones was a supplementary function. The Co-Chair also observed that there was no evidence in practice or in sources of international law of an obligation on States to regularly update their nautical charts, particularly so since many States lacked the necessary capacity to conduct regular hydrographic surveys.

217. With regard to the purpose of the nautical charts under international law, several members recalled that such charts were predominantly used for the safety of navigation and that the maritime boundaries delimitation was a concern that was secondary in nature. Other members questioned whether the Study Group could conclude that the safety of navigation was the primary function of the navigation charts. The need to distinguish between nautical charts used for seafaring purposes and those used for recording maritime zones was emphasized.

218. Members expressed agreement that there was no obligation for States under the United Nations Convention on the Law of the Sea to update nautical charts, once duly deposited with the Secretary-General, for the purposes of depicting basepoints, baselines or maritime boundaries. Several members noted that there was also insufficient State practice to support the existence of such an obligation. It was also recalled that some States had difficulties in preparing charts as they did not have dedicated hydrographic agencies. It was further stressed that the need for legal stability should not have any effect on the question of updating navigational charts. A question was raised as to whether it would be beneficial to encourage States to register their nautical charts, and to provide technical assistance to that end. A concern was raised that the fixed baselines approach together with the lack of an obligation to update baselines could pose hazards to the safety of navigation as charts might not reflect physical reality, potentially in contravention of the relevant international instruments, in particular the International Convention for the Safety of Life at Sea.[300]

219. The Co-Chair (Ms. Oral) reiterated that the purpose of the chapter was to examine the role of navigational charts and, specifically, whether there was an obligation for States to update them. She recognized that the issue was linked to the debate on fixed versus ambulatory baselines and noted that the preliminary observations in paragraph 214 of the issues paper – in chapter X, on possible loss or gain by third States – did not contravene the fixed baseline approach.

(k) Relevance of other sources of law

220. At the seventh meeting of the Study Group, held on 4 May 2023, the Co-Chair (Mr. Aurescu) introduced chapter XII of the additional paper, on the relevance of other sources of law. He recalled that the members of the Study Group had suggested at the seventy-second session (2021) of the Commission that the Co-Chairs explore sources beyond the United Nations Convention on the Law of the Sea and the 1958 Geneva Conventions.[301] The chapter therefore listed a number of potentially relevant international instruments. The

[300] International Convention for the Safety of Life at Sea, 1974 (London, 1 November 1974), United Nations, *Treaty Series*, vol. 1184, No. 18961, p. 2.

[301] Convention on the High Seas (Geneva, 29 April 1958), United Nations, *Treaty Series*, vol. 450, No. 6465, p. 11; Convention on the Continental Shelf (Geneva, 29 April 1958), *ibid.*, vol. 499, No. 7302, p. 311; Convention on the Territorial Sea and the Contiguous Zone (Geneva, 29 April 1958), *ibid.*, vol. 516, No. 7477, p. 205; and Convention on Fishing and Conservation of the Living Resources of the High Seas (Geneva, 29 April 1958), *ibid.*, vol. 559, No. 8164, p. 285.

preliminary observations, reflected in paragraph 280, were that their relevance to the topic was limited, although the fixed baselines solution would favour the proper implementation of some of the international instruments examined.

221. Some members agreed with the preliminary observations of the additional paper as to the limited usefulness of exploring other sources of law. It was noted that a large number of multilateral and bilateral international instruments referred to various maritime zones, and that it was practically unfeasible for the Study Group to exhaustively explore the matter. The central role of the United Nations Convention on the Law of the Sea was thus emphasized.

3. Future work of the Study Group

222. Members made various suggestions and outlined several options during their exchange of views concerning the working methods of the Study Group and future work on the topic.

223. First, it was underlined that a clearer road map was required to meet the expectations of States, including in determining the form and content of the Study Group's final report, expected to be issued in 2025, and the outcomes to be delivered. The prioritization of issues that the Commission was in a position to address was also recommended.

224. Second, some members suggested that the Study Group proceed to an operative phase and propose concrete solutions to practical problems caused by sea-level rise. It was accordingly suggested that the Study Group should contemplate providing some practical guidance to States, possibly through a set of conclusions.

225. Third, several members were in favour of preparing an interpretative declaration on the United Nations Convention on the Law of the Sea, which could serve as a basis for future negotiations between States parties. In that connection, reference was made to the precedent of the fourth Review Conference (1996) of the Parties to the Convention on the Prohibition of the Development, Production and Stockpiling of Bacteriological (Biological) and Toxin Weapons and on Their Destruction.[302] At the same time, it was stressed that the interpretation of treaties, including the United Nations Convention on the Law of the Sea, fell within the purview of States parties and the instrument's bodies. A view was expressed that in the light of inadequate State practice and insufficient scientific evidence, there was no need to reinterpret the existing regime on the United Nations Convention on the Law of the Sea. Another view was expressed that an interpretative declaration would not serve as a sufficient guarantee to the affected States in the future.

226. Fourth, the Co-Chairs stressed the importance of further exploring the issue of submerged territories, which had not been raised in 2021. Given that the issue was related both to the law of the sea and to statehood, they suggested that it be addressed in the Study Group's additional paper to the second issues paper, expected to be issued in 2024, and in the consolidated final report, expected to be issued in 2025.

227. With regard to the outcome of the Study Group's work, various proposals were made, including a draft framework convention on issues related to sea-level rise that could be used as a basis for further negotiations within the United Nations system, following the example of the United Nations Convention to Combat Desertification in Those Countries Experiencing Serious Drought and/or Desertification, Particularly in Africa.[303]

228. More generally, it was also suggested that any outcome of the Commission's work on the topic should guarantee the sovereign rights of States over their maritime spaces. It was recalled that, while the Commission's mandate allowed for promotion of the progressive development of international law, its work ought to be rooted within the existing international rules.

---

[302] Convention on the Prohibition of the Development, Production and Stockpiling of Bacteriological (Biological) and Toxin Weapons and on Their Destruction (London, Moscow and Washington, 10 April 1972), United Nations, *Treaty Series*, vol. 1015, No. 14860, p. 163.

[303] United Nations Convention to Combat Desertification in Those Countries Experiencing Serious Drought and/or Desertification, Particularly in Africa (Paris, 14 October 1994), United Nations, *Treaty Series*, vol. 1954, No. 33480, p. 3.

229. In the light of recent requests for advisory opinions addressed first to the International Tribunal for the Law of the Sea and then to the International Court of Justice, a view was expressed that the Study Group should exercise caution in considering issues addressed by other bodies.

230. In 2024, the Study Group will revert to the subtopics of statehood and the protection of persons affected by sea-level rise. In 2025, the Study Group will then seek to finalize a substantive report on the topic as a whole by consolidating the results of the work undertaken.

Chapter IX
Succession of States in respect of State responsibility

A. Introduction

231. At its sixty-ninth session (2017), the Commission decided to include the topic "Succession of States in respect of State responsibility" in its programme of work and appointed Mr. Pavel Šturma as Special Rapporteur.[304] The General Assembly, in its resolution 72/116 of 7 December 2017, took note of the decision of the Commission to include the topic in its programme of work.

232. The Special Rapporteur submitted five reports from 2017 to 2022.[305] The Commission also had before it, at the seventy-first session (2019), a memorandum prepared by the Secretariat providing information on treaties which may be of relevance to its future work on the topic.[306] Following the debate on each report, the Commission decided to refer the proposals for draft articles made by the Special Rapporteur to the Drafting Committee. The Commission heard interim reports and statements from the successive Chairs of the Drafting Committee on succession of States in respect of State responsibility at the sixty-ninth to seventy-third sessions (2017 to 2019, 2021 and 2022).

233. At its seventy-third session (2022), on 17 May 2022, the Commission decided, on the recommendation of the Special Rapporteur, to instruct the Drafting Committee to proceed with the preparation of draft guidelines on the basis of the provisions previously referred to the Drafting Committee (including those provisions provisionally adopted by the Commission at previous sessions), taking into account the debate held in the plenary on the Special Rapporteur's fifth report.

234. Also at its seventy-third session, the Commission provisionally adopted, with commentaries, draft guidelines 6, 10, 10 *bis* and 11, which had been provisionally adopted by the Drafting Committee in 2018 and 2021, as well as draft guidelines 7 *bis*, 12, 13, 13 *bis*, 14, 15 and 15 *bis*, which were provisionally adopted by the Drafting Committee in 2022. As a result of the change of form of the outcome, the Commission also took note of draft articles 1, 2, 5, 7, 8 and 9, as revised by the Drafting Committee to be draft guidelines.

B. Consideration of the topic at the present session

235. At the present session, the Commission had no report before it on the topic, as the Special Rapporteur was no longer with the Commission. At its 3621st meeting, on 10 May 2023, the Commission decided to establish a Working Group on the topic and appointed Mr. August Reinisch as Chair of the Working Group.

236. The Working Group held four meetings, on 14, 18, 19 and 20 July 2023.

237. The Working Group focused its discussion on considering the way forward for the topic. It considered whether the Commission should continue developing a text in the Drafting Committee and proceed to conclude the first reading of the draft guidelines, or whether it should pursue a different course, as suggested in the plenary in 2022, and convene a dedicated Working Group with a view to eventually producing a report on the topic to be adopted by the Commission. The Working Group expressed its deep appreciation to the former Special Rapporteur for his outstanding contribution to the topic.

238. In the course of a broad and inclusive discussion in the Working Group, which highlighted both merits and shortcomings of the earlier work carried out on the topic, two

---

304 At its 3354th meeting, on 9 May 2017. The topic had been included in the long-term programme of work of the Commission during its sixty-eighth session (2016), on the basis of the proposal contained in annex B to the report of the Commission (*Official Records of the General Assembly, Seventy-first Session, Supplement No. 10* (A/71/10)).

305 A/CN.4/708, A/CN.4/719, A/CN.4/731, A/CN.4/743 and Corr.1, and A/CN.4/751, respectively.

306 A/CN.4/730.

main trends emerged. According to one approach, it was preferable to proceed in an incremental manner such that the Working Group would be reconstituted at the seventy-fifth session (2024) to continue its deliberations on the way forward and with a clear mandate to take a decision, as far as possible within a defined time period and on the basis of a working paper to be prepared by the Chair of the Working Group. That paper should also situate the topic within a broader global framework, reflecting more comprehensively the diversity of State practice across regions.

239. The alternative approach was to take a decision, at the present session, to discontinue the present Special Rapporteur-led format of the work, and instead opt for a Working Group-driven process aimed at preparing a final report to be adopted by the Commission, for eventual submission to the General Assembly. The Working Group considered a proposal along such lines, which would have involved recommending the reconstitution of the Working Group with a new mandate, and possibly with a restricted membership, precisely to prepare such a final report on the topic, within a period of two years.

240. While the preponderance of views within the Working Group favoured the conversion of the present format into a Working Group-based process, with the goal of producing a final report as opposed to the adoption of draft guidelines, there was nonetheless a preference for the more incremental approach, whereby a decision on such a way forward would be taken only at the seventy-fifth session, so as to allow more time for reflection.

241. Accordingly, the Working Group decided to recommend that the Commission continue its consideration of the topic, but not proceed with the appointment of a new Special Rapporteur.

242. It further recommended that the Working Group be re-established at the seventy-fifth session of the Commission, with the present open-ended composition, with a view to undertaking further reflection on the way forward for the topic, taking into account the views expressed, and the options identified, in the Working Group at the current session.

243. Such further reflection should be undertaken on the basis of a working paper identifying the various complexities surrounding the provisions adopted by the Commission thus far and outlining the options open to the Commission, to be prepared by the Chair of the Working Group in advance of the seventy-fifth session of the Commission, in close collaboration with interested members of the Working Group.

244. It was recommended that the re-established Working Group should seek to make a recommendation with a view to the Commission taking a decision on the way forward at its next session.

245. At its 3648th meeting, on 27 July 2023, the Commission took note of the oral report of the Chair of the Working Group, including the recommendations contained therein.

246. Following consultations within the Bureau and among members, the Commission decided, at its 3655th meeting, on 3 August 2023, to appoint Mr. August Reinisch as Chair of the Working Group to be re-established at the seventy-fifth session and to report to the Commission for further deliberation and decision.

Chapter X
Other decisions and conclusions of the Commission

A. Special memorial meetings

247. At its 3641st meeting, held on 20 July 2023, the Commission convened a memorial meeting in honour of the memory of former members Mr. Gaetano Arangio-Ruiz, Mr. Guillaume Pambou-Tchivounda, Mr. Sompong Sucharitkul and Mr. Nugroho Wisnumurti.

248. At its 3652nd meeting, held on 3 August 2023, the Commission convened a memorial meeting in honour of the memory of former member Mr. João Clemente Baena Soares.

B. Inclusion of new topics in the programme of work

249. At its 3656th meeting, on 4 August 2023, the Commission decided to include the topic "Non-legally binding international agreements" in its programme of work and to appoint Mr. Mathias Forteau as Special Rapporteur.

C. Immunity of State officials from foreign criminal jurisdiction

250. At its 3621st meeting, on 10 May 2023, the Commission decided to appoint Mr. Claudio Grossman Guiloff as Special Rapporteur for the topic "Immunity of State officials from foreign criminal jurisdiction" to replace Ms. Concepción Escobar Hernández, who was no longer with the Commission. On 17, 18 and 19 July 2023, the Special Rapporteur held informal consultations on the topic, for which the Commission had completed its first reading of the draft articles at its seventy-third session (2022). The Commission awaits comments and observations of Governments to resume consideration at its seventy-fifth session (2024).

D. Programme, procedures and working methods of the Commission and its documentation

251. On 28 April 2023, the Planning Group was constituted for the present session.

252. The Planning Group held five meetings on 28 April and on 7, 14, 20 and 21 July 2023. It had before it the topical summary of the discussion held in the Sixth Committee of the General Assembly during its seventy-seventh session, prepared by the Secretariat (A/CN.4/755); General Assembly resolution 77/103 of 7 December 2022 on the report of the International Law Commission on the work of its seventy-third session; General Assembly resolution 77/110 of 7 December 2022 on the rule of law at the national and international levels; and the proposed programme budget for 2024, Programme 6, Legal affairs, subprogramme 3, concerning the progressive development and codification of international law. The Chair of the Planning Group presented an oral report on the work of the Planning Group at the current session to the Commission, at its 3648th meeting, on 27 July 2023. The Commission took note of the oral report.

1. Working Group on the long-term programme of work

253. At its 1st meeting, on 28 April 2023, the Planning Group decided to establish the Working Group on the long-term programme of work for the present quinquennium, and elected Mr. Marcelo Vázquez-Bermúdez as Chair. The Chair of the Working Group presented an oral report on the work of the Working Group, including on proposals for topics being considered, at the current session to the Planning Group, at its fourth meeting, on 20 July 2023. The Planning Group took note of the oral report.

2. Working Group on methods of work of the Commission

254. At its 1st meeting, on 28 April 2023, the Planning Group decided to reconstitute the Working Group on methods of work of the Commission, and elected Mr. Charles Chernor Jalloh as Chair. The Working Group held four meetings on 5 May and 12 and 13 July 2023.

255. The Working Group first held a general exchange of views on the working methods of the Commission, at which time several issues for possible future consideration by the Working Group were raised. These included: the possibility of developing rules of procedure for the Commission; the possibility of developing an internal practice manual on the working methods and procedures of the Commission; the question of possible limits on the length of interventions made in the plenary, as well as on Special Rapporteur reports; the membership size of the Drafting Committees; the possibility of developing guidance on the nomenclature of the texts and instruments adopted by the Commission, including the meaning of output on topics described as draft articles, draft conclusions, draft guidelines, and draft principles; the allocation of time for the deliberation of topics on the programme of the Commission; the question of participation in meetings of the Drafting Committees and Working Groups; the timing of the issuance and distribution of official documents including in the various official languages; the possibility of establishing some mechanism for reviewing the reception by Member States of the past products of the Commission; and the role of the Special Rapporteurs. Views were also expressed on how best to enhance the interaction with the Sixth Committee and other legal bodies, including expert bodies. It was stressed that the relationship between the Commission and the Sixth Committee should be given priority, through formal and informal contact, but that consideration should also be given to how to deepen cooperation with other legal bodies, including regional codification bodies; for example, by organizing regular intersessional virtual meetings, briefings and exchanges of view on topics of shared interest. Additional suggestions included the preparation of a code of conduct for members in relation to issues of conflict of interest and even the possibility of undertaking a review of the statute to address, *inter alia*, issues of representation including gender parity in composition. A further suggestion was that the Working Group undertake a review of the implementation of its prior reports, particularly those adopted in 1996 and 2011. The Working Group also adopted several procedural recommendations (see below).

256. The Chair of the Working Group presented an oral report on the work of the Working Group at the current session to the Planning Group at its 4th meeting, on 20 July 2023. The Planning Group took note of the oral report.

257. The Commission noted the decision of the Working Group to establish a standing agenda, which will serve to organize its work into the future, until the Working Group decides otherwise, composed of the following three items:

1. Revitalization of the working methods and procedures of the International Law Commission.

2. Relationship of the International Law Commission with the General Assembly and other bodies.

3. Other issues.

258. The above standing agenda items are the broad themes under which specific working methods issues concerning both the more internal and external aspects of the work of the Commission will be discussed and debated each year.

259. The Commission further endorsed the recommendations of the Working Group that a new reporting practice be adopted whereby a brief summary of the Working Group's deliberations will be included in the Commission's annual report to the General Assembly, and that from the seventy-fifth session, in 2024, onwards the Working Group will be designated as the "Working Group on methods of work and procedures of the Commission".

260. The Commission requests the Secretariat, under the guidance of the Chair, to prepare a draft of an internal practice guide, handbook or manual on the working methods and procedures of the Commission, containing relevant material drawn from volume I of the *Work of the International Law Commission* and the reports of the Commission addressing methods of work from 1996 and 2011, as well as proposals for improvement made by

members in the previous quinquennium, to be considered by the Working Group once it has concluded its current work on another report on working methods.

3. Work programme of the Commission for the remainder of the quinquennium

261. The Commission recalled its decision in 2011 that the Planning Group should cooperate with Special Rapporteurs to define, at the beginning of any new topic, a tentative schedule for the development of the topic over a number of years as may be required, and periodically review the attainment of annual targets in such schedule, updating it when appropriate.[307] The Commission further recalled that it was customary at the beginning of each quinquennium to prepare the Commission's work programme for the remainder of the quinquennium, setting out in general terms the anticipated goals in respect of each topic on the basis of indications by the Special Rapporteurs. It is the understanding of the Commission that the work programme has a tentative character, since the nature and the complexities of the work preclude certainty in making predictions in advance.

Work programme (2024–2027)

(a) *Immunity of State officials from foreign criminal jurisdiction*

2024

First (and final) report: discussing *inter alia* the comments received from Governments and possible amendments to the draft articles adopted on first reading.

Completion of the draft articles on second reading.

(b) *Succession of States in respect of State responsibility*

See chapter IX of the present report.

(c) *General principles of law*

2025

Fourth (and final) report: discussing *inter alia* the comments received from Governments and possible amendments to the draft conclusions adopted on first reading.

Completion of the draft conclusions on second reading.

(d) *Sea-level rise in relation to international law*

2024

Additional paper to the second issues paper relating to statehood and protection of persons.

2025

The Study Group will seek to finalize a substantive report on the topic as a whole by consolidating the results of the work undertaken.

(e) *Settlement of disputes to which international organizations are parties*

2024

Second report: analysis of the practice of the settlement of disputes between international organizations and States, as well as between international organizations; formulation of recommended practices for the settlement of such disputes.

2025

Third report: analysis of the practice of the settlement of disputes between international organizations and private parties; formulation of recommended practices for the settlement of such disputes.

Completion of the draft guidelines on first reading.

[307] *Yearbook ... 2011*, vol. II (Part Two), para. 378 (c).

2027

Fourth (and final) report: discussing, *inter alia*, the comments received from Governments and possible amendments to the draft guidelines adopted on first reading.

Completion of the draft guidelines on second reading.

(f) *Prevention and repression of piracy and armed robbery at sea*

2024

Second report: analysis of regional and subregional practice and initiatives for combating piracy and armed robbery at sea, as well as the resolutions of relevant international organizations, in particular the International Maritime Organization.

2025

Third report: analysis of trends in academic writings and the views of learned societies on the topic, as well as the resolutions of the General Assembly and Security Council.

Completion of the draft articles on first reading.

2027

Fourth (and final) report: discussing, *inter alia*, the comments received from Governments and possible amendments to the draft articles adopted on first reading.

Completion of the draft articles on second reading.

(g) *Subsidiary means for the determination of rules of international law*

2024

Second report: focusing on the function of subsidiary means, especially judicial decisions and their relationship to the sources of international law, namely treaties, customary international law and general principles of law. Possible consideration of the question of the unity and coherence of international law in relation to conflicting judicial decisions by different courts and tribunals.

Preliminary consideration of the memorandum by the Secretariat surveying the case law of international courts and tribunals, and other bodies, which could be particularly relevant for the future work on the topic of subsidiary means for the determination of rules of international law.

2025

Third report: analysis of teachings and other subsidiary means for the determination of rules of international law, *inter alia*, the work of public and private expert bodies and the resolutions of international organizations; any other miscellaneous issues arising from the study of subsidiary means and the input of States on the topic.

Completion of the draft conclusions on first reading.

2027

Fourth (and final) report: discussing, *inter alia*, the comments received from Governments, international organizations and others, and possible amendments to the draft conclusions adopted on first reading.

Completion of the draft conclusions on second reading.

4. Consideration of General Assembly resolution 77/110 of 7 December 2022 on the rule of law at the national and international levels

262. The General Assembly, in its resolution 77/110 on the rule of law at the national and international levels, *inter alia*, reiterated its invitation to the Commission to comment, in its report to the General Assembly, on its current role in promoting the rule of law. Since its sixtieth session (2008), the Commission has commented at each of its sessions on its role in promoting the rule of law. The Commission notes that the comments contained in paragraphs

341 to 346 of its 2008 report[308] remain relevant and reiterates the comments made at its previous sessions.[309]

263. The Commission recalls that the rule of law is of the essence of its work. The Commission's purpose, as set out in article 1 of its statute, is to promote the progressive development of international law and its codification.

264. Having in mind the principle of the rule of law in all its work, the Commission is fully conscious of the importance of the implementation of international law at the national level, and aims at promoting respect for the rule of law at the international level.

265. In fulfilling its mandate concerning the progressive development of international law and its codification, the Commission will continue to take into account the rule of law as a principle of governance and the human rights and sustainable development that are fundamental to the rule of law, as reflected in the preamble and Article 13 of the Charter of the United Nations and in the declaration of the high-level meeting of the General Assembly on the rule of law at the national and international levels.[310]

266. In its current work, the Commission is aware of "the interrelationship between the rule of law and the three pillars of the United Nations (peace and security, development, and human rights)",[311] without emphasizing one at the expense of the other. The Commission also welcomes recent developments addressing sustainable development and climate change, and the recourse to advisory proceedings, in particular, the General Assembly's request for an advisory opinion submitted by consensus to the International Court of Justice.[312]

267. In fulfilling its mandate concerning the progressive development and codification of international law, the Commission is conscious of current challenges to the rule of law, including the need to ensure gender parity in national and international institutions. In this regard, the Commission itself recognizes the need for gender parity in its own composition.

268. Recalling that the General Assembly has stressed the importance of promoting the sharing of national best practices on the rule of law,[313] the Commission wishes to recall that much of its work consists of collecting and analysing national practices related to the rule of law with a view to assessing their possible contribution to the progressive development and codification of international law.

269. The Commission particularly welcomes the decision of the General Assembly inviting Member States to focus their comments regarding the rule of law, during the

[308] *Yearbook ... 2008*, vol. II (Part Two), pp. 146–147.

[309] *Yearbook ... 2009*, vol. II (Part Two), p. 150, para. 231; *Yearbook ... 2010*, vol. II (Part Two), pp. 202–204, paras. 390–393; *Yearbook ... 2011*, vol. II (Part Two), p. 178, paras. 392–398; *Yearbook ... 2012*, vol. II (Part Two), p. 87, paras. 274–279; *Yearbook ... 2013*, vol. II (Part Two), p. 79, paras. 171–179; *Yearbook ... 2014*, vol. II (Part Two) and Corr.1, p. 165, paras. 273–280; *Yearbook ... 2015*, vol. II (Part Two), p. 85, paras. 288–295; *Yearbook ... 2016*, vol. II (Part Two), pp. 227–228, paras. 314–322; *Yearbook ... 2017*, vol. II (Part Two), pp. 149–150, paras. 269–278; *Official Records of the General Assembly, Seventy-third Session, Supplement No. 10* (A/73/10), paras. 372–380; *ibid., Seventy-fourth Session, Supplement No. 10* (A/74/10), paras. 293–301; *ibid., Seventy-sixth Session, Supplement No. 10* (A/76/10), paras. 304–312; and *ibid., Seventy-seventh Session, Supplement No. 10* (A/77/10), paras. 258–269.

[310] General Assembly resolution 67/1 of 24 September 2012 on the declaration of the high-level meeting of the General Assembly on the rule of law at the national and international levels, para. 41.

[311] Report of the Secretary-General on measuring the effectiveness of the support provided by the United Nations system for the promotion of the rule of law in conflict and post-conflict situations, S/2013/341, para. 70.

[312] General Assembly resolution 77/276 of 29 March 2023, entitled, "Request for an advisory opinion of the International Court of Justice on the obligations of States in respect of Climate Change". See International Tribunal for the Law of the Sea, Request for an advisory opinion submitted by the Commission of Small Island States on Climate Change and International Law, 12 December 2022; and Inter-American Court of Human Rights, Request for an advisory opinion on the climate emergency and human rights submitted by Chile and Colombia, 9 January 2023.

[313] General Assembly resolution 77/110 of 19 December 2022 on the rule of law at the national and international levels, paras. 2 and 19.

upcoming Sixth Committee debate at the seventy-eighth session of the General Assembly, on the subtopic "Using technology to advance access to justice for all".[314]

270. In this regard, the Commission notes that technological innovations may both pose challenges and provide opportunities for international law. For example, as evidenced by the work on the topic of prevention and repression of piracy and armed robbery at sea, which was considered in the present session, technology has changed the way in which these crimes are carried out. The Commission in its debate considered current and emerging technologies and the role that they may play in both combating piracy and armed robbery at sea, as well as facilitating the international cooperation essential to ensure justice and access to justice for those affected by these crimes. The Commission is consistently mindful of technological challenges faced by the various nations of the world and works to ensure that the outcomes of Commission topics are sufficiently inclusive and practical to be of greatest possible value now and in the future. Accordingly, the Commission wishes to reiterate the great value of input from States and international organizations, particularly on how they are using technologies to improve access to justice for all within their own States and within their international partnerships. The Commission stressed the importance of its website to disseminate its work.[315]

271. Bearing in mind the role of multilateral treaty processes in advancing the rule of law,[316] the Commission recalls that the work of the Commission on different topics has led to several multilateral treaty processes and to the adoption of a number of multilateral treaties.[317]

272. The Commission is of the view that the rule of law is greatly served when the law in such multilateral treaties may be supported by new technologies. In this regard, the Commission noted the reference by Mr. Miguel de Serpa Soares, Under-Secretary-General for Legal Affairs and United Nations Legal Counsel, in his statement of 11 May 2023 to the Commission,[318] that the legal regime under the United Nations Convention on the Law of the Sea continues to evolve, pursuant to General Assembly resolution 72/249 of 24 December 2017,[319] with the finalization of the text of an agreement on the conservation and sustainable use of marine biological diversity of areas beyond national jurisdiction which, *inter alia*, includes substantive provisions to further cooperation in capacity-building and the transfer of marine technology to strengthen the rule of law and help ensure the continued health of our global waters. The text of this agreement was subsequently adopted by the intergovernmental conference on 19 June 2023.[320]

273. In the course of the present session, in the first year in which the Commission returned to its usual working methods without the constraints of the COVID-19 pandemic, the Commission continues to make its contribution to the promotion of the rule of law, including by working on the topics in the programme of work for the present session: "General principles of law" (adopted on first reading at the present session); "Succession of States in respect of State responsibility"; "Sea-level rise in relation to international law"; "Settlement of disputes to which international organizations are parties"; "Prevention and repression of

---

314 *Ibid*., para. 23.

315 See section 11, below, and https://legal.un.org/ilc/.

316 General Assembly resolution 77/110 of 19 December 2022 on the rule of law at the national and international level, para. 8.

317 See, more specifically, *Yearbook ... 2015*, vol. II (Part Two), para. 294.

318 See United Nations Office of Legal Affairs, Statement by Mr. Miguel de Serpa Soares to the International Law Commission, Geneva, 11 May 2023, pp. 24–26.

319 General Assembly resolution 72/249 of 24 December 2017 on international legally binding instrument under the United Nations Convention on the Law of the Sea on the conservation and sustainable use of marine biological diversity of areas beyond national jurisdiction, paras. 1, 2, 6–9, and 23 (considering the recommendations in the Report of the Preparatory Committee (A/AC.287/2017/PC.4/2), established by General Assembly resolution 69/292 of 19 June 2015).

320 Intergovernmental conference on an international legally binding instrument under the United Nations Convention on the Law of the Sea on the conservation and sustainable use of marine biological diversity of areas beyond national jurisdiction, Agreement under the United Nations Convention on the Law of the Sea on the conservation and sustainable use of marine biological diversity of areas beyond national jurisdiction (A/CONF.232/2023/4).

piracy and armed robbery at sea"; and "Subsidiary means for the determination of rules of international law".

274. The Commission reiterates its commitment to the promotion of the rule of law in all of its activities.

5. Commemoration of the seventy-fifth anniversary of the International Law Commission

275. The Commission discussed the holding of the seventy-fifth anniversary session in Geneva in 2024 and agreed that during the first part of the session:

(a) there should be a solemn meeting of the Commission to which dignitaries, including the Secretary-General, the President of the General Assembly, the President of the International Court of Justice, the United Nations High Commissioner for Human Rights, and representatives of the host Government should be invited;

(b) there should be one and a half days of meetings with legal advisers of Ministries of Foreign Affairs dedicated to the work of the Commission;

(c) Member States, in association with regional organizations, professional associations, academic institutions and members of the Commission concerned, should be encouraged to convene national or regional meetings, which would be dedicated to the work of the Commission.

276. The Commission recommended that the Secretariat, in consultation with the Chair and Bureau of the seventy-fourth session for the remainder of 2023, and then in consultation with the Chair designate and Bureau designate for the seventy-fifth session in 2024, assist in making arrangements for the implementation of (*a*) and (*b*).

6. Honoraria

277. The Commission reiterates its views concerning the question of honoraria, resulting from the adoption by the General Assembly of its resolution 56/272 of 27 March 2002, which have been expressed in the previous reports of the Commission.[321] The Commission emphasizes that resolution 56/272 especially affects Special Rapporteurs, as it compromises support for their research. This is without prejudice to the establishment of the trust fund pursuant to paragraph 37 of resolution 77/103 of 7 December 2022.

7. Documentation and publications

278. The Commission underscored once more the unique nature of its functioning in the progressive development of international law and its codification, in that it attaches particular relevance to State practice and the decisions of national and international courts in its treatment of questions of international law. The Commission reiterated the importance of providing and making available all evidence of State practice and other sources of international law relevant to the performance of the function of the Commission. The reports of its Special Rapporteurs require an adequate presentation of precedents and other relevant data, including treaties, judicial decisions and doctrine, and a thorough analysis of the questions under consideration. The Commission stressed that it and its Special Rapporteurs

---

[321] See *Yearbook ... 2002*, vol. II (Part Two), pp. 102–103, paras. 525–531; *Yearbook ... 2003*, vol. II (Part Two), p. 101, para. 447; *Yearbook ... 2004*, vol. II (Part Two), pp. 120–121, para. 369; *Yearbook ... 2005*, vol. II (Part Two), p. 92, para. 501; *Yearbook ... 2006*, vol. II (Part Two), p. 187, para. 269; *Yearbook ... 2007*, vol. II (Part Two), p. 100, para. 379; *Yearbook ... 2008*, vol. II (Part Two), p. 148, para. 358; *Yearbook ... 2009*, vol. II (Part Two), p. 151, para. 240; *Yearbook ... 2010*, vol. II (Part Two), p. 203, para. 396; *Yearbook ... 2011*, vol. II (Part Two), p. 178, para. 399; *Yearbook ... 2012*, vol. II (Part Two), p. 87, para. 280; *Yearbook ... 2013*, vol. II (Part Two), p. 79, para. 181; *Yearbook ... 2014*, vol. II (Part Two) and Corr.1, p. 165, para. 281; *Yearbook ... 2015*, vol. II (Part Two), p. 87, para. 299; *Yearbook ... 2016*, vol. II (Part Two), p. 229, para. 333; *Yearbook ... 2017*, vol. II (Part Two), p. 150, para. 282; *Official Records of the General Assembly, Seventy-third Session, Supplement No. 10* (A/73/10), para. 382; *ibid.*, *Seventy-fourth Session, Supplement No. 10* (A/74/10), para. 302; *ibid.*, *Seventy-sixth Session, Supplement No. 10* (A/76/10), para. 317; and *ibid.*, *Seventy-seventh Session, Supplement No. 10* (A/77/10), para. 270.

are fully conscious of the need to achieve economies whenever possible in the overall volume of documentation and will continue to bear such considerations in mind. While the Commission is aware of the advantages of being as concise as possible, it reiterates its strong belief that an *a priori* limitation cannot be placed on the length of the documentation and research projects relating to the work of the Commission. It follows that Special Rapporteurs cannot be asked to reduce the length of their reports following submission to the Secretariat, irrespective of any estimates of their length made in advance of submission to the Secretariat. Word limits are not applicable to Commission documentation, as has been consistently reiterated by the General Assembly.[322] The Commission stresses also the importance of the timely preparation of reports by Special Rapporteurs and their submission to the Secretariat for processing and submission to the Commission sufficiently in advance so that the reports are issued in all official languages, ideally four weeks before the start of the relevant part of the session of the Commission. In this respect, the Commission reiterates the importance of Special Rapporteurs submitting their reports within the time limits specified by the Secretariat. Only on this basis can the Secretariat ensure that official documents of the Commission are published in due time in the six official languages of the United Nations.

279. On the other hand, the Commission called on the Secretariat to ensure that the documentation services involved in editing and translating documents increase their efficiencies, in particular, in ensuring the timely processing and circulation of Special Rapporteur reports from the original languages in which they are prepared and all the other official languages of the United Nations.

280. The Commission recognizes the particular relevance and significant value to the work of the Commission of the legal publications prepared by the Secretariat.[323] The Commission notes with appreciation the efforts of the Secretariat in desktop publishing, which greatly enhanced the timely issuance of such publications for the Commission, despite constraints due to lack of resources. The Commission expressed its appreciation for the issuance, at the beginning of the present quinquennium, of the tenth edition in English of *The Work of the International Law Commission*, which is a vital tool in the Commission's work, and urges that its early availability in the various official languages be ensured.

281. The Commission reiterated its firm view that the summary records of the Commission, constituting crucial *travaux préparatoires* in the progressive development and codification of international law, cannot be subject to arbitrary length restrictions. The Commission once more noted with satisfaction that the measures introduced at its sixty-fifth session (2013) to streamline the processing of its summary records had resulted in the more expeditious transmission to members of the Commission of the English version for timely correction and prompt release. The Commission once more called on the Secretariat to resume the practice of preparing provisional summary records in both English and French, and to continue its efforts to sustain the measures in question, in order to ensure the expeditious transmission of the provisional records to members of the Commission. The Commission further noted that the more recent practice of submitting to the members of the Commission the provisional records electronically for corrections to be made in track changes was working smoothly. The Commission also welcomed the fact that those working methods had led to the more rational use of resources and called on the Secretariat to continue its efforts to facilitate the preparation of the definitive records in all official languages, without compromising their integrity.

282. The Commission expressed its gratitude to all Services involved in the processing of documentation, both in Geneva and in New York, for their efforts in seeking to ensure timely and efficient processing of the Commission's documents, often under narrow time constraints. It emphasized that timely and efficient processing of documentation was

322 For considerations relating to page limits on the reports of Special Rapporteurs, see, for example, *Yearbook ... 1977*, vol. II (Part Two), p. 132, and *Yearbook ... 1982*, vol. II (Part Two), pp. 123–124. See also General Assembly resolution 32/151 of 9 December 1977, para. 10, and General Assembly resolution 37/111 of 16 December 1982, para. 5, as well as subsequent resolutions on the annual reports of the Commission to the General Assembly.

323 See *Yearbook ... 2007*, vol. II (Part Two), paras. 387–395. See also *Yearbook ... 2013*, vol. II (Part Two), para. 185.

essential for the smooth conduct of the Commission's work. The work done by all Services was all the more appreciated under the current conditions.

283. The Commission reaffirmed its commitment to multilingualism and recalled the paramount importance to be given in its work to the equality of the six official languages of the United Nations, which had been emphasized in General Assembly resolution 76/268 of 10 June 2022.[324]

284. The Commission expressed its gratitude for the continued efforts by the United Nations Library at Geneva to provide effective research support services, including the online information package and multilingual bibliographies that are prepared by the Library exclusively for the Commission, and expressed its gratitude for the briefings on library services and the guided tour of the Library and Archives it received in May 2023. The Commission commends the continuing efforts of the Library to maintain excellence in service despite the effects of protracted budget restrictions, which have begun to impact the capacity of the Library to implement its mandate and to adequately maintain its collections. The Commission noted that library services are essential to the functioning of the Commission and expressed concern that current budget restrictions may inhibit the Library's ability to provide specialized research assistance and to procure additional digital products and publications required to support the Commission during the closing of the Library building due to renovations. The Commission emphasized both the need to maintain the budget and staff resources of the Library and to limit as much as possible the impact of the renovations on the access to research spaces and the legal collection of the Library, especially during the Commission's seventy-fifth session. Finally, the Commission wished to encourage the continuing evolution of the United Nations Library at Geneva towards a research centre of excellence to build research capacity and to improve the accessibility and diversity of resources available to the Commission in the performance of its mandate.

8. *Yearbook of the International Law Commission*

285. The Commission reiterated that the *Yearbook of the International Law Commission* was critical to the understanding of the Commission's work in the progressive development of international law and its codification, as well as in the strengthening of the rule of law in international relations. The Commission took note that the General Assembly, in its resolution 77/103 of 7 December 2022, expressed its appreciation to Governments that had made voluntary contributions to the Trust Fund on the backlog relating to the *Yearbook of the International Law Commission*, and encouraged further contributions to the Trust Fund.

286. The Commission recommends that the General Assembly, as in its resolution 77/103, *express its satisfaction* with the remarkable progress achieved in recent years in catching up with the backlog of the *Yearbook of the International Law Commission* in all six languages, and *welcome the efforts* made by the Division of Conference Management of the United Nations Office at Geneva, especially its Editing Section, in effectively implementing relevant resolutions of the General Assembly calling for the reduction of the backlog; and *encourage* the Division of Conference Management to continue providing all necessary support to the Editing Section in advancing work on the *Yearbook*.

9. Trust fund on Assistance to Special Rapporteurs

287. The Commission notes with appreciation that, pursuant to paragraph 37 of General Assembly resolution 77/103 of 7 December 2022, the Secretary-General had established a trust fund to receive voluntary contributions for assistance to Special Rapporteurs of the International Law Commission or Chairs of its Study Groups and matters ancillary thereto. While reiterating the importance of ensuring necessary allocations for the Commission and its secretariat in the regular budget, the Commission appeals to Member States, NGOs, private entities and individuals to contribute to the trust fund, in accordance with the terms of the trust fund, including the need for the financial contributions not to be earmarked for

[324] See also General Assembly resolutions 69/324 of 11 September 2015; 71/328 of 17 September 2017; and 73/346 of 16 September 2019. See further General Assembly resolution 77/103 of 7 December 2022.

any specific activity of the International Law Commission, its Special Rapporteurs or Chairs of its Study Groups.

10. Assistance of the Codification Division

288. The Commission expressed its appreciation for the invaluable assistance of the Codification Division of the Secretariat in its substantive servicing of the Commission and the ongoing assistance provided to Special Rapporteurs and the preparation of in-depth research studies pertaining to aspects of topics presently under consideration, as requested by the Commission. In particular, the Commission expressed its appreciation to the Secretariat for the preparation of memorandums on prevention and repression of piracy and armed robbery at sea (A/CN.4/757); and on subsidiary means for the determination of rules of international law – elements in the previous work of the International Law Commission that could be particularly relevant to the topic (A/CN.4/759). The Commission also recognized the work of the Codification Division in providing texts in different languages to ensure the quality and representativeness of the work of the Drafting Committee.

11. Websites

289. The Commission expressed its appreciation to the Secretariat for the website on the work of the Commission, and welcomed its continuous updating and improvement.[325] The Commission reiterated that the website and other websites maintained by the Codification Division[326] constitute an invaluable resource for the Commission and for researchers of the work of the Commission in the wider community, thereby contributing to the rule of law and to the overall strengthening of the teaching, study, dissemination and wider appreciation of international law. The Commission welcomed the fact that the website on the work of the Commission included information on the current status of the topics on the agenda of the Commission, as well as links to the advance edited versions of the summary records of the Commission and the audio and video recordings of the plenary meetings of the Commission.

12. United Nations Audiovisual Library of International Law

290. The Commission once more noted with appreciation the extraordinary value of the United Nations Audiovisual Library of International Law[327] in promoting a better knowledge of international law and the work of the United Nations in the field, including the work of the Commission.

13. Consideration of the convening in the present quinquennium of the first part of a session of the Commission in New York

291. Further to paragraph 281 of the report of its seventy-third session (2022), in which the Commission recommended the holding of the first part of a session in New York during the next quinquennium with the view to enhancing its dialogue with the General Assembly to facilitate direct contact between the Commission and delegates of the Sixth Committee, the Commission takes note that it will not be able to meet at the United Nations Headquarters in New York due to the unavailability of conference rooms for the first part of its seventy-fifth (2024) or seventy-sixth session (2025). It therefore recommends that the first part of its seventy-seventh session (2026) be held in New York. The Commission requests the Secretariat to proceed with the necessary administrative and organizational arrangements to facilitate the holding of that part of the session in New York. Particular attention was drawn to the need to ensure access to sufficient conference and library facilities at Headquarters and electronic access to the resources and research assistance of the Library of the United Nations Office at Geneva. The need to ensure access and sufficient space for assistants to members of the Commission to attend meetings of the Commission was also emphasized.

---

325 http://legal.un.org/ilc.

326 In general, available from: http://legal.un.org/cod/.

327 http://legal.un.org/avl/intro/welcome_avl.html.

E. Date and place of the seventy-fifth session of the Commission

292. The Commission decided that its seventy-fifth session would be held in Geneva from 15 April to 31 May and from 1 July to 2 August 2024.

F. Cooperation with other bodies

293. At the 3639th meeting, on 18 July 2023, Judge Joan E. Donoghue, President of the International Court of Justice, addressed the Commission and briefed it on the recent judicial activities of the Court.[328] An exchange of views followed.

294. The Inter-American Juridical Committee was represented at the present session of the Commission by Mr. George Rodrigo Bandeira Galindo, member of the Committee, who addressed the Commission at the 3636th meeting, on 4 July 2023, and gave an overview of the activities of the Committee on various legal issues.[329] An exchange of views followed.

295. The African Union Commission on International Law was represented at the present session of the Commission by Ms. Hajer Gueldich, Chair of the Commission and Mr. Kevin Ferdinand Ndjimba, its General Rapporteur. They addressed the Commission at its 3637th meeting, on 6 July 2023, and gave an overview of the activities of the African Union Commission on various legal issues.[330] An exchange of views followed.

296. The Committee of Legal Advisers on Public International Law of the Council of Europe was represented at the present session of the Commission by Mr. Helmut Tichy, Chair of the Committee, and Mr. Jörg Polakiewicz, Legal Adviser to the Council of Europe, who addressed the Commission at its 3638th meeting, on 13 July 2023.[331] They focused on the current activities of the Committee in the field of public international law, as well of the Council of Europe. An exchange of views followed.

297. The Asian-African Legal Consultative Organization was represented at the present session of the Commission by Mr. Kamalinne Pinitpuvadol, the Secretary-General of the Organization, who addressed the Commission at its 3639th meeting, on 18 July 2023.[332] He briefed the Commission on the organization and provided an overview of its activities. An exchange of views followed.

298. On 4 July 2023, an informal exchange of views was held between members of the Commission and the International Committee of the Red Cross (ICRC) on matters of mutual interest. Welcoming remarks were made by Mr. Nils Melzer, Director, International Law, Policy and Humanitarian Diplomacy, ICRC, and opening remarks by Ms. Cordula Droege, Chief Legal Officer and Head of the Legal Division, ICRC, and Ms. Patrícia Galvão Teles, Chair of the Commission. A discussion was held on "Current challenges for the implementation of international law", moderated by Ms. Droege. Presentations were made on the topics "International humanitarian law and cyber operations during armed conflicts" by Mr. Tilman Rodenhäuser and Mr. Kubo Mačák, Legal Advisers, ICRC, and on "Subsidiary means for the determination of rules of international law" by Mr. Charles C. Jalloh, Special Rapporteur on the topic. Each set of presentations was followed by a discussion moderated by Ms. Droege. Concluding remarks were made by Mr. Melzer.

G. Representation at the seventy-eighth session of the General Assembly

299. The Commission decided that it should be represented at the seventy-eighth session of the General Assembly by its Chair, Ms. Patrícia Galvão Teles. The Chair during the first part of the session, Ms. Nilüfer Oral, will also attend.

[328] The statement is recorded in the summary record of that meeting.
[329] *Idem.*
[330] *Idem.*
[331] *Idem.*
[332] *Idem.*

H. International Law Seminar

300. Pursuant to General Assembly resolution 77/103 of 19 December 2022, the fifty-seventh session of the International Law Seminar was held at the Palais des Nations from 3 to 21 July 2023, during the present session of the Commission. The Seminar is intended for young jurists specializing in international law, and young professors or government officials pursuing an academic or diplomatic career in posts in the civil service of their countries.

301. Twenty-three participants of different nationalities, from all regional groups, took part in the session.[333] The participants attended plenary meetings of the Commission and specially arranged lectures, and participated in working groups on specific topics.

302. Ms. Patrícia Galvão Teles, Chair of the Commission, and Ms. Nilüfer Oral opened the Seminar. Mr. Markus Schmidt, Senior Legal Adviser to the United Nations Office at Geneva, was responsible for the administration, organization and conduct of the Seminar and served as its Director. Mr. Vittorio Mainetti, international law expert and consultant, acted as Coordinator, assisted by Ms. Kira Reitemeier and Ms. Nomungerel Jamsranjav, legal assistants.

303. The following lectures were given by members of the Commission: "Introduction to the work of the International Law Commission" by Mr. Mathias Forteau; "The contribution of the International Law Commission to the development of international law" by Mr. Dapo Akande; "Subsidiary means for the determination of rules of international law" by Mr. Charles C. Jalloh; "Particular customary international law" by Mr. George Rodrigo Bandeira Galindo; "The International Law Commission and the Sixth Committee" by Mr. Giuseppe Nesi; "General principles of law" by Mr. Marcelo Vázquez-Bermúdez; "The impact of the burden of proof on the overall determination of reparations in *Democratic Republic of the Congo v. Uganda* case (International Court of Justice 2022)" by Mr. Ivon Mingashang; "Immunity of State officials from foreign criminal jurisdiction" by Mr. Claudio Grossman Guiloff; "Prevention and repression of piracy and armed robbery at sea" by Mr. Yacouba Cissé; "Settlement of disputes to which international organizations are parties" by Mr. August Reinisch; "Legal aspects of Governmental representation at the United Nations" by Ms. Phoebe Okowa; and "The International Criminal Court and the issue of immunities" by Mr. Dapo Akande and Mr. Rolf Einar Fife. In addition, a round table was organized with four co-Chairs of the Study Group on the topic "Sea-level rise in relation to international law", Mr. Bogdan Aurescu, Ms. Patrícia Galvão Teles, Ms. Nilüfer Oral and Mr. Juan José Ruda Santolaria.

304. A lecture was given by Ms. Laurence Boisson de Chazournes, Professor at the University of Geneva, on "Prevention and settlement of disputes relating to the environment and climate change".

305. Participants visited the exhibition "100 years of Multilateral Cooperation in Geneva" at the United Nations Museum Geneva, led by Mr. Alex Renault, historian and adviser to the United Nations Library and Archives Geneva. Participants also visited the International Labour Organization (ILO), under the guidance of Mr. Remo Becci, Director of the ILO Archives, and attended two presentations given by Mr. Dražen Petrović, Registrar of the ILO Administrative Tribunal, on "International administrative tribunals", and Mr. Georges

---

333 The following persons participated in the Seminar: Ms. Meriem Agrebi (Tunisia); Mr. Manduul Alimaa (Mongolia); Mr. Gergó Barna Balázs (Hungary); Ms. Kezia Campbell-Erskine (Guyana); Mr. Stefano D'Aloia (Italy); Mr. Joel Diaz Rodriguez (Peru); Mr. Moussa Fadiga (Côte d'Ivoire); Mr. Natnael Fitsum Tekeste (Eritrea); Ms. Frida Fostvedt (Norway); Ms. Omnia Gadalla (Egypt); Ms. Bahareh Ghanoon (Islamic Republic of Iran); Ms. Randa Hasfura (El Salvador); Mr. Marvin Ikondere (Uganda); Ms. Natalia Jiménez Alegria (Mexico); Ms. Jolane T. Lauzon (Canada); Ms. Yasmine Luhandjula (Democratic Republic of the Congo); Mr. Neil Nucup (Philippines); Ms. Magma Sountouma (Togo); Ms. Dana Talic (Saudi Arabia); Ms. Ornela Flavia Vanzillotta (Argentina); Ms. Anita Yadav (India); Mr. Satomi Yanagidani (Japan); and Ms. Patricia Zghibarta (Republic of Moldova). The Selection Committee, chaired by Mr. Makane Moïse Mbengue, Professor of International Law at the University of Geneva, met on 3 May 2023 and selected 23 candidates from 105 applications.

Politakis, ILO Legal Adviser, on “ILO standard-setting”. They also visited the World Trade Organization (WTO) and attended presentations by Ms. Gabrielle Marceau, Senior Counsellor at the Research Division, and Mr. Juan Pablo Moya Hoyos, Dispute settlement Lawyer at WTO.

306. A day trip was organized to Lausanne to the Swiss Institute of Comparative Law, where a special programme was specifically designed, with the participation of Mr. Lukas Heckendorn Urscheler, Acting Director, Ms. Nathalie Matthey, Head of the Library, Mr. John Curran, Legal Adviser, Common Law, Ms. Ilaria Pretelli, Legal Adviser, Italian Law, Ms. Carole Viennet, Legal Adviser, French Law, and Mr. Henrik Westermark, Legal Adviser, Scandinavian Law.

307. Participants attended a workshop hosted by the University of Geneva on the topic “Unravelling waves: exploring climate change’s impact on the law of the sea and international water law”, with the participation of Ms. Laurence Boisson de Chazournes, Professor at the University of Geneva, Ms. Mara Tignino, Reader, University of Geneva, and Coordinator of the Platform for International Water Law/Geneva Water Hub, and Ms. Patrícia Galvão Teles, Ms. Nilüfer Oral, Mr. Mario Oyarzábal, Mr. Juan José Ruda Santolaria, members of the Commission. They also attended a conference on “Social justice and the future of ILO”, in honour of Mr. Francis Maupain, former ILO legal adviser, at the Graduate Institute of International and Development Studies, Geneva.

308. Two working groups, on “Identifying new topics for the International Law Commission” and “Regionalism and universalism in the work of the International Law Commission” were organized and participants were assigned to one of them. Two members of the Commission, Mr. Dapo Akande and Mr. George Rodrigo Bandeira Galindo, respectively, supervised and provided guidance to the working groups. Each group prepared a report and presented its findings during the last working session of the Seminar. The reports were compiled and distributed to all participants, as well as to the members of the Commission.

309. Participants also attended a session with the International Law Seminar Alumni Network. Ms. Verity Robson (alumna 2017), President of the Network, Mr. Moritz Rudolf (alumnus 2017), Vice-President of the Network, Ms. Mary Chong (alumna 2017), Vice-President of the Network, and Mr. Vittorio Mainetti, Secretary-General of the Network and Coordinator of the International Law Seminar, addressed the participants and presented the work of the Network.

310. The Republic and Canton of Geneva offered its traditional hospitality at the Geneva Hôtel de Ville. Seminar participants visited the Alabama room and the premises of the cantonal authorities, guided by Mr. Samy Bensalem, Deputy Head of Protocol of the Republic and Canton of Geneva.

311. The Chair of the Commission, the Director of the International Law Seminar and Mr. Marvin Ikondere (Uganda), on behalf of participants attending the Seminar, addressed the Commission during the ceremony of diplomas. Each participant was presented with a diploma.

312. The Commission noted with preoccupation that, in recent years, the finances of the International Law Seminar have been adversely affected by economic and financial factors, which in turn has had an impact on what the Seminar can offer in terms of stipends. The situation is now much better than it was in 2019, due to two large voluntary contributions the Seminar have now secured on a regular basis. However, the Seminar must nonetheless reflect on ways and means to broaden its financial basis in the future. In 2023, 16 fellowships were granted (15 for travel and subsistence, 1 for subsistence only).

313. Since its inception in 1965, 1,307 participants, representing 178 nationalities, have taken part in the Seminar. Some 797 participants have received a fellowship.

314. **The Commission stresses the importance it attaches to the Seminar, which enables young lawyers, especially those from developing countries, to familiarize themselves with the work of the Commission and the activities of the many international organizations based in Geneva. The Commission recommends that the General Assembly should again appeal to States to make voluntary contributions in order to secure the organization of the Seminar in 2024 with as broad participation as possible, and an adequate geographical distribution.**